Social
Modeling
Using the *i**
Framework

Xavier Franch • Julio Cesar Sampaio do Prado Leite • Gunter Mussbacher • John Mylopoulos • Anna Perini
Editors

Social Modeling Using the *i** Framework

Essays in Honour of Eric Yu

Springer

Editors
Xavier Franch
Universitat Politècnica de Catalunya (UPC)
Barcelona, Spain

Julio Cesar Sampaio do Prado Leite
Universidade Federal da Bahia (UFBA)
Salvador-Bahia, Brazil

Gunter Mussbacher
Electrical and Computer Engineering
McGill University
Montreal, QC, Canada

John Mylopoulos
University of Trento
Trento, Italy

Anna Perini
Fondazione Bruno Kessler
Trento, Italy

ISBN 978-3-031-72106-9 ISBN 978-3-031-72107-6 (eBook)
https://doi.org/10.1007/978-3-031-72107-6

This Springer imprint is published by the registered company Springer Nature Switzerland AG
The registered company address is: Gewerbestrasse 11, 6330 Cham, Switzerland

Eric Yu, Professor Emeritus, University of Toronto

Foreword

It is with great honor and appreciation that we present this book in celebration of Professor Eric Yu, whose distinguished career in academic research and teaching has shaped his field and inspired many researchers, practitioners, and students. Eric's scientific work is situated in the field of "requirements engineering" (RE), a field that addresses challenges in establishing artifacts, be they models, tools, or methods, that help capture, share, represent, analyze, negotiate, and prioritize requirements as a basis for design decisions and interventions.

Common challenges to RE include evolution of requirements, ambiguity and uncertainty, communication barriers, complexity, and size.

Eric's work has had a profound influence on addressing these as well as emerging challenges in RE, due to exceedingly complex and nonlinear dynamic dependencies between system components and their natural, technical, and social environment. The intertwining of requirements and their context, the interplay between the two worlds, is often intricate, complex, dynamic, and generative. In addressing this challenge, Eric's work on "strategic modelling," "social modelling," and "dynamic capability modelling" has been a beacon of intellectual rigor and innovative thinking.

In the early 1990s, and as part of his PhD thesis (advised by Professor John Mylopoulos), Eric designed the *i** framework. The objectives of this work were to facilitate the externalization of complex relationships among systems and stakeholders, to help stakeholders better understand their needs, and importantly to determine the rationale (the "why") and not just the "what" and the "how." The approach focuses on modelling the relationships between actors and their goals, tasks, and resources, emphasizing the strategic rationale behind goals. His article, emanating essentially from this work, "Towards Modelling and Reasoning Support for Early-Phase Requirements Engineering" in *Proceedings of the 3rd IEEE Int. Symposium on Requirements Engineering* (1997) received the Most Influential Paper Award at the 2007 Requirements Engineering Conference.

Over the years, and related to the IEEE Conference on Requirements Engineering, there have been regular workshops dedicated to the discussion of concepts, methods, techniques, tools, and applications associated with *i** and related goal modelling frameworks. The outputs from these workshops, together with Eric's over 200 publications as well as numerous publications from other authors on themes related to the *i** framework form a lasting source of materials in RE for the researchers of the future.

Eric has been on the Editorial Board of the *Requirements Engineering* journal (https://link.springer.com/journal/766), and I am personally grateful to him for his dedication, insights, and general support that, along with the rest of the Editorial Board members, helped ensure that the high standards of this journal have been constantly maintained.

The chapters in this book, contributed by colleagues of Eric, or by scholars who became influenced by Eric's work, are reflections on the characteristics of *i**, its variations in syntax, efforts toward standards, as well as the deployment of the framework in various real-world applications. To this end, the book represents a well-rounded exposition of Eric's work and its relevance to continuing challenges in RE.

We are deeply grateful to all the contributors for their insightful essays and to everyone who has made this Festschrift possible. This book will serve as a lasting tribute to Eric Yu and a source of inspiration for future scholars.

Editor-in-Chief Requirements
Engineering Journal, Athens
June 2024

Pericles Loucopoulos

Preamble

"It takes a village..."—African saying

Research is a collaborative enterprise. It has been my good fortune to be part of a community of like-minded researchers in the field of requirements engineering. I am greatly honored by this volume, which highlights some of the research results and current thinking that follow from the *i** modeling framework, a central focus of my life's work.

My own development in this field would not have been possible without the support and collaboration of many friends and research colleagues over the years. I am especially indebted to my doctoral advisor, Professor John Mylopoulos, who patiently guided me through my circuitous journey during my studies and has provided invaluable mentorship throughout my academic career. Without John's unwavering support, I would not have found the courage to persevere. I want to express my sincere gratitude to all.

My doctoral studies began with some tentative forays into the hot topic of the day—artificial intelligence. Under John's patient guidance, I eventually proposed *i** for modeling and analyzing software system requirements in a social context, inspired by ideas from AI multi-agent systems and theories of human organization. A turning point in my PhD journey, as I now recall, was when John posed this terrifying question: "Are you doing organization modeling or requirements modeling?" Shaking in my boots and contemplating the prospect of a premature end to my PhD career, I had to do some soul-searching about what it meant to do requirements engineering and how it related to the organization modeling that I was dabbling in.

Today, AI is once again the hot topic of the day. I believe we have some soul-searching to do once more. What does doing requirements engineering mean in light of the current wave of AI? With AI promising both unprecedented human flourishing and species extinction, the stakes could not be higher. Are we, as requirements engineers, up to the challenge?

Eric Yu

Preface

About 30 years ago, Eric Yu proposed in his PhD thesis, completed in 1995, to model and analyze stakeholders and their requirements for an IT system in terms of actors, their goals, and social interdependencies. The modelling language for the task was named *i** as a shorthand for "distributed intentionality." The results of Eric's thesis were published through papers presented at the 1st IEEE International Symposium on Requirements Engineering in 1993 [9], the 13th International Conference on Conceptual Modelling in 1994 [8], and the 3rd IEEE International Symposium on Requirements Engineering in 1997 [10], which won the Most Influential Paper Award 10 years later.

At that time, the benefits of conceptual modelling (knowledge representation techniques) and reasoning techniques in the design phases of software systems were already evident and already obtained on a practical level, so as to motivate, precisely in those years, the definition of standards for modelling languages in software engineering, such as UML.[1] However, it was necessary to model other entities to express the reasons for designing a new software system, its potential impact on the entire organization (social context in which it will come into use), as well as to analyze possible alternative ways to meet the goals of the involved stakeholders. Goal-oriented modelling was seen as an opportunity to address this need and motivated a large effort by the requirements engineering research community to develop goal-oriented requirements engineering (GORE) methods and techniques [1,5].

*i** is founded on the notions of actor for representing stakeholders, goal for representing stakeholder requirements, and strategic dependency relationships for representing social interdependencies among actors. The idea of modelling requirements as goals was adopted from Dardenne et al. [2] and Mylopoulos et al. [6] as well as the PhD thesis of Lawrence Chung, a contemporary PhD candidate with Eric at the University of Toronto. The seminal contribution of Eric's thesis has been the introduction of social actors and social dependencies into requirements models. This

[1] https://www.omg.org/spec/UML/

innovation means that for the first time, requirements problems were acknowledged to be social, rather than technical system problems.

While the whole area of goal-oriented requirements engineering has been systematically surveyed [3,4], the key source of knowledge on social modelling is the book *Social Modeling for Requirements Engineering* [7], which includes Eric's thesis as well as a series of chapters on *i** applications. Furthermore, the long-standing *i** workshop series reflects the wealth of research results in the *i** community.

To celebrate Eric Yu, on the occasion of his retirement, we organized a symposium which was colocated with the 31st IEEE International Requirements Engineering Conference in Hannover, Germany. The presentations by invitation aimed to give testimony to the impact of Eric's work during the last 30 years of research and practice in requirements engineering and reflected on future prospects. The chapters of this book have the same aim. In fact, several of them are extensions of symposium presentations.

Structure of This Book

The contents of the book are structured into five sections, relative to the relationship of each chapter to the *i** requirements modelling language. The first four sections cover retrospectives and reflections on *i**, empirical research studies on *i**, *i** modelling language variants, and applications of *i** to address open research challenges. The last section presents a vision on how *i** could foster the transition toward a new RE paradigm, i.e., RE as *Augmenting Aspiring Selves*, a paradigm that should better fit with the needs of RE for AI-based systems.

Retrospectives includes two chapters discussing experiences and lessons learned with work extending or using *i**. In particular, Chap. 2 presents experiences of Anna Perini and Angelo Susi in adopting and applying *i** in a series of research and R&D projects. These experiences involve many different domains ranging from Software Engineering to Multimedia and Agriculture. In several cases, *i** had to be extended in order to deal with the complexities of the domain. Chapter 3, authored by Daniel Amyot and Gunter Mussbacher, explains how *i** influenced the development of the Goal-oriented Requirement Language (GRL), first standardized by the International Telecommunication Union in 2008 as part of the User Requirements Notation (URN). It also reflects on similarities and differences between *i** and URN with respect to syntax, features, and supported analysis techniques.

Empirical Studies presents case studies evaluating *i** in different domains. In particular, Chap. 4 is authored by Gerhard Lakemeyer and Martin Liebenberg and concerns an application of a logic-based extension of *i** to a water management problem in megacities, in search of sustainable solutions. The paper emphasizes the great advantage of *i** to model and analyze social problems in non-IT stakeholder terms. Chapter 5 presents a proposal for know-how map models and is authored by Arnon Sturm. Know-how maps consist of know-how problems represented as *i** tasks and pointers to various knowledge sources that provide solutions to each problem. The proposal has been evaluated with human subjects who found that the models are easy to use and modify.

Variants includes chapters that report on variants of *i** that describe extensions in expressiveness or extensions motivated by particular domains. In particular, after 20 years of study and use, *i** was revisited in two workshops held during 2014 and 2015, respectively, and attended by researchers and users to discuss lessons learned and propose iStar 2.0. iStar 2.0 was drafted by Fabiano Dalpiaz, Xavier Franch, and Jennifer Horkoff and is presented in Chap. 6. Sotirios Liaskos, Shakil Khan, and John Mylopoulos co-authored Chap. 7, which proposes iStar T as an extension of iStar 2.0 that allows for greater variability with respect to tasks. iStar T models can be translated into Hierarchical Task Networks and Golog specifications enabling automated analysis of iStar T models. Safety requirements are key concerns for critical systems in domains such as Healthcare and Defense. In Chap. 8, Moniky Ribeiro, Jaelson Castro, and Maria Lencastre propose to integrate *i** with a safety analysis technique. The resulting method is illustrated with an insulin infusion pump system. Chapter 9, authored by John Mylopoulos, Daniel Amyot, and Amal Anda, discusses two variants of the social dependency concept, namely, the notions of commitment, adopted from Multi-Agent Systems, and that of obligation adopted from the Legal Domain. These have been used as core concepts to propose a language, named Azzurra, for business processes, and another, Symboleo, for legal contracts.

Applications describes applications of *i** in different domains. Alistair Sutcliffe authored Chap. 10, which focuses on "soft" requirements, such as ethical values, motivations, emotions, and beliefs. Soft requirements influence each other, as well as "hard" functional requirements, differently from hard requirements. The paper explores these differences through a case study concerning home-based support for senior citizens. Chapter 11 authored by Ana Lavalle, Alejandro Reina, Alejandro Maté, and Juan Trujillo adopts *i**'s social perspective to design a data analytics application for decision-makers. The proposed approach has been evaluated with a case study which suggests that *i** is better suited than conventional techniques for the integrated analysis of the social goals of decision-makers along with the technical goals of data specialists. In Chap. 12, Yves Wautelet and Manuel Kolp argue that the focus of businesses should shift from business-IT alignment (BITA) to digital-business alignment (DBA) where IT is replaced by the technologies of digital transformation, namely, the cloud, cybersecurity, AI, IoT, sustainability, and others. Moreover, they propose an *i**-centric framework to explore alternative ways of achieving digital-business alignment for each business. Ethicality requirements, such as transparency and explainability, came to the forefront of requirements engineering research largely due to the advent of AI systems. In Chap. 13, Renata Guizzardi, Glenda Amaral, Giancarlo Guizzardi, and John Mylopoulos present an ontology-based approach to eliciting ethicality requirements using *i**. The proposed approach is illustrated with an autonomous vehicle example.

Visions presents Eric's vision for the next generation of requirements engineering in Chap. 13 which sees requirements engineering being reconceptualized to focus not on the design of technical systems, but rather on augmenting the intelligence of its stakeholders with that of AI systems. A personal wellness app is used as motivating example.

Acknowledgments We would like to thank all authors of the book chapters for their contributions, as well as all reviewers who ensured the quality of the contributions. Without your dedication, this book would not have been possible. We also would like to thank Springer for their support in publishing these essays in honor of Eric Yu.

Barcelona, Spain — Xavier Franch
Salvador-Bahia, Brazil — Julio Cesar Sampaio do Prado Leite
Montreal, QC, Canada — Gunter Mussbacher
Toronto, ON, Canada — John Mylopoulos
Trento, Italy — Anna Perini

References

1. Antón, A.I., McCracken, W.M., Potts, C.: Goal decomposition and scenario analysis in business process reengineering. In: Advanced Information Systems Engineering: 6th International Conference, CAiSE'94 Utrecht, June 6–10, 1994 Proceedings 6. pp. 94–104. Springer, Berlin (1994)
2. Dardenne, A., Van Lamsweerde, A., Fickas, S.: Goal-directed requirements acquisition. Sci. Comput. Program. **20**(1–2), 3–50 (1993)
3. ElSayed, I.A., Ezz, Z., Nasr, E.: Goal modeling techniques in requirements engineering: a systematic literature review. J. Comput. Sci. **13**(9), 430–439 (2017)
4. Horkoff, J., Aydemir, F.B., Cardoso, E., Li, T., Maté, A., Paja, E., Salnitri, M., Piras, L., Mylopoulos, J., Giorgini, P.: Goal-oriented requirements engineering: an extended systematic mapping study. Requir. Eng. **24**(2), 133–160 (2019). https://doi.org/10.1007/s00766-017-0280-z
5. van Lamsweerde, A., Darimont, R., Massonet, P.: Goal-directed elaboration of requirements for a meeting scheduler: problems and lessons learnt. In: Second IEEE International Symposium on Requirements Engineering, March 27–29, 1995, York, pp. 194–203. IEEE Computer Society, Washington (1995). https://doi.org/10.1109/ISRE.1995.512561
6. Mylopoulos, J., Chung, L., Nixon, B.: Representing and using nonfunctional requirements: a process-oriented approach. IEEE Trans. Software Eng. **18**(6), 483–497 (1992). https://doi.org/10.1109/32.142871
7. Yu, E., Giorgini, P., Maiden, N., Mylopoulos, J.: Social Modeling for Requirements Engineering. The MIT Press, Cambridge (2010)
8. Yu, E.S.K., Mylopoulos, J.: From E-R to "A-R" — Modelling strategic actor relationships for business process reengineering. In: Loucopoulos, P. (ed.) Entity-Relationship Approach — ER '94 Business Modelling and Re-Engineering, pp. 548–565. Springer, Berlin (1994)

9. Yu, E.S.: Modeling organizations for information systems requirements engineering. In: [1993] Proceedings of the IEEE International Symposium on Requirements Engineering, pp. 34–41. IEEE, Piscataway (1993)
10. Yu, E.: Towards modelling and reasoning support for early-phase requirements engineering. In: Proceedings of ISRE '97: 3rd IEEE International Symposium on Requirements Engineering, pp. 226–235 (1997). https://doi.org/10.1109/ISRE.1997.566873

Contents

Part I
Retrospectives

*i** or Not *i**, This Was the Question

Anna Perini and Angelo Susi

Abstract We applied goal-oriented modelling with *i** in several projects in our 20-year or more research activities. In this chapter, we propose an a posteriori reflection and revisit our choice to use or not *i** in representative projects, in light of modelling language's qualities, which are well accepted in research literature. When performing requirements engineering for software systems, goal-modelling provided us conceptual tools for the analysis of alternative ways to reach domain stakeholders' goals and for making explicit their mutual dependencies. Thus we were able to experience the *pragmatic qualities* of the models we built. The integration of goal-oriented modelling with other elicitation and reasoning techniques was relevant to consolidate and validate requirements. In some cases, to increase the language's *domain appropriateness* quality, we extended the language adding new constructs. We shortly report about evaluation studies that have performed to assess quality properties of the proposed language's extensions. Concluding remarks on our experience are proposed.

1 Introduction

Goal-oriented modelling has emerged as a tool for software systems' requirements analysis since the 1990s [29, 30]. It represents a key element of the so-called Goal-Oriented Requirements Engineering (GORE), which includes methods and tools that exploit the notion of goals to elicit, model, analyze, and validate requirements.

GORE research led to the definition of extensions of goal-oriented modelling languages to enhance their expressiveness towards modelling different types of requirements, as well as the proposals of language formalization and reasoning tools to support requirements analysis, verification, and validation [10].

A. Perini · A. Susi (✉)
Fondazione Bruno Kessler, Trento, Povo, Italy
e-mail: perini@fbk.eu; susi@fbk.eu

X. Franch et al. (eds.), *Social Modeling Using the i* Framework*,
https://doi.org/10.1007/978-3-031-72107-6_1

Our contribution in the field of GORE started at the beginning of 2000, with the development of the *Tropos* methodology, a joint effort with the University of Trento and the University of Toronto, under the guidance of John Mylopoulos. The *Tropos* methodology [3, 27] is a model-driven agent-oriented software development methodology which guides the software development process from early requirements to implementation and testing [19]. The *Tropos* methodology has been demonstrated through applications to the development of agent-oriented software. Moreover, *Tropos*'s requirements engineering steps have been used in several industrial projects aiming at designing service-based systems. The modelling languages adopted in *Tropos* include *i** [30] and some UML diagrams. In this chapter we mainly refer to the *i** version, which is used in *Tropos*.

Specifically, in this chapter we revisit goal-oriented modelling applications with *i** that we have realized over the last 20 years or more in the context of different projects in which our research group was involved.

In all of these cases, we evaluated the opportunity to use or not *i** (i.e., answering the question "*i** or not *i**?"), taking the perspective of the requirements engineers or that of requirements engineering (RE) researchers. Each perspective brings different objectives, which lead to considering different properties as relevant for a modelling language and for the derived models. As requirements engineers, goal-modelling provided conceptual tools for the analysis of alternative ways to reach a goal and for making explicit actor's goals and mutual dependencies for their achievement. As researchers, enhancing the expressiveness of *i** allowed to model domain entities, such as norms and risks, which can be relevant to elicit appropriate requirements. Moreover, the integration of goal-oriented modelling with other elicitation and reasoning techniques was relevant to consolidate and evaluate requirements.

In this chapter, we present a critical reflection on representative projects, focusing on our choice of using *i**, in light of modelling language's qualities, which are well accepted in research literature, e.g., [12, 16].

Along the analyst's perspective, we revisit examples from past projects and highlight how *i** can fit with *domain appropriateness* and *audience appropriateness* qualities, which are factors that contribute to building models that can be comprehended by stakeholders and allow reaching deontic goals of modelling such as increasing stakeholders' awareness about the "as-is" situation and communicating the context of change captured by a "to-be" model.

Along the RE researcher's perspective, we first summarize why and how we enhanced the expressiveness of *i** by extending the visual modelling language with new elements. Second, we revisit successful experiences where we integrated goal-oriented modelling with other requirements elicitation techniques, as a different means to improve the quality of the collected requirements.

The rest of the chapter is structured as follows: in Sect. 2 we recall definitions proposed for models' and modelling languages' qualities and the perspectives that guide the described analysis of past projects; in Sect. 3 projects are revisited along the perspective of requirements analysts; the requirements engineering researchers' perspective is taken for the analysis presented in Sect. 4. Concluding remarks are presented in Sect. 5.

2 Model Qualities and Analysis's Perspectives

Since the early 1990s, visual modelling has been applied in the early development of software systems, as a complement to textual requirements specifications. At the same time, properties that these models have to satisfy in order to be considered good quality artifacts were defined [12, 16, 17].

Lindland et al.'s framework [16] and following extensions, such as the SEQUAL framework defined by Krogstie [12], build on semiotic theory. Figure 1 depicts the core idea of these quality frameworks. Quality aspects are identified following the relations between a *model* and the *conceptual modelling language* (i.e., guided by the goal: syntax correctness); between a model and the *domain* it will be used for (i.e., semantic, following validity and completeness goals); and between the model and the *audience* that will build, validate, or use the model (i.e., pragmatic, which includes achieving comprehension).

Achieving these qualities rests on the use of modelling languages that meet specific qualities. For the purpose of our reflection, we focus on the following, as defined in the SEQUAL framework: *domain appropriateness*, *comprehensibility appropriateness*, *audience appropriateness*, and *tool appropriateness*.[1] They are defined as follows:

- *Domain appropriateness* refers to the relation between the modelling language and the domain. Reducing temporarily or extending a language metamodel to include concepts that suit the domain is used to achieve this quality. Quality

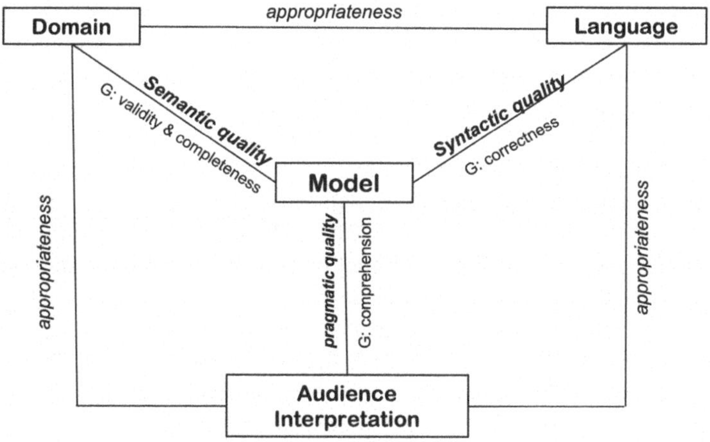

Fig. 1 Key concepts of the framework by Lindland et al. [16], extended in the SEQUAL framework [12]

[1] Notice that the SEQUAL framework proposes seven model's qualities and six modelling languages' qualities [12].

aspects of the visual notation, which were investigated by Moody [17] under semiotic clarity principles (i.e., symbol excess and symbol deficit), are also covered by the *domain appropriateness* quality.
- The three following qualities, *comprehensibility appropriateness*, *audience appropriateness*, and *tool appropriateness*, relate the language to the audience interpretation. Audience includes different types of stakeholders, namely, modellers, experts on automated reasoning techniques, and domain stakeholders. The first quality refers mainly to domain stakeholders' appropriateness, the *audience appropriateness* quality to modellers and their knowledge, and the *tool appropriateness* quality to the technical audience.

Empirical studies were performed to evaluate qualities of the *i** language, often comparing different variants of the language. For instance, comprehensibility of *i** models vs. UML use case models has been investigated in a family of controlled experiment with students [7]. Similarly in [18], we reported about two controlled experiments, aimed at comparing the comprehensibility, effectiveness, and modelling effort for requirements models of a self-adaptive system using *Tropos4AS*, an extension of *Tropos* for self-adaptive systems, in comparison with the *Tropos* notation. Liaskos in [15] describes a set of empirical studies with students, which aim at measuring and comparing the intuitiveness of different contribution link visualizations and semantics.

Differently, we use the qualities they propose as sort of criteria for a qualitative assessment of the use of *i** and its tools in different cases, performing an a posteriori analysis on the benefits of using *i** (*Tropos*) models in past projects. Specifically, we take the perspective of audience members, such as the generic domain stakeholders, who would like to have a problem solved (DS for short); the requirements engineer/analyst (REA), who aims at understanding a problem domain and elicits, analyzes, and validates requirements for a solution to be built; and the requirements engineering researcher (RER), who aims at providing effective and appropriate methods for domain understanding and requirements analysis, to better support REAs in doing their tasks. Visual modelling languages, which fit with language qualities, modelling tools, and automated reasoning tools, are part of the contribution that RERs can provide. These three perspectives are modelled in the *i** 2.0 model depicted in Fig. 2. Mutual dependencies between these actors are experienced in application projects, such as those aiming at designing (IT) solutions to specific application domain problems. For instance, the actor DS depends on the requirements analysts (REA) to have their needs understood, while the actor REA depends on the actor DS to validate requirements. Moreover, the actor REA depends on the actor researchers (RER) to get modelling languages that fit with *domain appropriateness*, *comprehensibility appropriateness*, *audience appropriateness*, and *tool appropriateness*, besides methodologies and guidelines which can help them doing their job. More generally, the actor REA depends on the researchers to get access to the needed elements to take an informed decision about which modelling language to use in a project, and how. Vice versa the actor RER depends on the actor REA to validate modelling method and models.

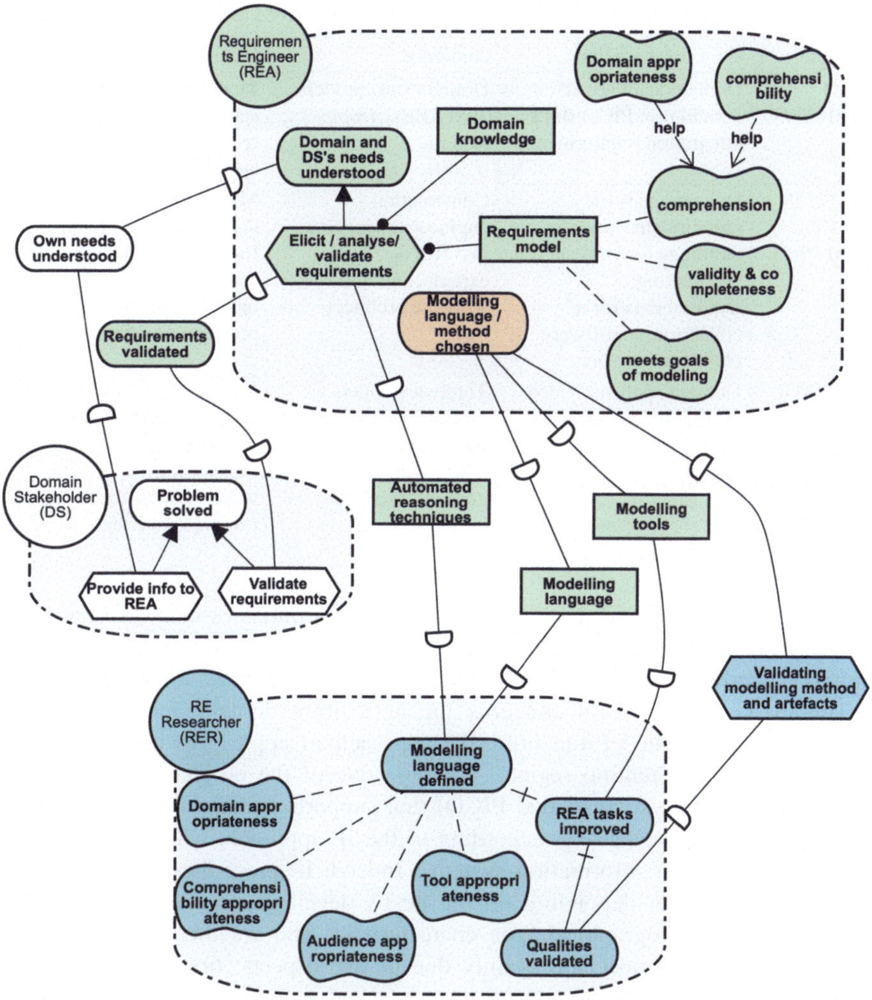

Fig. 2 *i** 2.0 model [5, 24] of the three perspectives, namely, DS (gray), REA (green), and RER (light blue)

3 RE Analyst's Perspective

We focus on three information technology application projects, which were conducted in different periods in the 20-year considered range (i.e., there is almost 10-year difference between the first and the next and almost 20 with respect to the third one). They concern different application domains, thus involving stakeholders with different skills and expectations. This offers us insights into the difference in audience characteristics when evaluating the modelling experience with *i**. Key information about the considered projects is summarized in Table 1, which reports

Table 1 A summary of the characteristics of the projects considered from the REA's perspective

Project	Goals of modelling	Audience	Means—comprehension
PICO 2000–2003	Domain analysis: IP agriculture; PICO-dss's integration requirements	Domain stakeholders. Two RERs, *Tropos* experts	Modelled only key domain actors; limited number of relationships. Participatory approach
MADE IN ITALY 2010–2013	Domain analysis: prefabricated wooden buildings for construction engineering; requirements for a collaborative software platform	Construction engineering experts; two REAs, *Tropos* experts, and one software architect	Mainly strategic dependency diagrams. Interviews with domain stakeholders to validate the model. Models discussed at project's meetings
ELEVATE 2019–2023	Domain analysis: video tutorial for SOP training	Three developers familiar with UML and one with *i** 2.0. Two REAs expert in goal-oriented analysis	Models with only key domain actors and strategic dependencies. Focus on the transition from as-is to to-be. Models discussed at project's meetings

the project's acronym and the time period, the main purposes of the GO analysis (i.e., deontic goals), features of the team involved in the GO analysis (column *Audience*), and strategies to help model comprehension (column *Means*).

The PICO project[2] [20] concerns the agriculture domain and in particular the so-called Integrated Protection (IP) approach in apple growing, one of the main crops in the Trentino region. The objective of the project was to develop a decision support system (called PICO) that supports technicians and producers to manage apple pest diseases according to the IP approach, which needed to be integrated with other information systems. Indeed, IP prescribes specific actions for pest management depending on the pest's development stage and on other factors including geographical area characteristics and weather conditions. The complexity of the project was mainly due to two aspects: first, the presence of domain stakeholders with specific competences and responsibilities and second the technical dimension concerning the study of natural plant protection techniques.

*i** looked as promising candidate language to help us understand the responsibilities and mutual dependencies of the domain stakeholders. Moreover, at that time we were learning how to use *i** and the OME[3] modeling tool, which was the current available *i** tool. Moreover, we were collaborating at the development of the *Tropos* methodology, thus resulting in a positive value for the *audience appropriateness* factor. During the project, we modelled the as-is situation and the to-be that included the PICO agent. This helped us (in the role of requirements engineers, REA) to elicit

[2] A research and innovation project funded by the Italian national government.

[3] http://istarwiki.org/tiki-index.php?page=OME

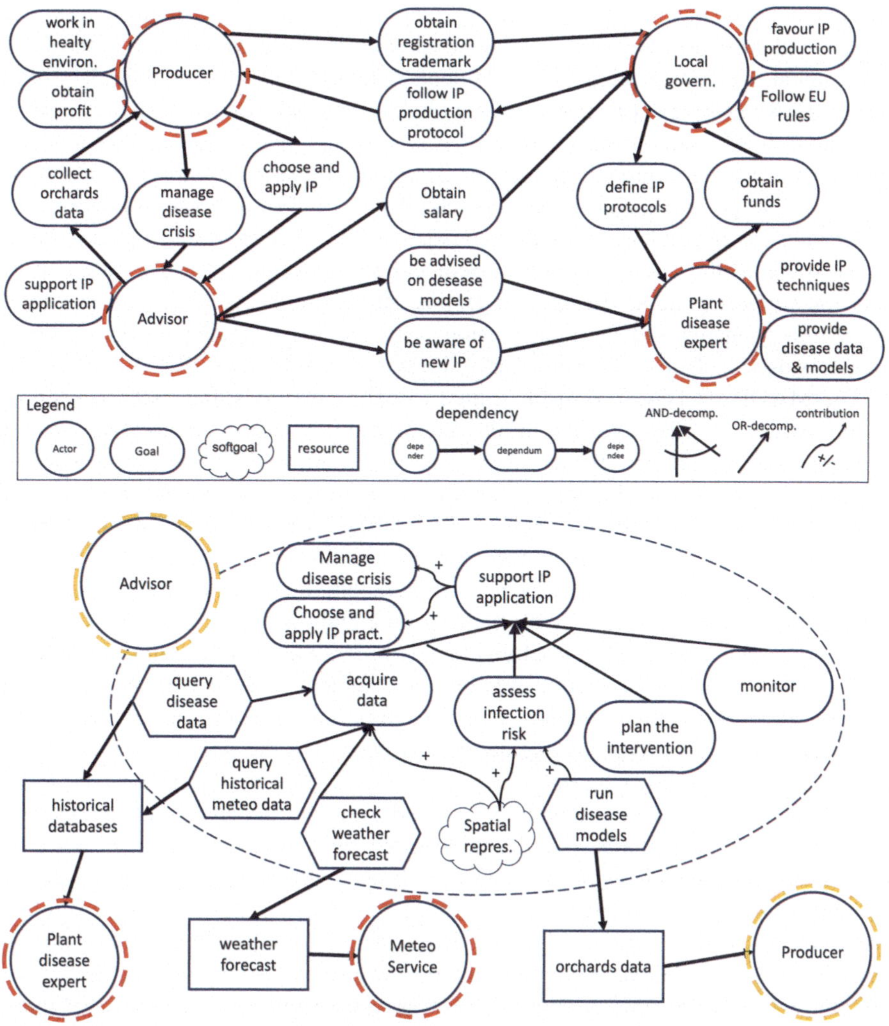

Fig. 3 Examples of as-is model in *Tropos* in the PICO project [20]. Mutual dependencies between four organizational roles (top), dependencies on external IT systems (dashed orange circles) during decision-making by the growers' Advisor (bottom)

system integration requirements and at the same time increased awareness of DSs about the mutual dependencies existing in their domain.

The complexity of the models we built was kept low. For instance, in the as-is situation domain model, we modelled four key actors (the actor `Producer`, `Local Government`, `Plant Disease Expert`, `Advisor`), with up to three mutual dependencies. An example is depicted in Fig. 3. This model provided an effective support during project's meetings with stakeholders for domain understanding since it helped to identify how key goals, like the goal `Favour IP production` of the local government, were motivating a chain of dependencies going through the other three actors (see `follow IP protocol`, in Fig. 3). Domain stakeholders became familiar with the *i** basic notation, and helped revise the model, and building other models, such as the strategic rationale model for describing the as-is situation of decision-making for IP pest management of the actor `Advisor`. From this model, we could understand the dependencies of the advisor from other system and human actors of the domain, thus helping elicit system integration requirements for the PICO decision support system. We applied *Tropos* till the architectural design, in which system components and their interaction were specified, adding UML sequence diagrams used in *Tropos*. A prototype of the system was developed [20].

The MADE IN ITALY project[4] aimed to define methods and tools to support a consortium of professionals in the creation of wooden super-elevations on existing buildings. These artifacts were supposed to be sold abroad, using wooden components prefabricated in Italy. Our role in the project concerned the elicitation of requirements for a software platform to facilitate partners' coordination during the entire life cycle of such engineering project, from the feasibility study to design, construction, and maintenance of these buildings' extensions. Given the large number of stakeholders, with their specific and different technical skills, the domain analysis presented several challenges to us, who were playing the role of REAs. Interviews, questionnaire, and domain document analysis were performed to create a glossary for this domain, to identify important artifacts and to understand key decisions in such type of engineering projects. On the basis of the collected information, we decided to build two GO models. The first model is the early requirements model with domain actors and strategic dependencies, as for the as-is situation. This model was complemented by a list of challenges reported by stakeholders, which were grouped according to four problem types, namely, communications; data; documents; and process management. The second is a late requirements model including the new software platform (system actor) with the new dependencies between domain actors and system actor, which represented domain actors' expectations about the software platform to be adopted for these construction projects. These models were built by two REAs familiar with *Tropos* and discussed with the software engineer working for the company responsible for developing the software platform. They were used in meetings with representatives of the different stakeholders to validate our understanding of their needs. Also in this case, the models used for the meetings with stakeholders contained between five and ten actors and between two and eight strategic dependencies.

[4] A project funded by MIUR. Project's deliverable, titled *L'Architettura delle Performance. LA 6.1_PL 35_Analisi del dominio*, in Italian. Available upon request.

The ELEVATE (E-LEarning with Virtual interAcTive Experience) project,[5] led by the company Delta Informatica, was aimed at building a tool suite at support of the development and management of interactive multimedia (IMM) exercises for online professional training on Standard Operating Procedure (SOP) in emergency management. Our role in the project was twofold: on one side we were expected to support the company in the elicitation of requirements for the ELEVATE tool suite and on the other side to define a methodology for the creation of IMM exercises with the ELEVATE tool suite and evaluate the effectiveness of such IMM exercises in SOP training [22]. Along the first objective, we first performed a GO analysis of the project's application domain to understand the role of the different domain stakeholders in SOP training when online and in-presence approaches are mixed [21]. This model helped understand the collaborative process that takes place when designing such training sessions and provided information about four specific roles of the users of the intended ELEVATE tool suite. This has served as a preliminary step to elicit key requirements for the ELEVATE tool suite and its companion methodology. Specifically, together with the team of developers, we derived a set of user story for each identified role, which guided the development of the tool suite following a SCRUM approach. In this case we opted for *i** 2.0 [5] and the modeller *piStar* [23]. Indeed, one of the company's software engineer was already familiar with *i** 2.0 and the *piStar* tool that were taught at that time in the RE course at the University of Trento.

Common to the three considered project is the complexity of the application domain, along two dimensions: the organizational dimension and the knowledge dimension, due to the specialized technical skills involved. Modelling stakeholders with their main goals and mutual dependencies in the *as-is* situation helped stakeholders to increase awareness about critical aspects, including the need of improving collaborative processes. It also supported us in understanding perceived challenges and needs. Modelling the *to-be* situation with changes obtained thanks to the introduction of a new software system helped capture and prioritize stakeholders' expectations and provided a rationale for the requirements of the system to be built. Looking a posteriori at the choice of using *i** (*Tropos*), we can state that putting in place strategies (means) that leverage on its *comprehensibility appropriateness*, *domain appropriateness*, and *audience appropriateness* qualities, we were able to build models that were comprehended by domain stakeholders.

4 Researcher's Perspective

From a researcher's perspective, a challenge we encountered in different projects regards the trade-off between *domain appropriateness* and *audience appropriateness*. To illustrate it we take examples from four projects. Table 2 summarizes

[5] An industrial innovation project funded by the Autonomous Province of Trento, Italy, within the framework *Legge Provinciale 6* (https://elevate.deltainformatica.eu/).

Table 2 Characteristics of the considered projects, from the researcher's perspective

Project	Goals of modelling	Audience	Means
RISCOSS 2012–2015	Organization and risk analysis in OSS domain	Risk experts and *Tropos* experts	*Tropos metamodel extension*: concepts related to risk modelling added in the *Tropos* metamodel
AMICO 2009–2010	Regulatory compliance in the Electronic Health Record domain	*Tropos* experts, organizational experts, and lawyers	*Tropos metamodel extension*: concepts related to norms added in the *Tropos* metamodel
ACUBE 2008–2011	Domain analysis for Ambient Assisted Living	IT researchers, HCI experts, and *Tropos* experts	*Integration at process level*: joint use of *Tropos* and Persona methodologies
ELEVATE COVID19 2020–2023	User feedback as means to assess stakeholders' goals	*Tropos* experts, researchers, and technologists	*Integration of metamodels*: connection of *Tropos*, GQM, and Business Intelligence metamodels

relevant information about them, namely, the project's acronym and the time period, the main purposes of the GO modelling, the RERs involved in the project (column *Audience*), and strategies (column *Means*) to address the most relevant between *domain appropriateness* and *audience appropriateness* qualities.

For the first two, namely, the RISCOSS and AMICO projects, priority was given to achieve *domain appropriateness*, which requested to consider enhancing the expressiveness of the language to include concepts belonging to the jargon of the two domains at the same level of abstraction of the *i** concepts. This was possible thanks to the work of researchers in the area of conceptual modelling. For the other two projects (ACUBE and ELEVATE COVID19), the different skills and knowledge of audience's members suggested addressing *audience appropriateness* by integrating *i** modelling with other methods.

RISCOSS (Risk and Cost of Open Source Software Adoption), a European research project [6], had the objective of specifying a methodology for the representation and reasoning on the risks and opportunities in adopting open-source software components in the implementation of a software system, especially in the case of large and critical systems. Several aspects had to be considered in this case: on the one side, the objectives of the company producing the software and the needs of the stakeholders that can be captured by *i** and, on the other side, the set of risks and the impact of risks on those objectives and needs. In this domain the risks are mainly due to the quality of the software or to the strong connection that is established when components from third parties must be included in a software system. The project aimed at providing decision-makers a modelling framework and related reasoning techniques that support combining the perspectives of goals and risks in the domain.

In the RISCOSS project, the *i** metamodel has been extended to represent the concepts of risk events and impact of the risk on the goals of the organization resulting in the *RiskML* language [26]. Specifically, the risk was represented as a concept that is composed by a risk *Event*, a *Situation*, in which an event can happen or not happen with a given probability, and a set of relationships between these two concepts to represent, for instance, the fact that a given situation can *Expose* or *Protect* from the event. The event is connected to the *i** goal concept with an *Impact* relationship describing the effect of the event on the different goals of the actors. In the project it was explicitly decided to avoid representing at this level of abstraction the concepts of "risk level" that are typical in the risk assessment domain but that are at a lower level of abstraction with respect to the other concepts that mainly focus on the structure of the organization and of the related risks. This choice represents a trade-off between the need of representing concepts that are domain specific to accomplish an *audience appropriateness* quality and the fact that some of these concepts are intrinsically not adequate to be represented at the same level of abstraction of the *i** language. The evaluation of the approach has been performed together with the risk experts of the industrial partners of the project, all of them involved in OSS-based software development. Experts have found particularly relevant and new the possibility of having a holistic vision on risks and their consequences throughout the entire organization, so confirming the *domain appropriateness* of the language extensions. Similar approaches to risk modelling have been proposed in literature such as in the case of the KAOS methodology [28] where the goal-oriented modelling language has been extended with the concept of obstacle as a means to represent possible risks impacting the satisfaction of goals, so resulting in a method that includes both the dimensions in a unified modelling framework.

The same considerations concerning the extension of the metamodel and language apply to the project AMICO, in which we took advantage of the *Nomos* language, an extension of *Tropos* with concepts related to norms, which was under development in the context of two PhD research works [11, 25].

The AMICO project focused on the social and health assistance of patients having serious and long-term health diseases such as cognitive problems. The objective was that of setting up an Electronic Health Record serving as knowledge hub for recording the conditions of the patients including medical screenings, relevant events, and health problems. Given the nature of the information collected and maintained in the system, it was of paramount importance to integrate the analysis of the corpus of norms related to privacy and security in the healthcare and social domain. This aspect led to consider the possibility to integrate the modelling of law and norms into the representation of the actors and goals of the domain.

In this case the important aspects to be represented were the relationships among the different actors and related goals impacted by the norms. Similarly to RISCOSS also in this case, the extension has been limited to a set of concepts to ensure the *domain appropriateness* and the *audience appropriateness* criteria. Specifically, the concepts of *Situation*, used to model events relevant for the norms, and *Norm* have been included in the metamodel, also distinguishing the different deontic characteristics of the norms defined by Hohfeld [8], namely, if the *Norm* concerns a *Right*, a *Duty*, a *Power*, or a *Liability* for an actor. Relationships have also been identified between the Situations and the Norms, between the different Norms and between the Norms and the Goals of the *Tropos* actors. This last type of relationship is the way to connect the normative concern in the domain to the organizational concern described via *Tropos*. Several other concepts exist in the legal domain, such as those describing the specific penalties in case of norm violations, that have not been represented in the extension to avoid mixing different levels of abstraction in the resulting modelling framework.

The resulting language also fits to criteria related to *audience appropriateness*. The concept of Norm and the characterization into Right and Duty, Power, or Liability allows the legal domain expert to recognize in her own jargon the kind of impacts the different norms in the domain have on the goals of the organization.

The appropriateness of the language for the purpose of understanding the impact of norms has been studied in an experiment with domain experts that had to decide how the new privacy rules introduced in European laws were influencing the goals of the organizations involved in the management of the Electronic Health Record systems [11].

Differently from the extensions introduced in RISCOSS and AMICO, in the projects ACUBE [13] and ELEVATE COVID19 [1], the strategy was to avoid any extension to *i** or *Tropos*. The aim instead was that of integrating the GO modelling and analysis with other requirements elicitation, modelling, and analysis techniques.

In ACUBE we designed a methodology and a tool to implement an Ambient Assisted Living framework to be introduced in critical environments, such as social residencies or private houses for patients affected by Alzheimer's disease. The framework was based on two layers: a set of heterogeneous sensors and IoT technologies for perception and actuation in the environment and an intelligent coordination system to implement a semiautomated decision-making layer on top of the sensors and actuators layer. The social nature of the project generated several concerns related to human computer interaction, privacy, and safety issues. These concerns were the stimulus for the deep analysis of the requirements of the actors (e.g., patients, families, nurses, doctors), of their needs in the context of the domain, and of the relationships among them.

In the project we used methods and concepts proposed in the user-centered design methodology. Specifically, we applied the method *Persona* [4] that focuses on the extraction and modelling of archetypes of the domain stakeholders along with their needs, goals, daily tasks, preferences, and desires, with the objective to design a concrete representation of the typical domain actors. The same information has been exploited to specify a model of the domain using *Tropos*. The use of the two methods allowed on the one side to extract and validate the characteristics of the different actors in the domain also thanks to the validation activities of the modelled Personas made with stakeholders in interviews and focus groups and, on the other side, to formalize the elicited and validated knowledge into *Tropos* actors, their internal goals, and their social interactions identified and modelled via *Persona*. It is interesting here to notice that *Persona* and *Tropos* share some of the concepts for the description of the characteristics of the actors (goals, activities, desires) so facilitating the integration of the two methods in a coherent methodology and analysis process [14].

In a follow-up research of the ELEVATE project, we explored how to design feedback channels for users of online training applications, such as that set up by the local government for instructing citizens about regulations during COVID-19 pandemic. In this context the online user feedback can provide a way to assess how the goals of the designers and developers of the training applications have been met. These goals include learning objectives, as well as functional goals of the software application. The objective of our research was to define a systematic method to derive requirements for user feedback channels from goals of the developers of such training applications. The proposed solution, called *GO+GQM* method, is an example of integration among metamodels of different modelling frameworks; in fact it combines *Tropos*'s early and late requirements models with Goal-Question-Metric (GQM) analysis [2], which has been extended with the concept of *Indicator* and *Indicator level* borrowed from Business Intelligence approaches [9]. In a nutshell, the *GO+GQM* method supports the developer for specifying online feedback channels as follows: Once a goal model of the app functionalities (i.e., a *Tropos* late requirements model) is built, a GQM analysis is performed on the functional goal with the purpose to identify questions the developer would like to answer by analyzing online user feedback. Metrics for a given question depends on the task that operationalizes a functional goal in the *Tropos* model. For instance, given the goal to have COVID-19 rules learned by interactive exercises that users of the training application can perform online, monitoring the number of accesses in a time period, or the number of users that completed the exercises successfully, or the average time spent on a piece of exercise helps assess to what extent the goal has been met. These monitor mechanisms are type of implicit user feedback that can complement explicit feedback channels through which users can state if they perceived the training experience as useful or not.

The *GO+GQM* method has been defined in the context of an action research described in [1]. The method has been applied to two different projects, and a first evaluation of quality in use, as perceived by developers, has been performed via a questionnaire distributed to the company's developers. Results have shown that the integration seems to be in line with the objective of *audience appropriateness* since it fits the way developers refer to the concepts related to the feedback management.

Summarizing the experience concerning the strategies used in the different projects, in RISCOSS and AMICO, the approach has been to identify concepts to be added to the *i** or *Tropos* modelling language extending the metamodel and the visual notation. This is a heavy approach since the extensions should be carefully designed in order to maintain a homogeneous modelling framework in terms of the level of abstraction of the new concepts that are introduced in the metamodel. In ELEVATE a lighter approach was adopted, consisting in the integration of different existing metamodels and their visual languages. Here attention has been posed to the level of abstraction of the different languages to precisely define the interactions among the metamodels. Finally, in ACUBE the decision was that of using different languages together with *i** to cover various modelling perspectives in the domain, leaving the integration among the different perspectives at the methodological and modelling process level. This approach is easier to be implemented if the different languages share bridging concepts as in the case of *Persona* and *Tropos* where the concepts of actor, goals, and activities/tasks have been the bridge.

5 Discussion

We have presented an analysis of our experience with *Tropos* and *i** in research and technological innovation projects. A recurring question we encountered can be expressed as follows: *should we use i* or not?* In the a posteriori reflection presented in this chapter, we have addressed this question from two different perspectives, namely, the requirements analysts and the RE researchers' perspectives. We referred to quality factors for the models and modelling languages, which have been proposed in the literature. We would like to highlight that it was not possible to adopt a systematic quantitative approach to this postmortem analysis, but rather a qualitative one. The results, while not claiming to be generalizable, can be summarized in terms of the following lessons learned.

The *comprehension* goal was a key objective in IT innovation projects in which we played the role of REAs, who had first to understand the domain and stakeholder needs. *i** concepts, such as that of role, goal, and dependency for goal achievement, were understandable by domain stakeholders. In this case, *domain appropriateness* was achieved by using a subset of the language constructs.

Audience appropriateness was relevant both in industrial and in research projects. In industrial projects, in which we mainly acted as REAs, the strategy was to use simple strategic dependency diagrams. This helped domain stakeholders to familiarize with the language and propose revisions when discussing as-is and to-be models. Differently, in research projects, the opportunity to exploit different skills and knowledge of audience members leads to different strategies, namely, to integrate *i** modelling with other requirements or analysis methods.

Domain appropriateness has been addressed in the considered research projects, by extending the *i** metamodel. This has been achieved thanks to the effort of researchers who paid attention to aspects of semantic coherence, reasoning tool support, and semiotic qualities (*comprehensibility appropriateness*) for the choice of the symbol notation for the new constructs. Moreover, empirical evaluation of the quality of the extended language was performed. That is, adopting the strategy of extending *i** with domain concepts generally turns out to require considerable effort, which can affect the *time-to-market* factor. On the other hand, this approach can lead to a more robust and generalizable requirements modelling solution, with respect to results obtained by integrating basic *i** modelling with other requirements elicitation and analysis method. The latter resulted to be the preferable strategy when *time-to-market* was an issue, and we could count on experts of the different methods collaborating in the project team.

Acknowledgments We would like to thank the many collaborators in the projects mentioned in this chapter and in particular Paolo Bresciani, Paolo Busetta, Daniele Dellagiacoma, Xavier Franch, Artem Gabbasov, Paolo Giorgini, Fausto Giunchiglia, Renata Guizzardi, Silvia Ingolfo, Chiara Leonardi, Mirko Morandini, John Mylopoulos, Loris Penserini, Luca Sabatucci, Alberto Siena, Eric Yu, and Massimo Zancanaro. We also thank the organizers of *i** 2023 and of its Celebratory Symposium in honor of Prof. Eric Yu and the anonymous reviewers of this chapter.

References

1. Astegher, M., Busetta, P., Gabbasov, A., Pedrotti, M., Perini, A., Susi, A.: Specifying requirements for collection and analysis of online user feedback. Requir. Eng. **28**(1), 75–96 (2023). https://doi.org/10.1007/S00766-022-00387-3
2. Basili, V.R.: Goal question metric paradigm. Encyclopedia of Software Engineering, pp. 528–532 (1994)
3. Bresciani, P., Perini, A., Giorgini, P., Giunchiglia, F., Mylopoulos, J.: Tropos: an agent-oriented software development methodology. Auton. Agents Multi Agent Syst. **8**(3), 203–236 (2004). https://doi.org/10.1023/B:AGNT.0000018806.20944.EF
4. Cooper, A., Reimann, R., Cronin, D.: About Face 3: The Essentials of Interaction Design. Wiley, Hoboken (2007). https://www.worldcat.org/oclc/263717431
5. Dalpiaz, F., Franch, X., Horkoff, J.: istar 2.0 language guide. CoRR abs/1605.07767 (2016). http://arxiv.org/abs/1605.07767
6. Franch, X., Kenett, R.S., Mancinelli, F., Susi, A., Ameller, D., Annosi, M.C., Ben-Jacob, R., Blumenfeld, Y., Franco, O.H., Gross, D., López, L., Morandini, M., Oriol, M., Siena, A.: The RISCOSS platform for risk management in open source software adoption. In: Damiani, E., Frati, F., Riehle, D., Wasserman, A.I. (eds.) Open Source Systems: Adoption and Impact - 11th IFIP WG 2.13 International Conference, OSS 2015, Florence, May 16–17, 2015, Proceedings. IFIP Advances in Information and Communication Technology, vol. 451, pp. 124–133. Springer, Berlin (2015). https://doi.org/10.1007/978-3-319-17837-0_12
7. Hadar, I., Reinhartz-Berger, I., Kuflik, T., Perini, A., Ricca, F., Susi, A.: Comparing the comprehensibility of requirements models expressed in use case and tropos: results from a family of experiments. Inf. Software Technol. **55**(10), 1823–1843 (2013)
8. Hohfeld, W.N.: Fundamental legal conceptions as applied in judicial reasoning. Yale Law J. **26**(8), 710–770 (1917). http://www.jstor.org/stable/786270
9. Horkoff, J., Barone, D., Jiang, L., Yu, E., Amyot, D., Borgida, A., Mylopoulos, J.: Strategic business modeling: representation and reasoning. Software Syst. Model. **13**(3), 1015–1041 (2014)
10. Horkoff, J., Aydemir, F.B., Cardoso, E., Li, T., Maté, A., Paja, E., Salnitri, M., Piras, L., Mylopoulos, J., Giorgini, P.: Goal-oriented requirements engineering: an extended systematic mapping study. Requir. Eng. **24**(2), 133–160 (2019). https://doi.org/10.1007/S00766-017-0280-Z
11. Ingolfo, S., Siena, A., Mylopoulos, J., Susi, A., Perini, A.: Arguing regulatory compliance of software requirements. Data Knowl. Eng. **87**, 279–296 (2013). https://doi.org/10.1016/j.datak.2012.12.004
12. Krogstie, J.: Model-Based Development and Evolution of Information Systems: A Quality Approach. Springer Science & Business Media, Berlin (2012)
13. Leonardi, C., Sabatucci, L., Susi, A., Zancanaro, M.: Ahab's leg: exploring the issues of communicating semi-formal requirements to the final users. In: Pernici, B. (ed.) Advanced Information Systems Engineering, 22nd International Conference, CAiSE 2010, Hammamet, June 7–9, 2010. Proceedings. Lecture Notes in Computer Science, vol. 6051, pp. 455–469. Springer, Berlin (2010). https://doi.org/10.1007/978-3-642-13094-6_35

14. Leonardi, C., Sabatucci, L., Susi, A., Zancanaro, M.: Design as intercultural dialogue: coupling human-centered design with requirement engineering methods. In: Campos, P.F., Graham, T.C.N., Jorge, J.A., Nunes, N.J., Palanque, P.A., Winckler, M. (eds.) Human-Computer Interaction - INTERACT 2011 - 13th IFIP TC 13 International Conference, Lisbon, September 5–9, 2011, Proceedings, Part III. Lecture Notes in Computer Science, vol. 6948, pp. 485–502. Springer, Berlin (2011). https://doi.org/10.1007/978-3-642-23765-2_34
15. Liaskos, S.: On the intuitive comprehensibility of contribution links in goal models: an experimental study. Empir. Software Eng. **29**(1), 26 (2024). https://doi.org/10.1007/S10664-023-10376-X
16. Lindland, O.I., Sindre, G., Solvberg, A.: Understanding quality in conceptual modeling. IEEE Software **11**(2), 42–49 (1994)
17. Moody, D.L.: The "physics" of notations: toward a scientific basis for constructing visual notations in software engineering. IEEE Trans. Software Eng. **35** (2009). https://api.semanticscholar.org/CorpusID:18149322
18. Morandini, M., Penserini, L., Perini, A., Marchetto, A.: Engineering requirements for adaptive systems. Requir. Eng. **22**(1), 77–103 (2017). https://doi.org/10.1007/S00766-015-0236-0
19. Nguyen, C.D., Perini, A., Tonella, P.: Goal-oriented testing for mass. Int. J. Agent Oriented Softw. Eng. **4**(1), 79–109 (2010). https://doi.org/10.1504/IJAOSE.2010.029810
20. Perini, A., Susi, A.: Developing a decision support system for integrated production in agriculture. Environ. Model. Softw. **19**(9), 821–829 (2004). https://doi.org/10.1016/J.ENVSOFT.2003.03.001
21. Perini, A., Susi, A., Gabbasov, A., Busetta, P., Dellagiacoma, D., Astegher, M., Pedrotti, M., Longato, M.: Using i* to understand the domain of video tutorial for online training. In: Guizzardi, R.S.S., Mussbacher, G. (eds.) Proceedings of the Thirteenth International iStar Workshop Co-located with 28th IEEE International Requirements Engineering Conference (RE 2020). CEUR Workshop Proceedings, vol. 2641, pp. 13–18. CEUR-WS.org (2020). https://ceur-ws.org/Vol-2641/paper_03.pdf
22. Perini, A., Schneider, K., Bertolli, L.M., Susi, A., Gabbasov, A., Busetta, P., Pedrotti, M.: Multimedia interactive exercises for online training. Multim. Tools Appl. **82**(25), 38319–38343 (2023). https://doi.org/10.1007/S11042-023-15157-8
23. Pimentel, J., Castro, J.: pistar tool - A pluggable online tool for goal modeling. In: Ruhe, G., Maalej, W., Amyot, D. (eds.) 26th IEEE International Requirements Engineering Conference, RE 2018, Banff, AB, Canada, August 20–24, 2018. pp. 498–499. IEEE Computer Society, Washington (2018). https://doi.org/10.1109/RE.2018.00071
24. Pimentel, J., Castro, J.: pistar tool–a pluggable online tool for goal modeling. In: 2018 IEEE 26th International Requirements Engineering Conference (RE), pp. 498–499. IEEE, Piscataway (2018)
25. Siena, A., Armellin, G., Mameli, G., Mylopoulos, J., Perini, A., Susi, A.: Establishing regulatory compliance for information system requirements: an experience report from the health care domain. In: Parsons, J., Saeki, M., Shoval, P., Woo, C.C., Wand, Y. (eds.) Conceptual Modeling - ER 2010, 29th International Conference on Conceptual Modeling, Vancouver, BC, November 1–4, 2010. Proceedings. Lecture Notes in Computer Science, vol. 6412, pp. 90–103. Springer, Berlin (2010). https://doi.org/10.1007/978-3-642-16373-9_7
26. Siena, A., Morandini, M., Susi, A.: Modelling risks in open source software component selection. In: Yu, E.S.K., Dobbie, G., Jarke, M., Purao, S. (eds.) Conceptual Modeling - 33rd International Conference, ER 2014, Atlanta, GA, October 27–29, 2014. Proceedings. Lecture Notes in Computer Science, vol. 8824, pp. 335–348. Springer, Berlin (2014). https://doi.org/10.1007/978-3-319-12206-9_28
27. Susi, A., Perini, A., Mylopoulos, J., Giorgini, P.: The tropos metamodel and its use. Informatica (Slovenia) **29**(4), 401–408 (2005)
28. van Lamsweerde, A., Letier, E.: Handling obstacles in goal-oriented requirements engineering. IEEE Trans. Software Eng. **26**(10), 978–1005 (2000). https://doi.org/10.1109/32.879820, https://doi.org/10.1109/32.879820

29. van Lamsweerde, A., Darimont, R., Massonet, P.: Goal-directed elaboration of requirements for a meeting scheduler: problems and lessons learnt. In: Second IEEE International Symposium on Requirements Engineering, March 27–29, 1995, York, pp. 194–203. IEEE Computer Society, Washington (1995). https://doi.org/10.1109/ISRE.1995.512561
30. Yu, E.S.: Towards modelling and reasoning support for early-phase requirements engineering. In: Proceedings of ISRE'97: 3rd IEEE International Symposium on Requirements Engineering, pp. 226–235. IEEE, Piscataway (1997)

From *i** to the User Requirements Notation

Daniel Amyot and Gunter Mussbacher

Abstract The *i** language enables the conceptual modelling and analysis of actors and goals, along intentional, social, and strategic dimensions. This chapter explains how *i** influenced the development of the Goal-oriented Requirement Language (GRL), first standardized by the International Telecommunication Union in 2008 as part of the User Requirements Notation (URN). In addition to a historical perspective on *i** and the creation of GRL, the chapter reflects on the differences and commonalities between *i** and URN in terms of syntax, features, and analysis capabilities. It further explores other extensions of URN that go beyond the standardized version, in support of aspects, legal compliance, feature modelling, time extensions, and others. The global impact of *i** on goal modelling is also assessed through the lens of URN.

1 Introduction

In requirements engineering, goal modelling enables describing systems and their stakeholders, together with their goals and various types of relationships. This usually enables reasoning about completeness and consistency at a high level of abstraction, as well as supporting the analysis of trade-offs among potential ways of meeting goals and of what-if scenarios. In his thesis, nearly three decades ago, Eric Yu [42] pioneered the development of the *i** Framework, with a graphical notation (Fig. 1) and analysis procedures. At the time, *i** enabled the modelling of the social dimension and intentionality in socio-technical systems and agent systems, especially during early requirements engineering activities. Different views

D. Amyot (✉)
University of Ottawa, Ottawa, ON, Canada
e-mail: damyot@uottawa.ca

G. Mussbacher
McGill University, Montreal, QC, Canada
e-mail: gunter.mussbacher@mcgill.ca

X. Franch et al. (eds.), *Social Modeling Using the i* Framework*,
https://doi.org/10.1007/978-3-031-72107-6_2

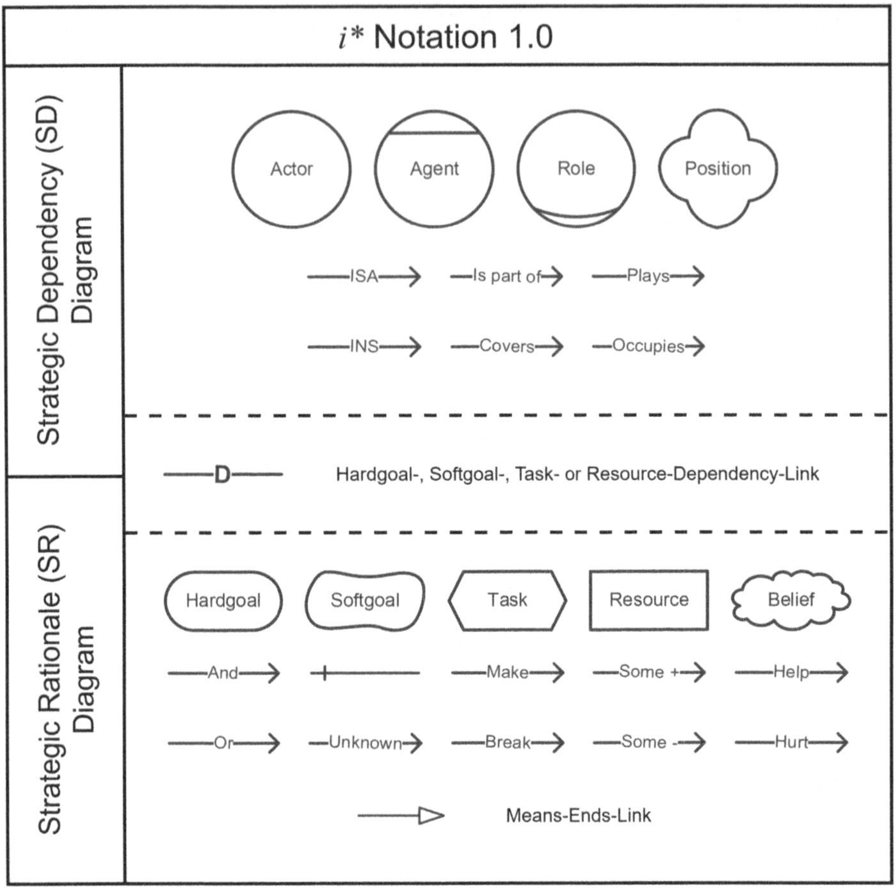

Fig. 1 Elements of the *i** notation (Siegbert v2 (own work), CC BY-SA 4.0, https://commons.wikimedia.org/w/index.php?curid=118255882)

of these models also supported the analysis of strategic dependencies and strategic rationales.

That framework was adopted by many researchers and users, and different variants and extensions of the original notation started to appear [26]. In particular, the *Goal-oriented Requirement Language* (GRL), which builds on the *i** Framework and on other concepts, was standardized in 2008 as part of ITU-T's *User Requirements Notation* (URN), with further revisions in 2012 and 2018 [29]. To this date, GRL remains the only international standard for goal modelling.

This chapter describes the origins and nature of GRL (Sect. 2) and explores how it relates to *i** both in terms of commonalities and differences, especially regarding syntaxes, features, and analysis capabilities (Sect. 3). It then explores important extensions to GRL that go beyond standard URN, in support of aspect-oriented modelling, legal compliance modelling and analysis, feature modelling, time extensions, and others (Sect. 4). The impact of *i** on GRL/URN and its community is further expanded in Sect. 5, before the chapter's conclusion in Sect. 6.

2 Goal-Oriented Requirement Language: Origins and Overview

This section describes the origins of GRL, as part of URN, in Sect. 2.1 and then gives an overview of the language in Sect. 2.2.

2.1 Historical Perspective

In the second half of the 1990s, several researchers at the University of Toronto (including Eric Yu and John Mylopoulos) developed two modelling notations that would form the basis of GRL, namely, the *Non-Functional Requirements* (NFR) Framework [18, 36] and the *i** Framework [42, 43]. GRL was meant to include some of the best concepts from these frameworks while keeping it small yet extensible.

The first version of GRL was produced by Lin Liu and Eric Yu, with input from Luiz Marcio Cysneiros, around 2000.[1] It proposed a graphical syntax based mainly on a subset of *i** that focused on intentional elements, links, and actors (for social modelling), supplemented with additional concepts supporting the kind of propagation-based analysis found in the NFR Framework. A textual syntax and an interchange XML schema were also proposed (with inputs from Daniel Amyot and Gunter Mussbacher, who were then researchers at Mitel, a telecommunications company).

Around the same period, a large Canadian telecommunication company (Nortel), heavily involved in international standardization activities, was looking for a new language that would enable standardization bodies to describe new wireless telephony services in an abstract way. They targeted a scenario/process language more abstract than the Message Sequence Charts (now UML sequence diagrams) used at the time. They became interested in the *Use Case Maps* (UCM) notation, mainly developed in the 1990s at Carleton University by Ray Buhr [15] with input from Ron Casselman [16] and Mark Vigder [41]. One advantage of UCM was that they decoupled behavior from the underlying structure of components.

UCM were also used in other companies including Mitel, which was also in favor of standardization. Mitel was using goal modelling for documenting architectural decisions, and researchers such as Tom Gray, Serge Mankovski, and Debbie Pinard suggested combining goal and scenario modelling as part of the proposal for a new standard, especially to support reflective systems (taking social aspects into

[1] See https://www.cs.toronto.edu/km/GRL/

consideration), and for feature personalization. Motorola also supported this way forward.

Requirements for the new combined *User Requirements Notation* (URN) language, developed first by Don Cameron (Nortel) and then by Daniel Amyot and Gunter Mussbacher (Mitel and then University of Ottawa), were first approved by ITU-T in 2003 as Recommendation Z.150, which was updated 8 years later [28]. The URN language description itself was first standardized in 2008 as Recommendation Z.151 [29], under the leadership of Amyot and Mussbacher, and with additional inputs from Eric Yu, Jennifer Horkoff, Jordi Cabot, Jason Kealey, Jean-François Roy, and others. The 2008 URN standard contains a definition of the abstract syntax with an integrated metamodel for goal and process/workflow modelling,[2] a graphical syntax for UCM and GRL, an XML-based interchange format, and modelling elements supporting the definition of analysis contexts. URN was revised in 2012 mainly to support indicators in GRL and to improve the execution mechanism of UCM models (called *traversal*). The 2018 version of the standard now includes a textual syntax for URN, similar to a programming language.

A more detailed overview of the UCM part of URN describes how it aligns with GRL [12]. Other historical details are also provided in a previous survey [7].

2.2 GRL Overview

The abstract syntax of GRL is shown in Fig. 2, whereas the concrete notation is shown in Fig. 3. The main concepts of GRL cover actors (stakeholders), intentional elements, and links. An *actor* is a holder of intentions that wants to achieve certain objectives or goals. Any entity that benefits from or is disadvantaged by a system may be modelled as an actor, regardless of whether it interacts with the system directly, indirectly, or not at all.

A *goal* is one kind of intentional element, together with tasks, resources, and beliefs. A goal may be a softgoal or a regular goal. The latter is differentiated from the former by having objective, agreed-upon criteria to determine the achievement of the goal. A *softgoal*, on the other hand, is often more vague and qualitative, as is often the case for nonfunctional concerns. A *task* describes an operationalization of a goal, i.e., what can be done to address the goal. Different tasks may be modelled for a goal, often with varying impacts on the goal and differing side effects on other goals. This allows for trade-off analysis among the tasks. The next type of intentional element is a *resource*, which captures something that needs to exist for a goal to be achieved or a task to be performed. GRL also supports the concept of a *belief*, meant to capture rationale for a task or goal. An intentional element may be

[2] https://github.com/JUCMNAV/projetseg-update/wiki/URNMetaModel

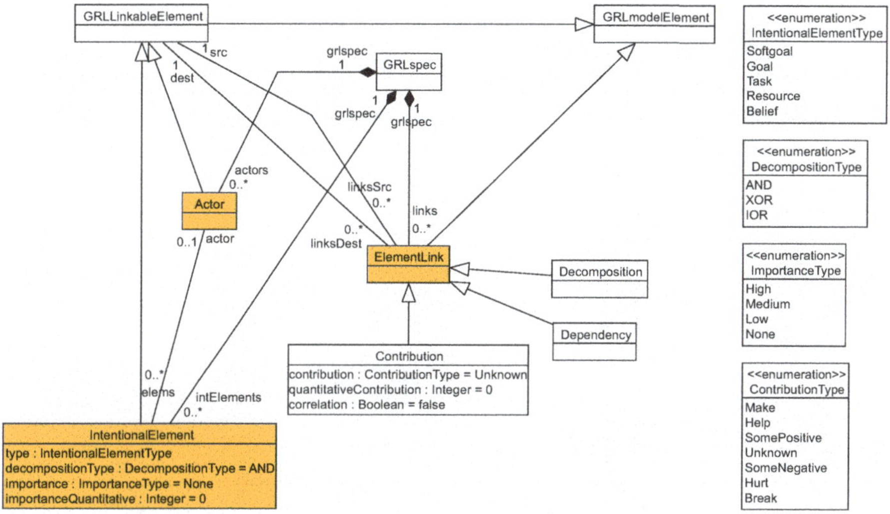

Fig. 2 Abstract syntax of GRL with key concepts highlighted

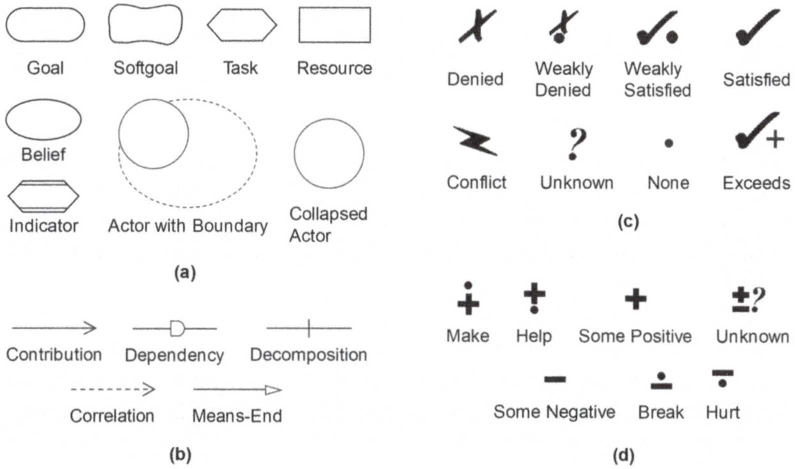

Fig. 3 Concrete notation of GRL. (**a**) GRL elements. (**b**) GRL links. (**c**) GRL satisfaction levels. (**d**) GRL contributions types

assigned a qualitative or quantitative *importance*, specifying the relative weight of the intentional element to the overall satisfaction of the element's actor.

Intentional elements are connected with each other by three types of links: contributions, decompositions, and dependencies. A *contribution* describes the positive or negative impact of one intentional element on another, either qualitatively with labels such as Help and Break or quantitatively within a range between −100 and 100. A contribution that describes a side effect is indicated in a GRL model

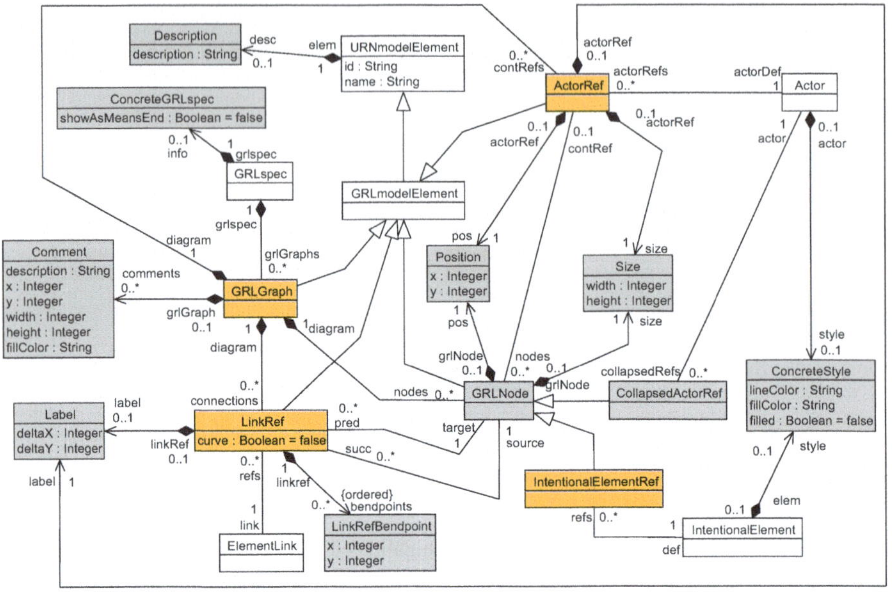

Fig. 4 Metaclasses supporting the concrete syntax of GRL with key concepts highlighted

with a *correlation* but otherwise acts like a contribution. A *decomposition* indicates that a parent intentional element is refined into a set of child intentional elements that either all (AND decomposition), at least one (OR decomposition), or exactly one (XOR decomposition) are required for the parent. The third type of link is a *dependency*, which is used for relationships of intentional elements from different actors but not for intra-actor relationships.

In addition to the core concepts of GRL, the abstract syntax in Fig. 2 includes a root class (*GRLspec*), containing all other GRL elements, and two abstract superclasses. The first, *GRLmodelElement*, captures common features across all GRL elements such as a name. The second, *GRLLinkableElement*, captures the ability to create links among GRL elements.

A GRL model may be visualized on several diagrams, which introduces additional concepts as shown in Fig. 4, which focuses on the metaclasses supporting the concrete syntax of GRL. A GRL diagram is called a *GRLGraph*. While the abstract syntax in Fig. 2 covers the definitions of core GRL model elements, a GRL diagram contains references to these definitions: an *ActorRef* references an actor, an *IntentionalElementRef* an intentional element, and a *LinkRef* a link. This allows the same GRL element to be used on several GRL graphs. The highlighted classes and the classes with gray background in Fig. 2 are solely needed for the visualization of GRL models.

In the URN standard, the semantics of GRL are specified with a set of detailed description of GRL analysis algorithms. In particular, the propagation of satisfaction values in a model, starting with an initial strategy, is covered in a *qualitative* algorithm (for qualitative satisfaction, importance, and contribution values), in a *quantitative* algorithm (for quantitative values), and in a *hybrid* algorithm (with qualitative contribution values mapped to quantitative values). These algorithms are further detailed and illustrated by Amyot et al. [9]. Figure 5 shows the concepts needed in support of these analyses. A *strategy* is a set of evaluations, where each *evaluation* assigns an initial satisfaction value to an intentional element. This initial value can either be qualitative (*qualitativeEvaluation*) or quantitative (*evaluation*). Furthermore, strategies may be grouped. Figure 6 shows the result of evaluating a strategy on a GRL model using a hybrid propagation algorithm,

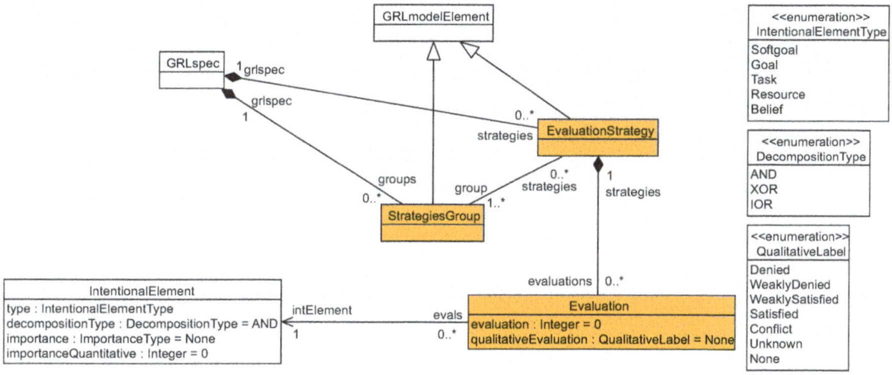

Fig. 5 Semantic domain of GRL in support of model evaluation with key concepts highlighted

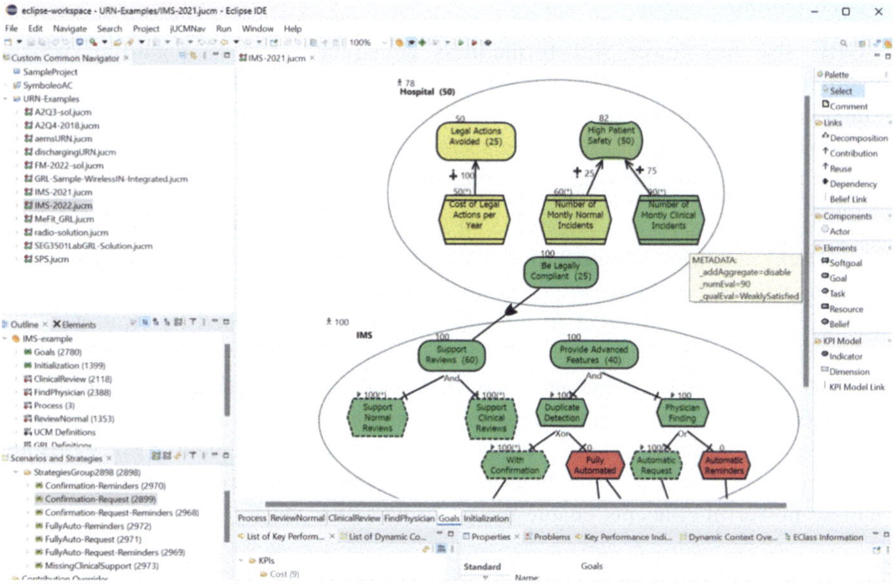

Fig. 6 Hybrid evaluation of a strategy in a GRL model, using the jUCMNav tool

using the jUCMNav[3] plug-in for Eclipse. The strategy's initial quantitative values are annotated with (*), and the greener the intentional element, the higher its satisfaction level. Since the last version of the standard, GRL's semantics has also been formalized by mapping GRL models to constraint satisfaction problems [23].

3 *i** and URN: Commonalities and Differences

GRL and *i** overlap substantially in form and intent. In particular, they both support:

- Basic actors
- The same types of intentional elements, including beliefs
- Intentional links: AND and OR decompositions, dependencies, and qualitative contributions
- Qualitative satisfaction values

They can hence both describe strategic dependency and strategic rationale views of goal models. There are also elements of the *i** Framework (see Fig. 1) that are not found in GRL:

- Advanced actor types (Agent, Role, and Position), which were considered less important in the application domains targeted by ITU-T
- Inter-actor links other than dependencies (ISA, Is part of, Plays, INS, Covers, Occupies), as there is only one type of actor in GRL
- A separate means-end link, subsumed in GRL by other links (e.g., Make contribution)

GRL also has fewer well-formedness constraints than *i** regarding which intentional elements can be connected by specific intentional links. Note that GRL, being extensible, can however capture the missing *i** elements/links and cover the additional well-formedness constraints should the need arise [8].

Standard GRL also provides new concepts not found in *i**:

1. Simple additions inspired from the NFR Framework and others include *correlation links*, qualitative/quantitative *importance* attributes for intentional elements (both explained in the previous section), as well as graphical comments.
2. GRL *strategies*, explained in the previous section, proposed by Roy et al. in 2006 [39].
3. *URN links*, which enable any pair of GRL/UCM modelling elements to be connected with a typed linked, as well as *metadata*, which are name-value pairs that can be used to annotate or stereotype modelling elements (Fig. 7). Both were provided in 2008. Together with user-defined well-formedness constraints, these powerful concepts enable the profiling and extension of GRL for specific

[3] https://github.com/JUCMNAV/projetseg-update/wiki/

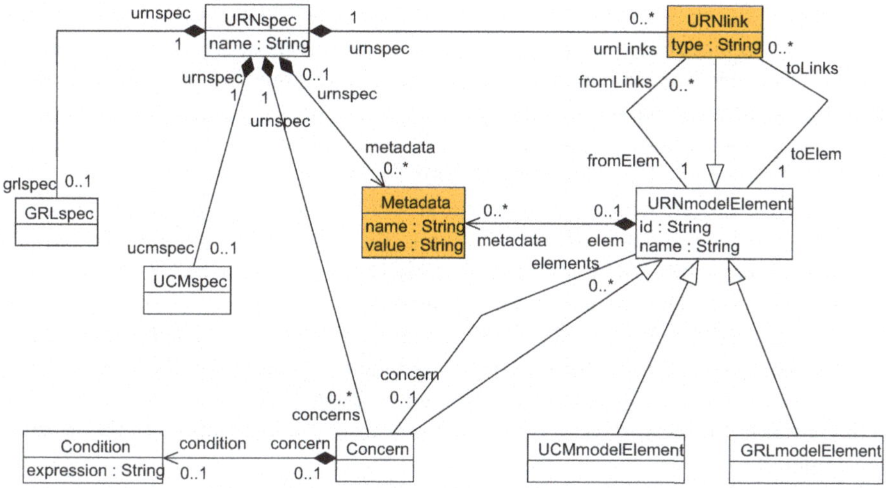

Fig. 7 URN links and metadata, which enable domain-specific profiles of GRL

domains [8], with past applications to healthcare, legal compliance, safety, and others. They also enable more formal consistency, completeness, and alignment analysis between the goal view in GRL and the process view in UCM [12].

4. In the 2012 edition of the URN standard, GRL was further extended with *indicators*, with a new symbol found in Fig. 3a. An indicator is a GRL model element that converts an observable value from the real world into a GRL satisfaction value (between −100 and 100). One example of a *conversion* is interpolations based on target, threshold, and worst-case parameters. Indicators, based on the work of Pourshahid and Chen [38] between 2007 and 2009, enable dealing with concrete values that stakeholders understand (e.g., in units such as meters and Euros) while normalizing these values against expectations in a way that integrates the results with existing propagation algorithms. Indicators also turn GRL models into monitoring and dynamic adaptation engines that can be fed external values, e.g., in adaptive systems.
5. *Qualitative indicators* were added in the 2012 edition of the URN standard based on work from Mussbacher, Kealey, Tremblay, and others [11]. Unlike regular indicators, which are continuous and numerical, qualitative indicators enable providing an explicit mapping between enumerated domain-specific values (e.g., bad, average, good, excellent) and quantitative GRL values (0, 33, 67, 100) or qualitative GRL satisfaction values.
6. *Contribution changes*, also added in 2012 [10], enable GRL contributions in a model to be overridden with different values in a given context, even when strategies are applied. As contribution levels are often difficult to specify precisely, this language feature helps assessing the impact of different contributions within one model, without the need for separate models.

Furthermore, standard GRL includes analysis capabilities not available for *i** in terms of *quantitative and hybrid* propagation algorithms, which exploit GRL's qualitative scales for contribution, satisfaction, and importance values (Figs. 2 and 5). Quantitative analysis enables more precise results than qualitative analysis, assuming that the model values can be obtained reliably. This results from the research of Roy and Ghanavati in 2006–2008 [9, 39].

Last but not least, while *i** has only a graphical concrete syntax, two concrete syntaxes exist for standard GRL in addition to the XML-based interchange format. A *textual syntax* for URN was added in 2018 based on work by Kumar and Mussbacher [31]. The textual syntax addresses scalability issues of large URN models that are difficult to handle with the graphical syntax and graphical editors.

Note that most of the additions to *i** included in standard GRL are however absent from the iStar 2.0 language, released in 2016 [19], which is much closer to the initial *i** Framework but provides a more formal underpinning in the form of a metamodel.

4 Beyond the URN Standard

Many extensions exist for URN that go beyond the URN standard including aspect-oriented modelling, legal compliance modelling and analysis, feature modelling, time extensions, and others.

1. In 2010, Mussbacher [35] incorporated *aspect-oriented modelling* concepts in URN with the Aspect-oriented User Requirements Notation (AoURN). Aspects address the issue of crosscutting concerns in models and programs. A crosscutting concern cannot be properly encapsulated with traditional decomposition techniques and has a widespread impact on many modelling elements, leading to poor separation of concerns and evolution problems. AoURN supports the encapsulation of crosscutting concerns in URN models (including GRL models) and their subsequent composition with the help of semantics-based matching.
2. In 2013, Ghanavati [25] introduced *Legal-URN*, a URN profile dedicated to capturing legal requirements with an extension to GRL and legal processes with an extension to UCM. The profile includes traceability links that enable compliance analysis between organization and legal models and between processes and legal goal models.
3. In the same year, Shamsaei [40] added support for *families of goal models*, akin to software product lines. This model family idea was further generalized, first by Palmieri [37] in 2015 and then by Alwidian [6] with union models in 2020.

4. In 2014, Liu et al. [34] integrated *feature modelling* with goal modelling supported by a single evaluation mechanism for both types of models. Feature models (AND/OR trees) are considered a special case of goal models (AND/OR graphs), and mandatory/optional feature links are mapped onto GRL contributions. Cross-tree feature constraints are expressed with OCL constraints in URN.
5. In 2015, Georg et al. [24] connected URN goal and scenario models with *activity theory*, a psychological paradigm. Activity theory helps understand the relationships between a system, the system's evolving context, and the system stakeholders. The developed URN profile and methodology allow for impact assessment of proposed system changes on social elements in the system, captured with a GRL view.
6. In 2017, Aprajita [14] considered the time dimension in GRL models with TimedGRL. *TimedGRL* enables the evaluation of a system over a longer period of time instead of a single snapshot in time. This extension allows, e.g., time-based functions to be defined for contribution values and intentional elements to be added to and removed from a model at different times.
7. In 2018, Duran [22] added the notion of *relative contributions* for reusability together with related evaluation enhancements. Relative contributions are needed to be able to combine independently developed *reusable goal models* where it cannot be assumed that these goal models adhere to the same assumptions when defining contribution values.
8. In the same year, Akhigbe [1, 2] developed a method for goal-oriented *regulatory intelligence* based on a GRL extension, with an integration between evaluated goal models and business intelligence applications.
9. Also in 2018, Fan and Anda [23] formalized GRL models with the help of *arithmetic semantics*. This work was then further extended to combined feature and goal models [13] to support *model optimization* in the context of adaptive systems.
10. In 2019, Alkaf et al. [3] proposed a forward *slicing* technique for URN models to address maintenance issues. The technique helps maintainers better understand how changes propagate within UCM models and between GRL and UCM models.
11. In 2020, Lessard et al. [32] created a GRL profile that captures the concepts found in *Service-Dominant Logic*, a recognized perspective on value creation in modern economies. A companion set of heuristics for eliciting requirements for service systems was shown to produce more requirements that were relevant, hence improving completeness during elicitation.
12. In 2021, Hassine et al. [27] provided a *game-theoretic semantics and method* for GRL, enabling the reconciliation of interacting stakeholders (captured as GRL actors) through reasonable trade-offs. Zero-sum game theory in GRL was further explored by Krishna in 2022 [30].

13. In 2022, Alwidian [5] extended GRL in a framework aiming to support *emotion*-oriented goals in early requirements elicitation. Concurrently, the same year, Alkhomsan et al. [4] also explored the adaptation of GRL for emotions modelling, with a healthcare case study.
14. In 2023, Daun et al. [20] extended GRL to model *human robot collaborations* while exploiting this extension to support analyzing safety threats in such collaborations.
15. In 2024, Chaudemar et al. [17] transformed GRL into a *mission description language* by extending it to better address the mission-based design of unmanned aerial vehicle (UAVs) and the analysis of stakeholder satisfaction under different degradation scenarios.

This non-exhaustive list of extensions to standard GRL, which spans nearly 15 years, highlights the diversity of the application domains as well as the originality of the scientific and practical solutions that were indirectly triggered by the existence of Eric Yu's *i**.

5 Impact of *i** on URN

Eric Yu's most cited publications related to GRL based on Google Scholar metrics are *Evaluating goal models within the goal-oriented requirement language* published in the *International Journal of Intelligent Systems* [9] with 380+ citations and *Designing information systems in social context: a goal and scenario modelling approach* published in *Information Systems* [33] with 248+ citations. The latter is the first and still one of the few publications that provide a methodology for using GRL and UCM during design. It still influences much more recent methodologies, including the one from Dongmo and Van der Poll [21], released in 2023.

The impact of Eric Yu's work is global, as can be seen from the Scopus statistics based on the following search query, performed in April 2024:

```
TITLE-ABS-KEY ( ( GRL AND
    ("goal-oriented" OR URN OR "User Requirements Notation" )
    OR "Goal-oriented Requirement Language" )
  AND ( EXCLUDE ( DOCTYPE , "cr" ) ) )
```

The search result included 150 publications authored by over 160 people from 25 countries. Even though half of these publications are in the computer science area, many other disciplines are also covered, as can be seen in Fig. 8. The distribution of papers over the last 22 years is illustrated in Fig. 9.

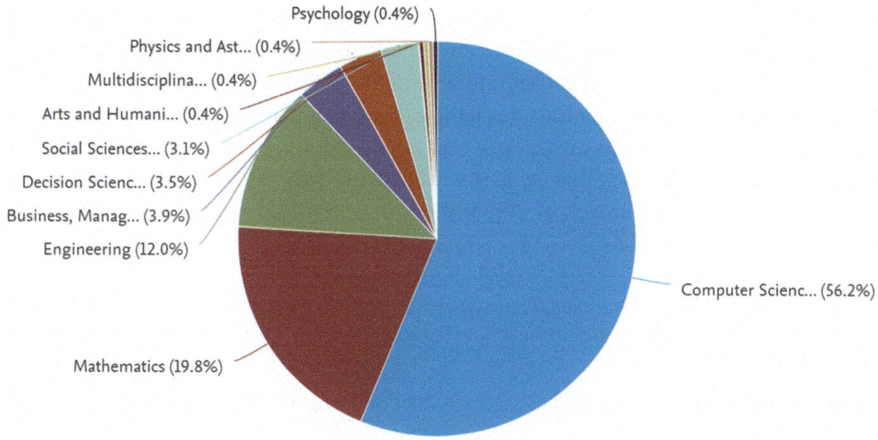

Fig. 8 Distribution of GRL publications over disciplines

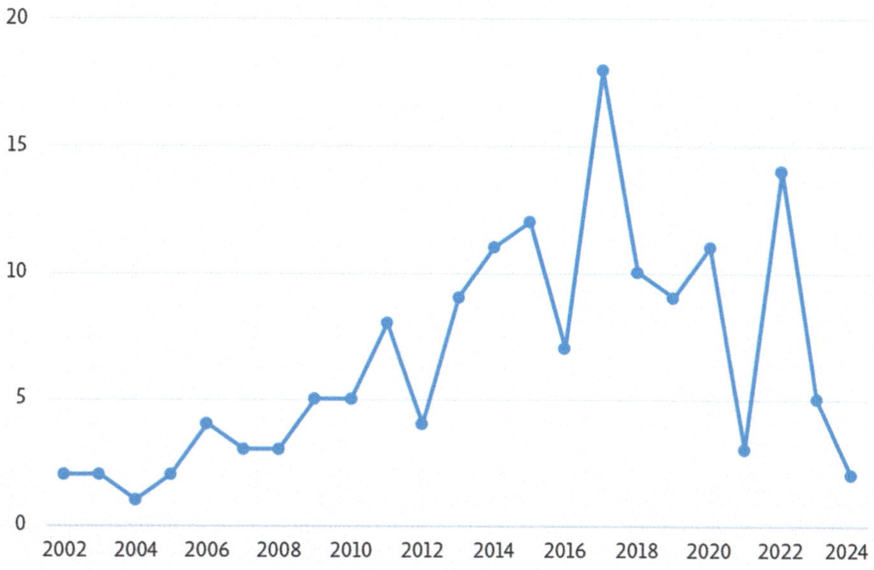

Fig. 9 Distribution of GRL publications over years

6 Conclusion

Yu's i^* Framework had a profound influence on the development of the Goal-oriented Requirement Language. The latest version of URN (2018) [29] remains the only international standard for goal modelling. This chapter (i) gave a historical perspective on i^* and the creation of GRL; (ii) reflected on their differences and commonalities in terms of syntax, features, and analysis capabilities, with a focus on six GRL concepts not found in *i** or iStar 2.0, in addition to more comprehensive analysis capabilities and a textual concrete syntax; and (iii) further explored 15 other extensions of URN/GRL that go beyond the standardized version, e.g., in support of aspects, legal compliance, feature modelling, time extensions, and diverse domain-specific profiles. The global impact of *i** on goal modelling is also assessed through the lens of URN, showing the immense reach of Yu's work through more than 150 publications from more than 160 authors in at least 25 countries and over two decades.

Acknowledgments We wish to extend our sincere gratitude to Prof. Eric Yu for his collaboration over the years. We also thank the organizers of iStar 2023 and of its Celebratory Symposium in honor of Prof. Eric Yu.

Competing Interests D. Amyot and G. Mussbacher are supported by their respective NSERC Discovery grants.

References

1. Akhigbe, O.S.: A Goal-Oriented Method for Regulatory Intelligence. PhD thesis, University of Ottawa (2018). https://ruor.uottawa.ca/handle/10393/38253
2. Akhigbe, O., Amyot, D., Richards, G., Lessard, L.: GoRIM: a model-driven method for enhancing regulatory intelligence. Software Syst. Model. **21**(4), 1613–1641 (2022). https://doi.org/10.1007/s10270-021-00949-z
3. Alkaf, H.S., Hassine, J., Binalialhag, T., Amyot, D.: An automated change impact analysis approach for User Requirements Notation models. J. Syst. Software **157** (2019). https://doi.org/10.1016/j.jss.2019.110397
4. Alkhomsan, M.N., Baslyman, M., Alshayeb, M.: Toward emotion-oriented requirements engineering: a case study of a virtual clinics application. In: 2022 IEEE 30th International Requirements Engineering Conference Workshops (REW), pp. 48–56 (2022). https://doi.org/10.1109/REW56159.2022.00017
5. Alwidian, S.: Towards extending the goal-oriented requirements language with emotion-oriented goals to support socio-technical systems. In: Proceedings of the 25th International Conference on Model Driven Engineering Languages and Systems: Companion Proceedings, pp. 306–311 (2022). https://doi.org/10.1145/3550356.3561547
6. Alwidian, S., Amyot, D.: "Union is power": analyzing families of goal models using union models. In: Proceedings of the 23rd ACM/IEEE International Conference on Model Driven Engineering Languages and Systems, pp. 252–262. ACM, New York (2020). https://doi.org/10.1145/3365438.3410963
7. Amyot, D., Mussbacher, G.: User Requirements Notation: the first ten years, the next ten years. J. Software (JSW) **6**(5), 747–768 (2011). http://www.jsoftware.us/vol6/jsw0605-1.pdf
8. Amyot, D., Horkoff, J., Gross, D., Mussbacher, G.: A lightweight GRL profile for i* modeling. In: Advances in Conceptual Modeling - Challenging Perspectives, pp. 254–264. Springer, Berlin (2009). https://doi.org/10.1007/978-3-642-04947-7_31
9. Amyot, D., Ghanavati, S., Horkoff, J., Mussbacher, G., Peyton, L., Yu, E.: Evaluating goal models within the Goal-oriented Requirement Language. Int. J. Intel. Syst. **25**, 841–877 (2010). https://doi.org/10.1002/int.v25:8

10. Amyot, D., Shamsaei, A., Kealey, J., Tremblay, E., Miga, A., Mussbacher, G., Alhaj, M., Tawhid, R., Braun, E., Cartwright, N.: Towards advanced goal model analysis with jUCMNav. In: Advances in Conceptual Modeling, pp. 201–210. Springer, Berlin (2012). https://doi.org/10.1007/978-3-642-33999-8_25
11. Amyot, D., Rashidi-Tabrizi, R., Mussbacher, G., Kealey, J., Tremblay, E., Horkoff, J.: Improved GRL modeling and analysis with jUCMNav 5. In: 6th International $i*$ Workshop, vol. 978, pp. 137–139. CEUR Workshop Proceedings (2013). https://ceur-ws.org/Vol-978/paper_26.pdf
12. Amyot, D., Akhigbe, O., Baslyman, M., Ghanavati, S., Ghasemi, M., Hassine, J., Lessard, L., Mussbacher, G., Shen, K., Yu, E.: Combining goal modelling with business process modelling: two decades of experience with the User Requirements Notation standard. Enterp. Model. Inf. Syst. Archit. **17**, 2:1–38 (2022). https://doi.org/10.18417/emisa.17.2
13. Anda, A., Amyot, D.: An optimization modeling method for adaptive systems based on goal and feature models. In: Proceedings of the Tenth International Model-Driven Requirements Engineering Workshop (MoDRE), pp. 10–20 (2020). https://doi.org/10.1109/MoDRE51215.2020.00008
14. Aprajita: TimedGRL: Specifying goal models over time. Master's thesis, McGill University, Canada (2017). https://escholarship.mcgill.ca/concern/theses/5425kd25m
15. Buhr, R.J.A.: Use Case Maps as architectural entities for complex systems. IEEE Trans. Software Eng. **24**(12), 1131–1155 (1998). https://doi.org/10.1109/32.738343
16. Buhr, R.J.A., Casselman, R.S.: Use Case Maps for Object-Oriented Systems. Prentice Hall, Hoboken (1996)
17. Chaudemar, J.-C., Aïello, O., de Saqui-Sannes, P., Poitou, O.: Mission-based design of UAVs. Syst. Eng. (2024). https://doi.org/10.1002/sys.21754
18. Chung, L., Nixon, B.A., Yu, E., Mylopoulos, J.: Non-Functional Requirements in Software Engineering, vol. 5. Springer Science & Business Media, Berlin (2000). https://doi.org/10.1007/978-1-4615-5269-7
19. Dalpiaz, F., Franch, X., Horkoff, J.: iStar 2.0 language guide. CoRR, abs/1605.07767 (2016). http://arxiv.org/abs/1605.07767
20. Daun, M., Manjunath, M., Jesus Raja, J.: Safety analysis of human robot collaborations with GRL goal models. In: Conceptual Modeling, pp. 317–333. Springer, Berlin (2023). https://doi.org/10.1007/978-3-031-47262-6_17
21. Dongmo, C., Van der Poll, J.A.: An improved user requirements notation (URN) models' construction approach. Systems **11**(6) (2023). https://doi.org/10.3390/systems11060301
22. Duran, M.B.: Reusable Goal Models. PhD thesis, McGill University, Canada (2018). https://escholarship.mcgill.ca/concern/theses/vx021h44b
23. Fan, Y., Anda, A.A., Amyot, D.: An arithmetic semantics for GRL goal models with function generation. In: International Conference on System Analysis and Modeling, pp. 144–162. Springer, Berlin (2018). https://doi.org/10.1007/978-3-030-01042-3_9
24. Georg, G., Mussbacher, G., Amyot, D., Petriu, D., Troup, L., Lozano-Fuentes, S., France, R.: Synergy between activity theory and goal/scenario modeling for requirements elicitation, analysis, and evolution. Inf. Software Technol. **59**, 109–135 (2015). ISSN 0950-5849. https://doi.org/10.1016/j.infsof.2014.11.003
25. Ghanavati, S.: Legal-URN Framework for Legal Compliance of Business Processes. PhD thesis, University of Ottawa, Canada, 2013. https://doi.org/10.20381/ruor-2935
26. Gonçalves, E., Castro, J., Araújo, J., Heineck, T.: A systematic literature review of iStar extensions. J. Syst. Software **137**, 1–33 (2018). ISSN 0164-1212. https://doi.org/10.1016/j.jss.2017.11.023
27. Hassine, J., Kroumi, D., Amyot, D.: A game-theoretic approach to analyze interacting actors in GRL goal models. Requir. Eng. **26**, 399–422 (2021). https://doi.org/10.1007/s00766-021-00349-1
28. ITU-T: Recommendation Z.150 (02/11) User Requirements Notation (URN) - Language requirements and framework (2011). http://www.itu.int/rec/T-REC-Z.150/en

29. ITU-T: Recommendation Z.151 (10/18) User Requirements Notation (URN) – Language definition (2018). http://www.itu.int/rec/T-REC-Z.151/en
30. Krishna, A.: GRL goal analysis using zero-sum game theory. Intel. Dec. Technol. **16**(3), 575–588 (2022). https://doi.org/10.3233/IDT-220031
31. Kumar, R., Mussbacher, G.: Textual user requirements notation. In: System Analysis and Modeling (SAM 2018), pp. 163–182. Springer, Berlin (2018). https://doi.org/10.1007/978-3-030-01042-3_10
32. Lessard, L., Amyot, D., Aswad, O., Mouttham, A.: Expanding the nature and scope of requirements for service systems through service-dominant logic: the case of a telemonitoring service. Requir. Eng. **25**(3), 273–293 (2020). https://doi.org/10.1007/s00766-019-00322-z
33. Liu, L., Yu, E.: Designing information systems in social context: a goal and scenario modelling approach. Inf. Syst. **29**(2), 187–203 (2004). ISSN 0306-4379. https://doi.org/10.1016/S0306-4379(03)00052-8
34. Liu, Y., Su, Y., Yin, X., Mussbacher, G.: Combined propagation-based reasoning with goal and feature models. In: 2014 IEEE 4th International Model-Driven Requirements Engineering Workshop (MoDRE), pp. 2736 (2014). https://doi.org/10.1109/MoDRE.2014.6890823
35. Mussbacher, G.: Aspect-oriented User Requirements Notation. PhD thesis, University of Ottawa, Canada (2010). https://doi.org/10.20381/ruor-13301
36. Mylopoulos, J., Chung, L., Nixon, B.A.: Representing and using nonfunctional requirements: a process-oriented approach. IEEE Trans. Software Eng. **18**(6), 483–497 (1992). https://doi.org/10.1109/32.142871
37. Palmieri, A., Collet, P., Amyot, D.: Handling regulatory goal model families as software product lines. In: Advanced Information Systems Engineering, pp. 181–196. Springer, Berlin (2015). https://doi.org/10.1007/978-3-319-19069-3_12
38. Pourshahid, A., Amyot, D., Peyton, L., Ghanavati, S., Chen, P., Weiss, M., Forster, A.J.: Business process management with the User Requirements Notation. Electron. Commer. Res. **9**, 269–316 (2009). http://dx.doi.org/10.1007/s10660-009-9039-z
39. Roy, J.-F., Kealey, J., Amyot, D.: Towards integrated tool support for the User Requirements Notation. In: System Analysis and Modeling: Language Profiles, pp. 198–215. Springer, Berlin (2006). https://doi.org/10.1007/11951148_13
40. Shamsaei, A., Amyot, D., Pourshahid, A., Braun, E., Yu, E., Mussbacher, G., Tawhid, R., Cartwright, N.: An approach to specify and analyze goal model families. In: System Analysis and Modeling: Theory and Practice, pp. 34–52. Springer, Berlin (2013). https://doi.org/10.1007/978-3-642-36757-1_3
41. Vigder, M.: Applying formal techniques to the design of concurrent systems. PhD thesis, Carleton University, Canada (1992). https://doi.org/10.22215/etd/1992-02275
42. Yu, E.S.K.: Towards modelling and reasoning support for early-phase requirements engineering. In: 3rd IEEE International Symposium on Requirements Engineering (ISRE'97), pp. 226–235 (1997). https://doi.org/10.1109/ISRE.1997.566873
43. Yu, E.S., Giorgini, P., Maiden, N., Mylopoulos, J.: Social Modeling for Requirements Engineering. MIT Press, Cambridge (2011)

Part II
Empirical Studies

*i** for Sustainability: A Case Study in Urban Management

Gerhard Lakemeyer and Martin Liebenberg

Abstract As the world is striving for more sustainability, the emerging megacities face enormous multi-stakeholder problems with complex trade-offs with overlapping as well as conflicting goals and multiple mutual interdependencies. Based on our earlier research on logic-based *i** extensions toward simulation and knowledge management, we pursue the question whether *i**-based analyses can help to understand and compare possible strategies in such settings. In this chapter, we summarize experiences from a case study concerning water management in megacities. It once again demonstrates the usefulness of the *i** modeling language and supporting tools as a foundation for fruitful discussions with non-IT stakeholders but also points to refinements of language concepts and analysis tools that promote deeper understanding and clarify positions and issues toward finding sustainable solutions.

1 Prologue by Gerhard Lakemeyer

This contribution to Eric Yu's Festschrift has taken a different turn from what was initially intended. The original title of the chapter was "*i** for Sustainability: Case Studies in Urban Management and Smart Farming Ecosystems." Matthias Jarke was supposed to be a co-author and write about a recent project, where *i** was used to model the interaction of stakeholders in smart farming ecosystems. In fact, the chapter was supposed to be an elaboration of a presentation we both gave in September 2023 in Hannover, Germany, at the Celebratory Symposium in honor of Eric as part of the 16th International *i** workshop. Tragically, Matthias fell ill in early 2024 and passed away in March of the same year. Sadly, his part of the chapter never got written. Matthias' sudden passing has been a shock to all of us and a tremendous loss for the information systems community at large. It is with deep sorrow that we dedicate this short chapter to him.

G. Lakemeyer (✉) · M. Liebenberg
RWTH Aachen University, Aachen, Germany
e-mail: gerhard@kbsg.rwth-aachen.de

X. Franch et al. (eds.), *Social Modeling Using the i* Framework*,
https://doi.org/10.1007/978-3-031-72107-6_3

So now we can only report on one case study that demonstrates the use of *i** in the context of sustainability. In particular, we show how *i** is capable of capturing the intricate interdependencies of stakeholders involved in managing water resources in megacities. For more details we refer the reader to [1]. For those who are interested in the other case study, we refer the reader to [5].

2 Modeling Water Resource Management in Megacities with *i**

Megacities are generally characterized as cities with a population of at least ten million people. Especially those megacities located in developing countries such as India are faced with serious problems as their infrastructure often cannot keep up with the enormous population growth. Part of the problem are vast areas of informal housing (aka slums), which are not properly connected to the water grid and even less so to the sewer system, resulting in bad conditions for waste disposal and various forms of pollution. In addition, water is often contaminated by industrial production and even agriculture within urbanized areas [6].

The interaction and underlying processes of the many stakeholders in megacities involving water supply or usage are still largely poorly understood. In order to arrive at a better understanding, we, together with Klaus Baier from the Chair of Engineering Geology and Hydrology at RWTH Aachen University, embarked on a project called SIKAMUS [1] in order to model the various stakeholders and their interdependencies and simulate the underlying processes. For the modeling part, *i** 's strategic rationale (SR) diagrams turned out to be ideal, and for the simulation part, we chose ConGolog [3], a programming language based on the situation calculus [8], which allows for the composition of complex concurrent actions. Fortunately, we did not have to start from scratch, but could rely on previous work in our group that developed SNet, which combined *i** and ConGolog in order to model and simulate the interaction of stakeholders in interorganizational networks [4]. In the following we briefly describe the changes to *i** and the SNet framework that we think are needed to faithfully capture the application scenario outlined above.

The changes we propose for *i** are perhaps best illustrated and motivated by an example. Figure 1 depicts (in a simplified form[1]) some of the interdependencies and interactions between water users and local water suppliers in a megacity like Hyderabad. The triangle in this diagram is an element from an *i** extension proposed by SNet called precondition-effect element. In the example, the task "complain about quality" fulfills the precondition "local discontent with water supply." Under the semantics originally given by SNet, this would immediately trigger the effect (task) "gather affected people," which is not what is intended in

[1] Besides simplifying the application scenario, the diagram also leaves out dependency links usually found in *i**, and agents are depicted using the "Role" symbol.

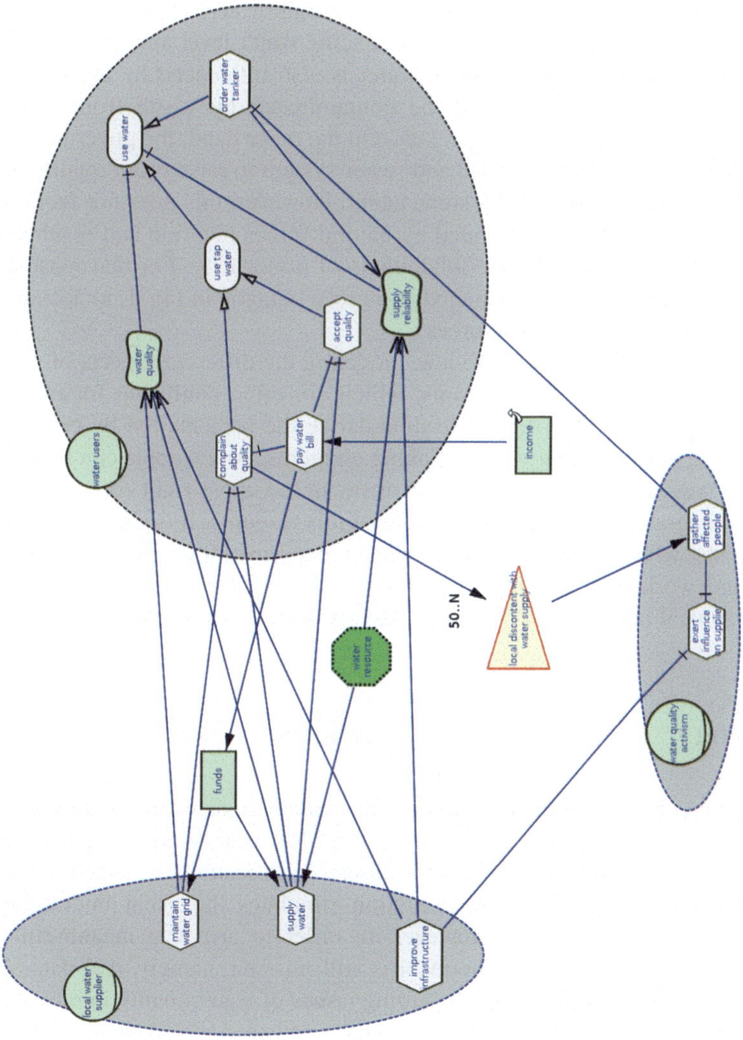

Fig. 1 A small example model of water usage in a megacity

this scenario. Instead the effect should only be triggered if a certain number of agents (here: at least 50) have complained about water quality. In order to model such a threshold, we decided to extend the semantics of preconditions by decorating the edge leading into the precondition by a numeric range in a way similar to what can be found in UML diagrams. Here "50..N" stands for "at least 50."

Another peculiar feature not normally found in applications of *i** is the concept of *nature*, in particular, natural resources like groundwater, which is affected by natural phenomena like rain and floods influencing water level and quality, among other things. In addition, the quality of water is also influenced by agents within a megacity. For instance, water can be contaminated by waste from informal households as well as production processes. On the other hand, the government can decide to build or extend a water grid and sewer system to raise water quality. In *i** resources are typically provided by some agent. However, this does not seem to fit resources like water, which is provided by natural forces like rain and is otherwise influenced by other agents like the inhabitants of a megacity. For that reason, we decided to add a novel element, depicted as a green octagon in Fig. 1, to account for the special category of natural resources.

From a representational point of view, modeling the different aspects of megacities tends to lead to huge *i** diagrams, which are often confusing for users. To overcome this problem, we propose to modularize the presentation by connecting separate diagrams using what we call linking elements. An example can be seen in the "income" resource of Fig. 1, where an arrow in the upper right corner indicates a link to the diagram describing the provider of this resource. It is also worth noting that geologists, who by and large have little IT expertise, found it very natural to construct and work with *i** diagrams. This can be attributed in part to the very intuitive graphical notation of *i** but also the modularization mentioned above.

3 Turning *i** Diagrams into Simulations

With an *i** model of the interdependencies and interactions of the stakeholders in a megacity in hand, we can in principle use the SNet framework to automatically generate ConGolog programs (with appropriate modifications to account for the newly introduced features), whose execution simulates the agent interaction as prescribed by the *i** diagrams. However, in order to arrive at meaningful and realistic simulations, a critical component is still missing, namely, real data about actual locations and their properties regarding issues of water quality in megacities.

Over many years geologists from Aachen have gathered such data about groundwater quality, water management, and urban growth in megacities like Hyderabad (India), Guangzhou (China), and Yogyakarta (Indonesia) [7, 9, 10].

From this data a semantic geodatabase was built and stored as an OWL database [2]. It contains information about land-use units, where each of them represents a piece of land in a megacity. In short, the information is about what a particular piece of land is used for, what kind of housing and workplaces are placed on it, and what is

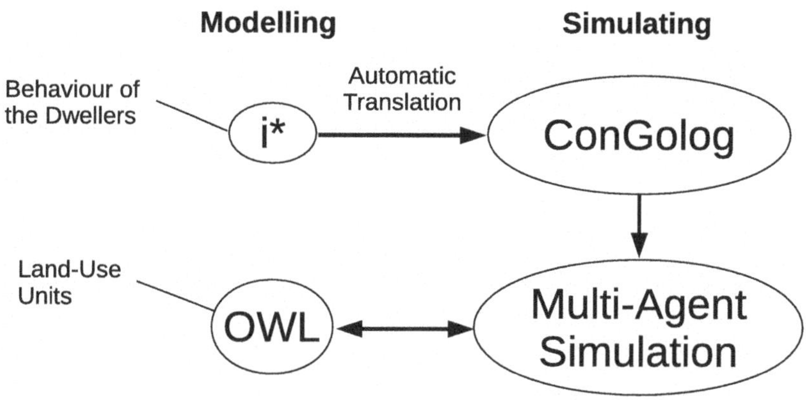

Fig. 2 A sketch of the SNet simulation environment augmented by an OWL database

located in its neighborhood. In addition, geological properties of the land are stored as well.

Figure 2 shows a rough sketch of our simulation environment. In order to run a simulation, agents need to be instantiated. Among other things, this means that they are assigned a name, their roles and values specifying how softgoals should be considered when fulfilling tasks and goals. Furthermore, the OWL data is used to situate each agent within a megacity, also telling the simulation framework what surrounds the agent. For more details we refer to [1].

4 Conclusion

This ends our brief excursion into *i**'s role in trying to model and understand water resource management in megacities. If nothing else it has yet again demonstrated the power and versatility of *i** in areas far beyond those it was intended for originally. It also shows Eric's foresight and vision when he conceived *i** decades ago. Thank you, Eric, for your groundbreaking contributions to the field.

References

1. Baier, K., Mataré, V., Liebenberg, M., Lakemeyer, G.: Towards integrated intentional agent simulation and semantic geodata management in complex urban systems modeling. Comput. Environ. Urban Syst. **5**, 47–58 (2015)
2. Bechhofer, S., van Harmelen, F., Hendler, J., Horrocks, I., McGuinness, D.L., Patel-Schneider, P.F., Stein, L.A.: OWL Web Ontology Language Reference (2004)
3. De Giacomo, G., Lespérance, Y., Levesque, H.J.: ConGolog, a concurrent programming language based on the situation calculus. Artif. Intel. **121**(1–2), 109–169 (2000)

4. Gans, G., Lakemeyer, G., Jarke, M., Vits, T.: SNet: a modeling and simulation environment for agent networks based on i* and ConGolog. In: Advanced Information Systems Engineering, pp. 328–343. Springer, Berlin (2006)
5. Jarke, M., Koren, I., Piller, F.T., Elmaraghy, H.: Introduction to the minitrack on data spaces for sustainability and resilience in manufacturing. In: Bui, T.X. (ed.) 56th Hawaii International Conference on System Sciences, HICSS, pp. 3641–3642. ScholarSpace, 2023.
6. Kraas, F., Aggarwal, S., Coy, M., Mertins, G. (eds.): Megacities: Our Global Urban Future. Springer, Berlin (2014)
7. Putra, D., Baier, K.: Impact of urbanization on groundwater recharge – the example of the Indonesian Million City Yogyakarta. In: UN Habitat – United Nations Settlement Programs: Fourth session of the World Urban Forum, Nanjing, China, Documentations of Germany's Contribution to a Sustainable Urban Future (2008)
8. Reiter, R.: Knowledge in Action: Logical Foundations for Specifying and Implementing Dynamical Systems. The MIT Press, Massachusetts (2001)
9. Wakode, H., Baier, K., Jha, R., Azzam, R.: Analysis of urban growth using Landsat TM/ETM data and GIS – a case study of Hyderabad, India. Arab. J. Geosci. **7**(1), 109–121 (2014)
10. Wehrhahn, R., Bercht, A.L., Krause, C.L., Azzam, R., Kluge, F., Strohschön, R., Wiethoff, K., Baier, K.: Urban restructuring and social and water-related vulnerability in megacities – the example of the urban VIllage of Xincún, Guangzhou (China). Die Erde **139**(3), 227–249 (2008)

From Goal Models to Know-How Mapping

Arnon Sturm

Abstract Technology domains such as engineering evolve at a fast pace. To keep up to date with such domains, there is a need for researchers and practitioners to effectively and efficiently manage that knowledge. To address the challenge, this work proposes mapping out relevant know-how that is more accessible so all stakeholders can contribute. During the last decade, we have adopted the design science approach to develop a goal-oriented knowledge mapping approach called ME-MAP. We define the syntax and semantics of the language to facilitate the construction of maps and the reasoning on such maps. A series of evaluations indicated that the maps produced were easy to follow, allowed continuous evolution, facilitated easy modification through modularity capabilities, further supported reasoning about know-how, provided adequate expressiveness, and enabled searching know-how. We believe that such a knowledge mapping approach can further improve resource (knowledge) utilization, reduce "reinventing the wheel" phenomena, and further create links across communities.

1 Introduction

Engineering and technology domains are developing at a fast pace. To stay on top of a field, researchers and practitioners alike require effective and efficient management of the fast-growing knowledge landscape [7, 10]. Researchers need to have a good overview of technical problems in a domain and understand how well existing solutions can address those problems. They want to identify gaps in the current state of the art, guide their research activities, and offer alternative solutions. Practitioners want to quickly learn about the methods and techniques available so that they can choose to adopt or adapt those that will meet their specific needs.

One way to address the needs of knowledge management is through knowledge mapping. "A knowledge map—whether it is an actual map, knowledge "yellow

A. Sturm (✉)
Ben-Gurion University of the Negev, Beer-Sheva, Israel
e-mail: sturm@bgu.ac.il

X. Franch et al. (eds.), *Social Modeling Using the i* Framework*,
https://doi.org/10.1007/978-3-031-72107-6_4

pages", or cleverly constructed database—points to knowledge, but it does not contain it. It is a guide not a repository" [3]. Using a know-how framework, stakeholders can explore problems and solutions within a domain and their qualification properties. Having such maps would reduce the effort required to explore domains.

The research reported here proposes complementing the usual narrative and descriptive literature reviews, reports, and surveys in such technical domains with a structured know-how map called the means-ends maps (ME-MAP). The map takes advantage of the centrality of the means-ends relationship in technology domains and offers concepts and relationships to capture rationales and supporting evidence. The emphasis on the means-ends relationship is based on the observation that in developing novel technology systems that offer specific utilities to stakeholders, designers aim to provide solutions (means) that meet the relevant goals (ends) of the client and other stakeholders. By highlighting means-ends relationships, the ME-MAP can potentially provide a unifying view of a body of technical knowledge. With respect to available techniques for knowledge mapping, ME-MAP consists of limited modeling constructs that ease its learning and usage. It also provides a semantic mapping that can be used for reasoning and allows for continuous updates. The work reported here summarizes the research that we have performed during the last decade.

The chapter is organized as follows: In Sect. 2 we introduce the ME-MAP approach. In Sect. 3 we present the evaluation of the approach. In Sect. 4 we discuss the reasoning capabilities supported by the ME-MAP approach. In Sect. 5 we demonstrate the way we envision the search of know-how in ME maps. Finally, in Sect. 6 we conclude.

2 ME-MAP in a Nutshell

The ME-MAP approach draws its core concepts from the goal-oriented requirements engineering (GORE) paradigm [21]. In particular, we adopt concepts from the *i** framework, a language that includes at its core the means-ends relationships.[1] We first tested the approach's applicability using *i** as is [5] and evaluated its usage [18]. We then examined and refined the notation while applying our ME mapping approach to several technical domains [16, 20]. The proposed approach is expected to map out a domain, provide an overview of the identified problems and their properties, and offer a systematic review of proposed solutions to problems and associated properties, as well as those that discuss open issues. In the following, we list the key principles that led to the design of the ME-MAP approach.

[1] We focused on the goal-task models of *i**.

- **Ease of Use:** The language should be easy to use by users with different backgrounds. Thus, we decided on a limited number of concepts and relationship types.
- **Expressiveness:** The language expressiveness should not cover actual technical knowledge. Rather, language constructs are used to characterize and index knowledge sources. We focus on the expressiveness to differentiate between alternative solutions.
- **Reasoning:** The language should include precise semantics for its constructs to allow appropriate reasoning.
- **Process Support:** The approach should offer constructs that guide knowledge elicitation and modeling, such as guiding the modeler to look out for alternative solution approaches, as well as identifying properties that help distinguish between alternatives.

2.1 ME-MAP Syntax

In the following, we present the elements and links included in the proposed ME-MAP language and further illustrate the language constructs with examples from an analysis of a comprehensive survey article presenting the domain of business process variability modeling [9].

The visualization constructs of the language include the following:

- A **Task** is a key element in the means-ends hierarchy. A Task can be interpreted either as a problem or as a solution depending on its location within the hierarchy. A Task is named with a concise verb phrase. Tasks are graphically depicted as rectangular shapes. In Fig. 1, the task *Specify BP (Business Process)* is a problem that should be addressed, whereas the task *Specify BP Families* is a high-level solution for that problem.
- A **Quality** expresses a property that is desired for a task. In an ME map, a quality is depicted as an ellipse and is typically named using adverbial or adjectival phrases or quality nouns (e.g., "-ilities"). For example, in Fig. 1, *Accessibility* and *Executability* are qualities, which further characterize how a solution that supports the *Specify BP Families* task should be designed. A quality can be associated with a task or be linked to another quality independently of a specific task (we refer to this link later on).
- The ***achieved-by*** link represents the means-ends relationship. The arrow points from the "end" to the "means." For example, in Fig. 1, *Model Multiple Variants Jointly* is a means to accomplish *Model Variability*. The link indicates an alternative for achieving an end. Drilling down the map, the *Model Multiple Variants Jointly* task can be achieved either by approaches such as *Model Variability by Extension* or by *Model Variability by Restriction*.
- The ***consists-of*** link indicates that a task has several sub-parts; all are required for the parent task to be accomplished. For example, in Fig. 1, *Use Algorithm*

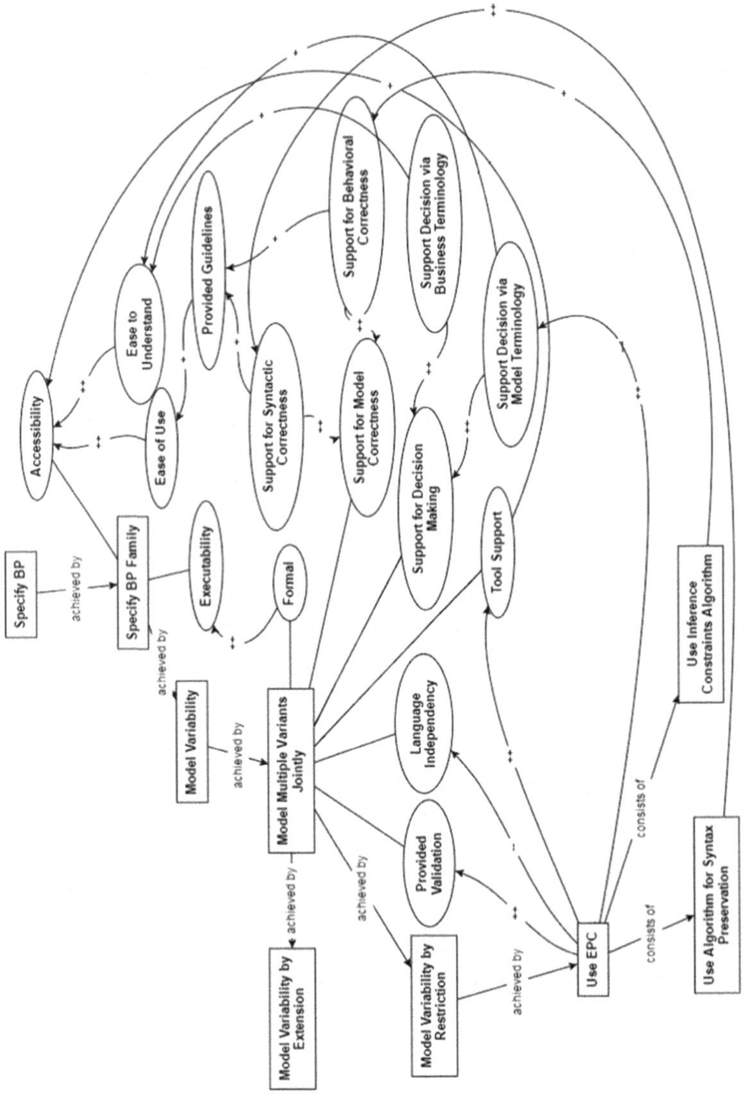

Fig. 1 A partial ME map of the business process variability modeling domain

for Syntax Preservation and *Use Inference Constraints Algorithm* need to be addressed when referring to *Use EPC*.

- The **association** link (an unlabeled and nondirectional link) indicates the desirable qualities for a given task. As mentioned, qualities associated with tasks should be taken into account when identifying and evaluating alternative ways for accomplishing the task. For example, in Fig. 1 the *Model Multiple Variants Jointly* task is associated with a number of qualities such as *Provided Validation, Language Independency*, and *Support for Correctness*. The tasks *Model Variability by Restriction* and *Model Variability by Extension* are alternative solutions for the *Model Multiple Variants Jointly*. The qualities associated with *Model Multiple Variants Jointly* should be addressed by each alternative solution independently, either by themselves or by tasks that further refine the solutions.
- The **contribution** link (a curved arrow) indicates a contribution toward a quality. Contributions can originate from a task or a quality and are always directed to a quality. The contribution ranges from strong negative (–) to strong positive (++). The contribution "polarity" and strength is determined subjectively by the map creator based on the available evidence. For example, in Fig. 1, *Use C-EPC* contributes positively to *Provided Validation* and negatively to *Language Independency*. Optionally, a contribution link may have a validity attribute to indicate how the contribution was determined (this is not shown visually). A quality can contribute to another quality. In such cases, the quality further elaborates and clarifies the other quality. For example, in Fig. 1 the quality *Ease of Use* is linked to the *Accessibility* quality, indicating that when a solution addresses the *Ease of Use* quality, then the solution also contributes to addressing the *Accessibility* quality.

All the concepts mentioned above should be associated with at least one reference to the knowledge sources and can be associated with contexts that can offer additional information on the environment or setting in which the concept is discussed.

2.2 ME-MAP Semantics

An ME map represents the hierarchy and links among the tasks with qualities. The semantics refers to the set of all possible sub-maps (or instances) that satisfy the constraints the original map imposes. That is, an instance consists of a set of interrelated tasks and qualities to achieve the task of the map while satisfying its constraints. For further defining the semantics, we set the following: Tasks except for the root task are *target* tasks for *achieved-by* or *consists-of* links. A quality can be associated with a task or supported by a task (via a contribution link, perhaps indirectly).

Definition 1 (Sub-map) For an ME map, $MEM = \langle \mathcal{T}, \mathcal{Q}, \mathcal{L}nk, \mathcal{L} \rangle$ ($\mathcal{T}$, a set of tasks; $\mathcal{Q}$, a set of qualities; $\mathcal{L}nk$, a set of links; $\mathcal{L}$, a set of labels), a sub-map of MEM is an ME map MEM'=$\langle \mathcal{T}', \mathcal{Q}', \mathcal{L}nk, \mathcal{L}\rangle$ where $\mathcal{T}' \subseteq \mathcal{T}, \mathcal{Q}' \subseteq \mathcal{Q}$, and $\mathcal{L}nk' \subseteq \mathcal{L}nk$.

Let $MEM = \langle \mathcal{T}, \mathcal{Q}, \mathcal{L}nk\rangle$ be an ME map. A legal instance of MEM is a *sub-map* $MEM' = \langle \mathcal{T}', \mathcal{Q}', \mathcal{L}nk'\rangle$ of MEM that satisfies the following constraints:

1. **Quality constraint**: $\mathcal{Q}'$ does not include dangling qualities.
2. *achieved-by* **link constraint**: A task can be achieved by only one task being selected from a set of alternatives. That is, the *achieved-by* links impose an *xor* constraint on the involved links. Formally:
   For a task $t \in \mathcal{T}$ and $S = \{t \xrightarrow{achieved-by} t_i \in \mathcal{L}nk\}$:
   $t \in \mathcal{T}' \iff (\exists i : t \xrightarrow{achieved-by} t_i \in (\mathcal{L}nk' \cap S)$ and $\forall j \neq i : \alpha = t \xrightarrow{achieved-by} t_j \in S \Rightarrow \alpha \notin \mathcal{L}nk')$.
3. *consists-of* **link constraint**: If a task belongs to an instance, then its involved *consists-of* links should also be part of that instance. That is, *consists-of* links impose an *and* constraint on the involved links. Formally:
   For a task $t \in \mathcal{T}'$, and $\beta = t \xrightarrow{consists-of} t_i$: $\beta \in \mathcal{L}nk \rightarrow \beta \in \mathcal{L}nk')$
4. **Association link constraint**: For each task $t \in \mathcal{T}'$, if $t \xrightarrow{assoc} q \in \mathcal{L}nk$, then $q \in \mathcal{Q}' \wedge t \xrightarrow{assoc} q \in \mathcal{L}nk'$
5. **Contribution link constraint**: For $t_1,\ t_2 \in \mathcal{T}', q \in \mathcal{Q}', t_2 \xrightarrow{assoc} q \in \mathcal{L}nk'$, a contribution path $q \xrightarrow{cont[l_1]} q_1, q_1 \xrightarrow{cont[l_2]} q_2, \ldots, q_{n-1} \xrightarrow{cont[l_n}]q_n$, and either $t_1 \xrightarrow{assoc} q \in \mathcal{L}nk$ or $t_1 \xrightarrow{cont[l]} q \in \mathcal{L}nk$. Then:

   (a) $q_i \in \mathcal{Q}',\ i = 1, n$ and $q_i \xrightarrow{cont} q_{i+1} \in \mathcal{L}nk', \forall i = 1, n-1$.
   (b) $t_1 \xrightarrow{cont} q \in \mathcal{L}nk \implies t_1 \xrightarrow{cont} q \in \mathcal{L}nk'$

   A detailed discussion on the ME-MAP semantics can be found in [11, 12].

3 Evaluation

We evaluated the approach by two means: (1) we tested the ability to develop useful ME maps, and (2) we examined the hypothesis that know-how mapping, using ME-MAP, better facilitates analysis of technological domains compared to a literature review.

3.1 Evaluating the Development of ME Maps

To evaluate the development of ME maps, we were interested in (H1) validating whether the ME map provides sufficient expressiveness to map out domain knowledge, (H2) examining how easy it is to map out domain knowledge using the ME

Table 1 Perceived quality of ME-MAP

Goals	Avg
(H1) Validate whether ME-MAP provides sufficient expressiveness to map out domain knowledge	4.08
(H2) Examine how difficult or easy it is to map out domain knowledge using an ME-MAP	4.64
(H3) Check whether the mapping using ME-MAP provides insights into the understanding of a domain	3.74
(H4) Explore whether ME-MAP supports the positioning of a research agenda	4.32

map, (H3) checking whether a performed mapping that uses ME-MAP provides insights in the domain reviewed, and (H4) exploring whether the ME-MAP helps in positioning a research agenda. All hypotheses were checked following a structured questionnaire.

The evaluation involved graduate students within a research method course with the following procedure: (1) The ME-MAP was taught in class for 3 hours. (2) The students were divided into 11 groups (of 4/5 students each) and selected a domain of their choice. Each student mapped out five papers in the domain, and the group was then required to create a coherent map of that domain. This was done as part of the assignments in the course. During the period of mapping out the domains, students were given the opportunity to consult with the course instructor to clarify issues regarding the usage of the approach. (3) Finally, we ask them to anonymously complete a reflective questionnaire. The questionnaire had several questions for each of the set hypotheses.

Table 1 summarizes the average results on a scale of 1 (low) to 5 (excellent). The results indicate that (H1) ME-MAP expressiveness is sufficient, (H2) ME-MAP is easy to use, and (H4) ME-MAP facilitates positioning a research agenda. However, (H3) using ME-MAP provides limited new insights. A detailed discussion appears in [17].

3.2 Evaluating the Comprehension of ME Maps

The next evaluation we performed was to test the benefits of ME-MAP for domain comprehension. Toward that end, we conducted a controlled experiment. The main objective of the controlled experiment was to evaluate the effectiveness of ME maps in understanding technical domain knowledge by comparing it to a widely used technique—a textual summary. We compared the effectiveness of the two approaches in terms of comprehension, the relative time it takes users to reach that comprehension, and their confidence regarding their comprehension.

The experiment design was of two factors: the method (ME-MAP vs. textual summary) and the domain (design patterns and sentiment analysis). We developed both the maps and the textual summaries for both domains. In developing these

Table 2 Correctness results

	SA		DP	
Category	ME-MAP	Textual summary	ME-MAP	Textual summary
Identifying solutions	0.68 (0.22)	0.68 (0.22)	**0.64 (0.25)**	0.46 (0.21)
Identifying problems	0.85 (0.26)	**0.88 (0.23)**	0.51 (0.30)	**0.62 (0.19)**
Evaluating alternatives	**0.75 (0.19)**	0.52 (0.16)	**0.69 (0.14)**	0.62 (0.16)
Total	**0.76 (0.16)**	0.68 (0.15)	**0.62 (0.17)**	0.57 (0.11)

artifacts, we verified that these are information equivalent, particularly concerning the comprehension questions we devised. Following that design, each participant used both methods with different domains to avoid the learning effect. We recruited 35 participants (senior undergraduate or graduate students) who received monetary compensation for their participation. The experiment took place in several occasions; in each of these, a short training on ME-MAP was introduced, followed by the major tasks. In those tasks, the participant received either an ME map for a domain or a textual summary of that domain and answered ten questions for each domain. The questions were classified into three themes: identifying solutions, identifying problems, and evaluating alternatives. Next, the participants filled a post-questionnaire reflecting their experience and perceptions.

Table 2 presents the results of the compression correctness (i.e., how well the participants answer a set of questions). The table shows the average results and the standard deviation in brackets. The bold-type numbers indicate the best results among the two methods. In general, the results indicate that the ME-MAP method is beneficial when trying to explore different technology-related domains. With respect to comprehension, in most categories, the use of ME-MAP allows the participants to reach a better understanding of the domain (answer the questions correctly), especially when identifying solutions and evaluating alternative solutions. The improvement over the textual summary was statistically significant when identifying solutions in the design patterns domain, where the map has more links and fewer tasks than the sentiment analysis domain map. The success in understanding the domains can be explained by the abstraction or the simplification that ME-MAP provides over the textual summary. This is manifested by condensed text description, structured knowledge, and organization of the know-how in a more convenient way, that is, all related knowledge gathered and presented in one place. In the textual summary, the knowledge is spread throughout the entire text. Simplification through abstraction was also discussed in [6], where the authors suggest that in order to increase accessibility to a large amount of information, it has to be pre-structured and this should be explained to the stakeholders. The visualization of such structured information may help in understanding relations between information elements and searching for relevant information. This is actually what has been done when using ME-MAP. Overall, the results confirm our conjectures with respect to comprehension, which are supported by Larkin and Simon [8] who claim that the graphic visual presentation offers an

Table 3 Time results: average time in minutes

	SA		DP	
Category	ME-MAP	Textual summary	ME-MAP	Textual summary
Identifying solutions	5:28 (2:35)	**4:25 (1:31)**	7:31 (3:26)	**6:27 (2:55)**
Identifying problems	4:40 (2:18)	**4:03 (1:12)**	6:37 (4:03)	**4:53 (2:29)**
Evaluating alternatives	7:30 (03:43)	**4:35 (2:06)**	7:34 (3:26)	**5:27 (1:49)**
Total	17:39 (5:56)	**13:21 (3:38)**	21:42 (8:01)	**16:48 (5:00)**

additional dimension that facilitates better comprehension. The cognitive fit theory [19] also supports the findings as the comprehension task consisted of questions related to know-how, which are explicitly represented with the ME-MAP, and thus, only minimal mental transformation is required. This is further supported by the perception of the participants, as they mentioned that the ME-MAP provides a short and focused summary that is easy to navigate, mainly in the case of the sentiment analysis map where the map had a tree-like structure. However, when the map layout was complex with many links, as in the case of the design pattern map, it seems that the participants perceived it as a burden on the understanding of the domain and it negatively affected their results in the case of identifying problems. This is also aligned with the mentioned theories, as additional mental transformation is required in order to handle the multiple links. With respect to the time aspect, we revisited the results reported in [13] and found errors in the analysis. Table 3 presents the adjusted analysis. Here again, the results consist of the average and standard deviation in brackets. The results indicate that using ME-MAP increases the time to explore the domain, especially in evaluating alternative solutions where the results were statistically significant in both domains. We attribute this to the participants' limited experience with ME-MAP (in particular, with respect to textual summaries) and the need to carefully navigate among the links. Concerning the confidence aspect, the results indicate that the confidence of the participants was higher when working with the textual summary. Textual representation in its nature contains more details than the map, which helps build confidence (at the cost of spending more time reading and inferencing). In addition, most participants had very little knowledge, if at all, of the map structure, and the short explanation we provided as part of the experiment was not enough for them to feel confident in their knowledge of the map structure, yet it was enough for achieving more correct answers. The details regarding that evaluation can be found in [13].

4 Reasoning

ME maps should be supported with reasoning capabilities. Maps without reasoning capability enable the construction of erroneous maps that may be left without practical use due to the difficulty of producing useful knowledge. As maps grow in size, their semantic analysis is error-prone and time-consuming [1]. In addition, reasoning facilitates the reclamation of the maps as well as searching them. In the following, we first list desired reasoning capabilities from ME maps (based on our own analysis) and then elaborate on the implementation of several of those capabilities.

4.1 Desired Reasoning Capabilities

Finding instances refers to producing a *legal instance* (a sub-map) from an ME map. It helps stakeholders to get alternative solutions (i.e., instances) for problems in light of their qualities. Finding instances helps stakeholders to check the feasibility of the solutions specified in a map.

Verifying Consistency refers to the identification of consistency problems, which make the ME map useless since it cannot admit any legal instance (as defined in Sect. 2.2).

Detecting Conflicts ME maps include positive and negative contributions (links) with various strengths. Therefore, a quality could receive different types of contributions (positive and negative) of various strengths, resulting in conflicts. The reasoning task at hand receives as input an ME map and produces information about the conflicts detected. Such conflicts, unlike a consistency problem, do not prevent the existence of instances (following the proposed semantics). Nevertheless, conflicts highlight that there are different (maybe contradictory) results regarding the contributions of certain tasks to some qualities. Hence, an identification of conflicts helps in detecting (1) *controversy issues* or (2) *mapping mistakes*.

Deducing of Implied Constraints Deducing implied constraints between map elements can help stakeholders by highlighting implicit constraints that can arise from interactions of links in the map.

Extracting a Core Map A *core map* is a map whose elements are part of all legal instances. The importance of a *core map* is that it highlights the important elements (tasks and qualities) of an ME map. These elements should be considered in every solution.

Checking Legal Instances This task takes an instance/partial instance and checks whether the given instance is legal or whether the partial instance can be completed to a legal instance. This task can help in checking the feasibility of different complete or partial instances. It may also serve for validation or testing of a map. If there are reasonable instances that are not legal, or if there are non-reasonable legal instances, the ME map is inadequate.

Finding Information Gaps Finding information gaps may raise potential *open problems* that need to be considered. Moreover, getting information about potential omissions improves the map's quality.

Ranking Solutions The number of instances of an ME map can be very large. Usually, stakeholders differentiate between instances in light of their qualities. Thus, ranking the instances based on these qualities addresses this need.

Abstraction As ME maps grow in size, they become increasingly large and complex. Therefore, modification or understanding of such maps becomes nontrivial tasks due to the many interdependencies that may exist. In essence, the abstraction is a simplification of maps by removing details that are deemed to be unimportant. Abstraction helps in dealing with the complexity and scalability, improves the map understandability, and might support the validation tasks by comparing to existing *higher-level* ME maps. As shown in [4], a major challenge in abstraction is recomputing the *hiding information* in the context of the remaining, *non-hidden* elements. For example, removing contribution links between two non-hidden qualities might require the existence of one link whose label is the composition of the labels of the removed links.

4.2 Implementation of Reasoning Capabilities

We now introduce the implementations of some of the reasoning capabilities we mentioned above: creating instances, checking consistency, extracting a core map, and abstraction.

To implement most of these capabilities, we utilized the constraint programming approach by translating the ME maps into a Constraint Satisfaction Problem (CSP). Then, the desired properties can be verified using a constraint solver [15]. Specifically, we encode the semantics of an ME-MAP into a set of variables and constraints with finite domains. The translation reflects the semantics, which is defined as a possible choice from the elements of an ME map. Therefore, a set of integer variables with domain 0 or 1 represents a selection of ME map tasks and links. A variable assigned a value of 1 means that the corresponding task or link is selected in the instance. If it is assigned zero, it implies that the corresponding task or link is not selected in that instance.

In such a translation, every task and link is represented by a variable of type integer whose domain is either [1, 1] for the root variable or [0, 1] for the later element variables. The domain [1, 1] enforces the root variable to get a *one* assignment in every solution. This reflects the semantics that requires the root task to appear in every instance. A variable with a domain [0, 1] can be assigned *zero*, meaning that its element is not selected in the instance, or *one*, which means that the element will be included in the instance. The constraints for the *achieved-by* semantics are specified as follows: A task can be achieved by only one task. Hence, if a task is selected, its variable is assigned *one*; then only one of the *achieved-by* variables can be satisfied. This means that the sum of all *achieved-by* variables (related to a specific task) should be equal to *one*. Similarly, for the *consists-of* link, if the variable of a task is assigned *one*, then also the involved *consists-of* variables should be assigned *one*. Note, if an *achieved-by*/*consists-of* variable is assigned *one*, then the related task variables should be assigned *one*. These constraints enforce the fact that *achieved-by*/*consists-of* links cannot appear without the involved tasks.

It should be noted that CSP translation does not consider the quality links (associations and contributions), as these do not affect the aforementioned problems due to the semantics we defined. Such problems can be caused only by the interaction between *achieved-by* and *consists-of* links. From the solution produced by the CSP solver, a legal instance for an ME map can be determined uniquely. The solution provides the tasks with their *achieved-by* and *consists-of* links. Then, the qualities can be derived from the ME map. The contribution links can also be determined from the map according to contribution semantics. A contribution link appears in the instance only if its source belongs to the instance and also if it contributes directly or non-directly to a quality of a task that also belongs to the instance.

4.2.1 Creating a Legal Instance

The input to this task is an ME map (ME) and a set of selected tasks (S) that the user aims to include in the solution. The algorithm for creating a legal instance applies a CSP solver after setting the variable of every task $t \in S$ to [1,1]. In case there is a solution, a legal instance will be based on it.

The algorithm works as follows: First, a solution sol is created. Next, an instance I is initialized by ME. Then, following the solution, the algorithm removes all elements and links from I whose assignments in sol are equal to zero. This step results in an instance I (possibly not legal), which includes (1) a set of tasks with their *achieved-by* and *consists-of* links, (2) all qualities of I tasks with their association link, and (3) a set of qualities and contribution links. At this stage, I includes tasks, *achieved-by* and *consists-of*, and quality links to achieve a legal instance. However, it might include additional illegal qualities and contribution links. The next step of the algorithm removes from I all these illegal qualities and contribution links.

4.2.2 Checking Consistency

Checking consistency is done using an off-the-shelf CSP solver. The constraint solver searches for an assignment for all variables without violating the constraints. Failing to find such an assignment means that the map is inconsistent. Yet, producing a legal instance does not mean that the map is consistent. It is possible that there exists a variable with zero assignment in all possible instances. Therefore, in case the constraint solver returns a possible instance, the consistency property should be checked separately with respect to each task by setting the task domain to [1, 1]. In case no legal assignment is found, the map is inconsistent.

4.2.3 Extracting a Core Map

In the case of core maps, the algorithm first computes the *core tasks*. Then, it checks for each task t if there is a solution to the corresponding CSP model with $domain(t) = [0]$. No solution means that t must be satisfied in every legal instance and hence belongs to the core map. Next, the core map is completed based on the *core tasks*.

4.2.4 Abstraction

As mentioned before, abstraction refers to the simplification of a map. In Fig. 2 we demonstrate the meaning of abstraction by means of synthetic examples. Figure 2a shows an original ME map. Figure 2b contains only *achieved-by* links between T and $\{T_6, T_7, T_8, T_{11}\}$. However, the sub-map in Fig. 2a does not include *achieved-by* paths between T and these four tasks. Therefore, the map may mislead the user

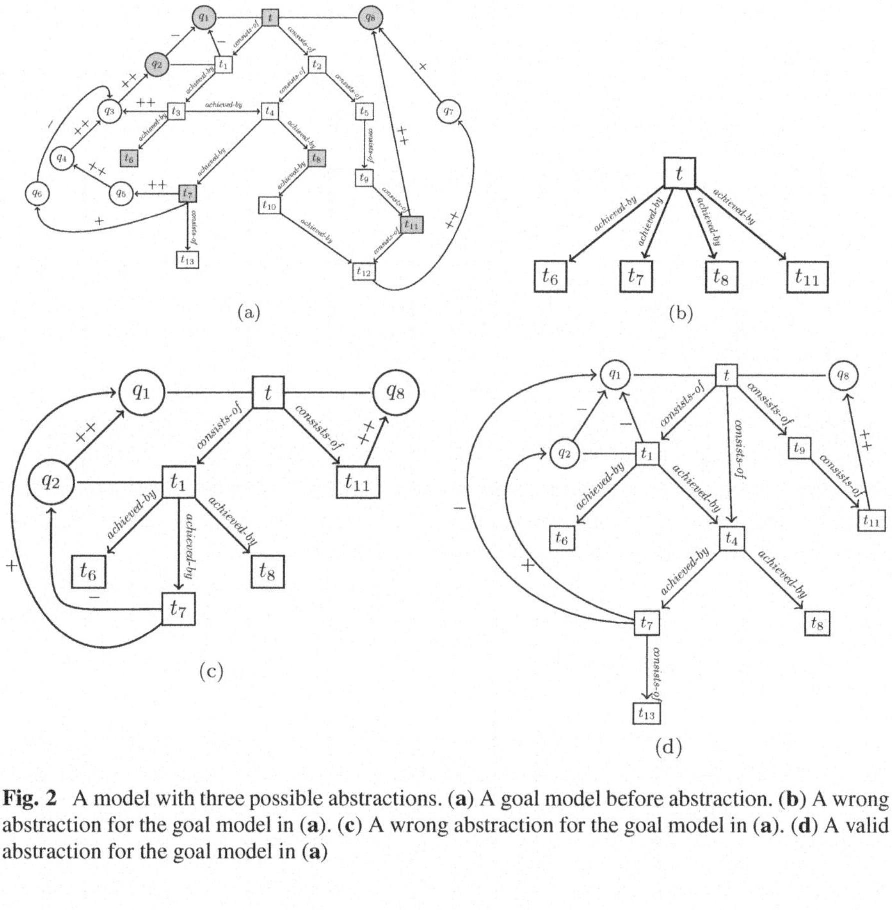

Fig. 2 A model with three possible abstractions. (**a**) A goal model before abstraction. (**b**) A wrong abstraction for the goal model in (**a**). (**c**) A wrong abstraction for the goal model in (**a**). (**d**) A valid abstraction for the goal model in (**a**)

because $\{T_6, T_7, T_8\}$, and T_{11} are not alternatives (direct or indirect) to achieving T. Moreover, due to the *xor* constraint of the *achieved-by* link, only one of these tasks can appear in any legal solution. In contrast, a legal solution in the original map may contain T_8 and T_{11}.

In Fig. 2c, the total cumulative contribution of t_7 to q_2 and q_1 is $+$ and $-$, respectively. Moreover, the task T_4 cannot be eliminated from the abstract maps. The task T requires T_1 and (indirectly) T_4 for achieving T_8 : $T \xrightarrow{consists-of} T_2, T_2 \xrightarrow{consists-of} T_4$. Removing T_4 results in the loss of this link.

Figure 2d shows a correct abstraction. On the one hand, the abstracted map contains the elements selected by the user and omits some other elements included in the original map. On the other hand, it retains the semantic properties of the original map. For example, for the *achieved-by* links between T_1 and T_4, there is a corresponding *achieved-by* path in the original map.

The algorithm we devised receives as an input a map and a list of elements the user aims to include in the abstraction. First, we construct a task graph, and then we abstract *achieved-by* and *consists-of* links, following Rule 1.

For a removable task $\boldsymbol{t_r}$, $l \in$ {achieved-by, consists-of}

$$t_1 \xrightarrow{l} \boldsymbol{t_r},\ \boldsymbol{t_r} \xrightarrow{l} t_2, \ \xRightarrow{\boldsymbol{replace-by}} t_1 \xrightarrow{l} t_2 \qquad \text{(Rule 1)}$$

For a removable quality $\boldsymbol{q_r}$ and implied contribution values l_1 and l_2

$$e \xrightarrow[L_1]{\text{cont}[l_1]} \boldsymbol{q_r},\ \boldsymbol{q_r} \xrightarrow[L_2]{\text{cont}[l_2]} q \ \xRightarrow{\boldsymbol{replace-by}} e \xrightarrow{\text{cont}[\min(l_1,l_2)]} q \qquad \text{(Rule 2)}$$

Next, we construct a quality graph and apply an abstraction over the contribution links. In particular, new contribution links are generated based on the original ones, following Rule 2. In addition, this generation requires the computation of contribution values.

We evaluate the abstraction mechanisms by two complementary methods. We checked the comprehension (via question answering) through a controlled experiment (not reported here) of ME abstracted maps vs. the original ones and found that the understanding of a domain increases when using the abstracted ME map. The reasoning regarding checking consistency in ME maps also greatly improved with respect to the time it took to detect the related problems.

5 Searching for Know-How

The motivation to establish ME-MAP was to increase knowledge accessibility. Thus, after considering the development of ME maps, their comprehension, and the reasoning support for improving their quality, there is a need to refer to the capabilities of retrieving the knowledge. In that sense, we anticipate a large set

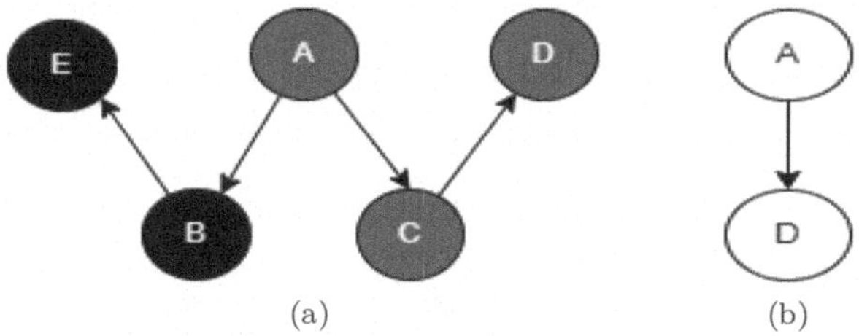

Fig. 3 An example of a map graph (**a**) and a query graph (**b**)

of ME maps in which one should search for the relevant know-how. Nowadays, searching for knowledge is mostly done textually using search engines. Yet, the outcomes of such search results are of limited accuracy, that is, many nonrelevant answers are being retrieved leading to a low efficiency of the search. To address this limitation, we suggest taking advantage of the underlying structure of the know-how (ME-MAP), which resembles the means-ends relationship. Using that structure, we are able to query it more precisely. The population of the ME maps can be regarded as graph that can now be searched using various techniques. Thus, we adapt a graph algorithm for searching ME maps and explore its effectiveness. In this work, we adopt the approach of querying the maps via (tiny) maps. See Fig. 3.

Having the graphs of both the maps and the query, we defined the problem as searching a similar path within a map graph that gains the highest similarity to that of the query graph. By finding a similar path, we assume that the map in which such a path exists is relevant to the query map. To address this problem, we devised an Iterative Greedy Search Algorithm (IGSA) that adopts the similarity considerations that appear in [14] and refers to label matching (match among labels), structure matching (in terms of links), semantic matching (in terms of labels' semantic similarity and links' semantics, e.g., synonyms and related concepts), and type matching.

We demonstrate the execution of the search algorithm using the example above. In the first stage, the IGSA searches for the most similar node in the graph that fits the first node "A" in the query graph. Next, the algorithm tries to find the most similar adjacent nodes (the number of nodes is set as a parameter). In the example, the most similar nodes to the "D" node in the query are "B" and "C." Since both nodes have low similarity value, they advance to the next step without advancing to the next query node. Therefore, the algorithm searches for the most similar nodes that are the neighbors of the nodes "B" and "C." The result of that search yields the paths of $A \rightarrow B \rightarrow E \; and \; A \rightarrow C \rightarrow D.$

In this example, there are no more nodes to explore; thus the algorithm terminates and calculates the path similarity. The results indicate that the path ending with "D" fits the most.

We also evaluate the quality and efficiency of the algorithm. For that we defined several categories of query complexity and referred to the following metrics:

- Accuracy-related metrics
  - **Mean Reciprocal Ranks (MRR)** indicate whether the right path (E-MRR) and graph (D-MRR) were retrieved, respectively.
  - **recall@N** determines whether the expected result appears within the top *N* results.
- Efficiency-related metrics
  - The **time** it took the search algorithm to return a result in seconds.

Applying the search algorithm with 10 queries over 200 ME maps resulted in high efficiency and acceptable accuracy (E-MRR = 0.525, D-MRR = 0.775, Recall@10 = 0.8, time $<$ 30 msec). For detailed results see [2].

6 Summary

In this chapter, we summarize a research project on know-how mapping that resulted in a new approach—ME-MAP. The research includes the development of a mapping language (along with defined syntax and semantics) and its evaluation. It further enhances the language with capabilities to reason about ME maps and to search for know-how in such maps. With respect to *i**, ME-MAP adopts a subset of its concepts to ease its usage and provide the semantics needed for knowledge mapping and reasoning, which were missing from *i**, as it meant for system analysis rather than domain/knowledge mapping. We envision that the approach, accompanied by its supporting tools, will increase the accessibility to know-how and fertilization among communities. In the future, more examination of the approach is required. In addition, with the advancements in natural language processing and large language models, it is appealing to check the automatic generation and population of ME maps.

Acknowledgments The work was carried out by many collaborators: Sadra Abrishamkar, Maxim Bragiloski, Michael Elhadad, Daniel Gross, Yifat Makias, Azzam Maraee, Soroosh Nalchigar, Jumana Nassour, Moran Shamshila, Roni Stern, Jian Wang, and of course *Eric Yu* who inspired this project. The research was partially funded by the Israel Science Foundation (ISF) #495/14.

References

1. Balaban, M., Maraee, A.: Finite satisfiability of uml class diagrams with constrained class hierarchy. ACM Trans. Softw. Eng. Methodol. **22**(3), 1–42 (2013)
2. Bragilovski, M., Stern, R., Sturm, A.: How do I find reusable models? Softw. Syst. Model. **23**, 85–102 (2023)

3. Davenport, T.H., Prusak, L.: Working Knowledge: How Organizations Manage What They Know. Harvard Business Review Press, Brighton, 2000
4. Egyed, A.: Automated abstraction of class diagrams. ACM TOSEM **11**(4), 449–491 (2002)
5. Gross, D., Sturm, A., Yu, E.S.K.: Towards know-how mapping using goal modeling. In: Proceedings of the 6th International *i** Workshop 2013, vol. 978, pp. 115–120. CEUR-WS.org (2013)
6. Keller, T., Tergan, S.-O.: Visualizing Knowledge and Information: An Introduction, pp. 1–23. Springer Berlin Heidelberg, Berlin (2005)
7. Kim, S., Suh, E., Hwang, H.: Building the knowledge map: an industrial case study. J. Knowl. Manage. **7**(2), 34–45 (2003)
8. Larkin, J.H., Simon, H.A.: Why a diagram is (sometimes) worth ten thousand words. Cogn. Sci. **11**(1), 65–100 (1987)
9. La Rosa, M., Van Der Aalst, W.M.P., Dumas, M., Milani, F.P.: Business process variability modeling: a survey. ACM Comput. Surv. **50**(1), 1–45 (2017)
10. Lee, J., Fink, D.: Knowledge mapping: encouragements and impediments to adoption. J. Knowl. Manage. **17**(1), 16–28 (2013)
11. Maraee, A., Sturm, A.: Formal semantics and analysis tasks for ME-MAP models. In: 11th International Conference on Research Challenges in Information Science, RCIS, pp. 234–243. IEEE, Piscataway (2017)
12. Maraee, A., Sturm, A.: Reasoning methods for me-maps - A CSP based approach. In: 12th International Conference on Research Challenges in Information Science, RCIS, pp. 1–11. IEEE, Piscataway (2018)
13. Nassour, J., Elhadad, M., Sturm, A., Yu, E.: Evaluating the comprehension of means-ends maps. Softw. Syst. Model. **18**(3), 1885–1903 (2019)
14. Reinhartz-Berger, I.: Towards automatization of domain modeling. Data Knowl. Eng. **69**(5), 491–515 (2010)
15. Rossi, F., Van Beek, P., Walsh, T.: Handbook of Constraint Programming. Elsevier, Amsterdam (2006)
16. Sturm, A., Gross, D., Wang, J., Yu, E.S.K.: Analyzing engineering contributions using a specialized concept map. In: Joint Proceedings of the CAiSE 2014 Forum and CAiSE 2014 Doctoral Consortium, vol. 1164. CEUR, pp. 89–96. CEUR-WS.org (2014)
17. Sturm, A., Gross, D., Wang, J., Yu, E.S.K.: Means-ends based know-how mapping. J. Knowl. Manage. **21**(2), 454–473 (2017)
18. Sturm, A., Yu, E.S.K., Abrishamkar, S.: Know-how mapping - A goal-oriented approach and evaluation. In: Proceedings of the Enterprise, Business-Process and Information Systems Modeling - 18th International Conference, BPMDS, 22nd International Conference, EMMSAD, vol. 287. LNBIP, pp. 272–286. Springer, Berlin (2017)
19. Vessey, I.: Cognitive fit: a theory-based analysis of the graphs versus tables literature. Decis. Sci. **22**(2), 219–240 (1991)
20. Wang, J., Sturm, A., Gross, D., Yu, E.S.K.: Know-how mapping: From i* to me-maps. In: Proceedings of the 7th i* Workshop, vol. 1157. CEUR Workshop Proceedings. CEUR-WS.org (2014)
21. Yu, E.S.K., Giorgini, P., Maiden, N.A.M., Mylopoulos, J.: Social Modeling for Requirements Engineering. Cooperative Information Systems. MIT Press, Cambridge (2011)

Part III
Variants

Definition and Use of iStar 2.0

Fabiano Dalpiaz, Xavier Franch, and Jennifer Horkoff

Abstract The *i** modeling language was introduced to fill the gap in the spectrum of conceptual modeling languages, focusing on the intentional (*why?*), social (*who?*), and strategic (*how? how else?*) dimensions. *i** has been applied in many areas, e.g., healthcare, security analysis, and e-commerce. Although *i** has seen much academic application, the diversity of extensions and variations can make it difficult for novices to learn and use it in a consistent way. This chapter introduces the iStar 2.0 core language, evolving the basic concepts of *i** into a consistent and clear set of core concepts, upon which to build future work and to base goal-oriented teaching materials. This chapter presents a more comprehensive illustrative example compared to the paper that first introduced iStar 2.0.

1 Note from the Authors

In 2016 we released the first version of the iStar 2.0 standard, a result of a multi-year standardization process within the *i** community. Here, in honor of the retirement of Prof. Eric Yu, we are presenting the 2016 version of the iStar 2.0 standard (see our arXiv preprint [3]), with a new example and more extensive explanations.

F. Dalpiaz (✉)
Utrecht University, Utrecht, The Netherlands
e-mail: f.dalpiaz@uu.nl

X. Franch
Universitat Politècnica de Catalunya, Barcelona, Spain
e-mail: xavier.franch@upc.edu

J. Horkoff
University of Gothenburg, Chalmers University of Technology, Göteborg, Sweden
e-mail: jenho@chalmers.se

X. Franch et al. (eds.), *Social Modeling Using the i* Framework*,
https://doi.org/10.1007/978-3-031-72107-6_5

2 Motivation and Overview

The *i** language was presented in the mid-1990s [11] as a goal- and actor-oriented modeling and reasoning framework. It consists of a modeling language along with reasoning techniques for analyzing created models. *i** was quickly adopted by the research community in fields such as requirements engineering and business modeling. Benefiting from its intentionally open nature, multiple extensions of the *i** language have been proposed (see [7] for an *i** review), either by slightly redefining some existing constructs, by detailing some semantic issues not completely defined in the seminal proposal, or by proposing new constructs for specific domains.

This flexible use of *i** has been fruitfully employed by researchers, who were able to benefit from a consolidated modeling and reasoning approach while tailoring it to their needs. However, this use has also some drawbacks. The most critical is the difficulty to spread the framework outside the experts' community:

- *Newcomers* find it hard to learn the intricacies of the language.
- *Educators* do not have a shared body of knowledge to teach.
- *Practitioners* are not provided with an established reference for using *i** in their projects.
- *Technology providers* cannot easily determine which are the core constructs to be implemented and the techniques to apply on top of those constructs.

As a response to the need of balancing the framework's open nature and a possible solution to the aforementioned adoption problems, researchers in the *i** community explored different directions: on the one hand, the formulation of *i** metamodels looking for a well-defined baseline to serve as shared understanding of *i** constructs [1, 8] and, on the other hand, the definition of interchange formats for integrating models built according to different *i** variants [2, 9]. However, in spite of different follow-up actions (e.g., using a meta-modeling development and configuration platform such as ADOxx to implement the metamodel [6]), none of these proposals were widely adopted by the entire *i** community, leaving the aforementioned adoption problems still open.

Given this lack of success of individual initiatives, the *i** research community started a joint endeavor to identify a widely agreed upon set of core concepts in the *i** language. The main goal was to keep open the ability to tailor the framework while agreeing on the fundamental constructs. This chapter summarizes the outcomes of the first iteration of the *i** standardization process. To clearly distinguish this core language from its predecessors, we name it **iStar 2.0**.[1]

The community discussed this language in several meetings and discussions starting in a dedicated 1-day meeting before the ER'14 conference in Atlanta (October 2014). At the subsequent community meeting at CAiSE'15 in Stockholm

[1] The language is spelled iStar instead of *i** to allow better indexing through search engines.

(at the iStar teaching workshop, iStarT, June 2015), it was decided that a smaller group of researchers (the authors of this chapter) would guide the process, making concrete proposals and processing the inputs of the rest of the community. An initial draft of the core was discussed both at the iStar Workshop colocated with RE'15 (August 2015) and in another dedicated 1-day meeting before ER'15 in Stockholm (October 2015). The obtained feedback has been incorporated into the chapter. A preliminary version was distributed among the researchers that participated in this process (December 2015), who provided a last round of comments, considered in this version (May 2016).

Each of the following five sections (Sects. 3–7) addresses a particular category of language constructs as presented in most *i** sources, for example, the i* wiki.[2] For each category, the chapter lists the concepts that are included in iStar 2.0, with a definition, necessary comments, concise examples, and the graphical representation. The focus of this chapter is on concepts and relationships; methodological possibilities are mentioned only briefly.

Several aspects are excluded from this first version of iStar. Among them, we mention the ontological definition of constructs (e.g., what is a goal?), visual representation (e.g., what is an effective graphical notation?), wording conventions (e.g., passive voices in goals), and methodological issues (e.g., when can a model be considered final?). Such issues should be addressed by the iStar community in future work.

Illustrative Example We illustrate the concepts of iStar 2.0 using a running example concerning the organization of a university course in a fictional university where course coordinators are responsible for a course while being assisted by lecturers, who deliver the lectures, and by the exam board and their examiners who prepare exams and do the marking. We will introduce iStar concepts gradually, slowly building up the example. In Fig. 1 we show a view of the example in order to give readers an early idea of the capabilities of iStar 2.0. A more complete version of this iStar 2.0 model, that includes the expanded actors Course lecturer and Examiner, can be found in the online appendix [5]. This example has been created using the online piStar tool [10].[3]

Organization Section 3 introduces the notion of actor and distinguishes between three types of actors. Section 4 presents the links in iStar 2.0 for relating actors. Section 5 describes the intentional elements that characterize the actors. Section 6 discusses the dependencies that socially relate the actors. Section 7 explains how the intentional elements can be linked. Section 8 details how to create different views of an iStar 2.0 model. Section 9 shows the metamodel of the language. Finally, we conclude and present future directions in Sect. 10.

[2] http://istarwiki.org

[3] piStar available at https://www.cin.ufpe.br/~jhcp/pistar/

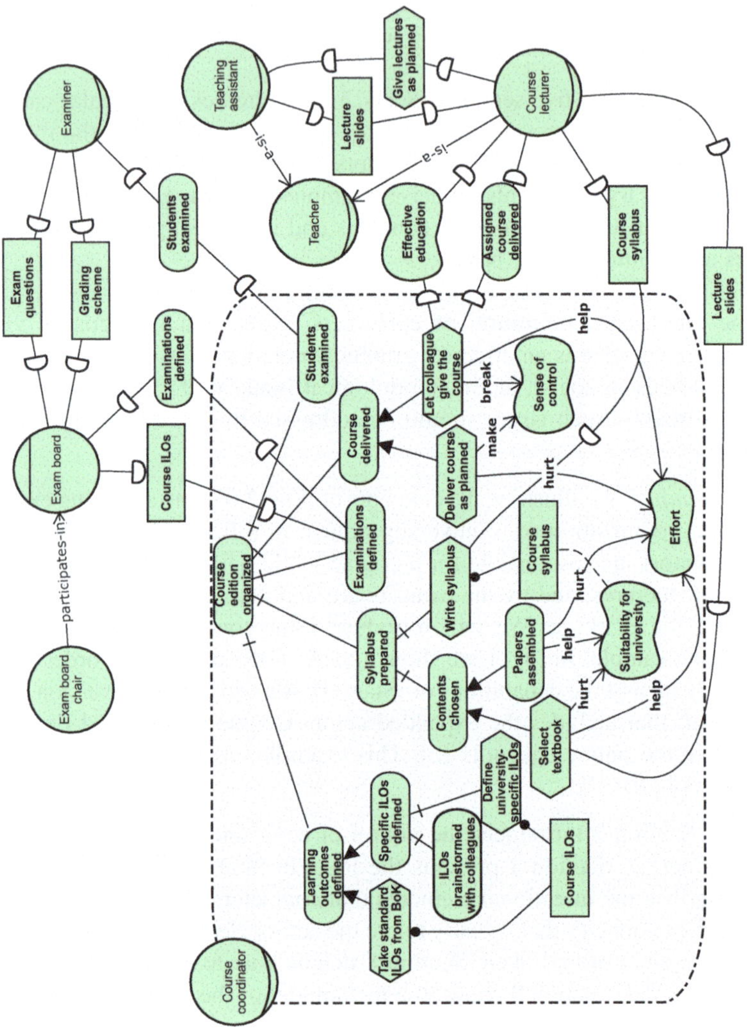

Fig. 1 A preview of the Course Organization scenario as captured in iStar 2.0

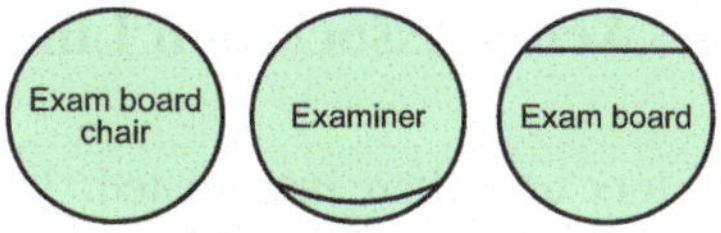

Fig. 2 Examples of actor, role, and agent

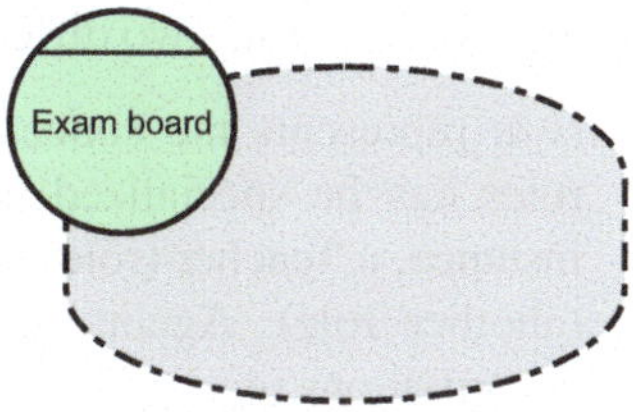

Fig. 3 Example of the visual representation of an actor boundary

3 Actors and Actor Types

Actors are central to the social modeling nature of the language. *Actors* are active, autonomous entities that aim at achieving their goals by exercising their know-how, in collaboration with other actors. In iStar 2.0, two types of actors are distinguished:

- *Role*: an abstract characterization of the behavior of a social actor within some specialized context or domain of endeavor. Examples in our illustrative scenario are Course coordinator, Teacher, and Examiner.
- *Agent*: an actor with concrete, physical manifestations, such as a human individual, an organization, or a department. Examples are: Exam board (one unit within our reference university), University of XYZ, Mike White.

Whenever distinguishing the type of actor is not relevant, either because of the scenario at hand or the modeling stage, the notion of generic *actor*—without specialization—can be used in the model. For example, we can denote Exam board chair as an actor to say that we do not know yet whether it refers to a specific individual (who holds this position for an indefinite time) or a characterization of a role.

Actors are represented graphically as circles. In the case of agent, a straight line is added in the top part of the actor circle. For a role, a curved line is added in the lower part. The graphical notation follows the mnemonic guidelines that the original *i** adopts.[4] Figure 2 illustrates the notation.

Actors' intentionality is made explicit through the *actor boundary*, which is a graphical container for their intentional elements (see Sect. 5) together with their interrelationships (see Sect. 7). Figure 3 shows the graphical representation of an actor boundary; elements and relationships will appear inside the gray area.

[4] These symbols are stylized depictions of a person wearing a hat and viewed from different angles. The Agent symbol is the frontal view where the name of the agent appears on the face. The Role symbol is an overhead view so that the label on the hat is visible.

4 Actor Association Links

Actors are often interrelated. In iStar 2.0, this is captured via actor links that define/describe these relationships. Actor links are binary, linking a single actor to a single other actor. Two different types of actor links have been defined:

- *is-a*: represents the concept of generalization/specialization in iStar 2.0. Only roles can be specialized into roles, or general actors into general actors. For instance, a Teacher (role) can be defined as a specialization of a Course lecturer (another role). Agents cannot be specialized via is-a, as they are concrete instantiations (e.g., Mike White cannot be another agent).
- *participates-in*: represents any kind of association, other than generalization/specialization, between two actors. No restriction exists on the type of actors linked by this association. Every actor can *participate-in* multiple other actors. Depending on the connected elements, this link takes different meanings. Two typical situations are the following:
  - When the source is an agent and the target is a role, this represents the *plays* relationship, i.e., an agent plays a given role. For instance, Mike White plays the role of Examiner in Fig. 4.
  - When the target is an agent, this will often represent the *part-of* relationship. For instance, the Exam board chair is part of the Exam board.

Actor association links are represented using arrows in the diagram. The arrowhead identifies the target (the participated actor or the superclass, respectively). A label identifying the type of link must be included. Figure 4 shows the graphical representation of the examples mentioned above.

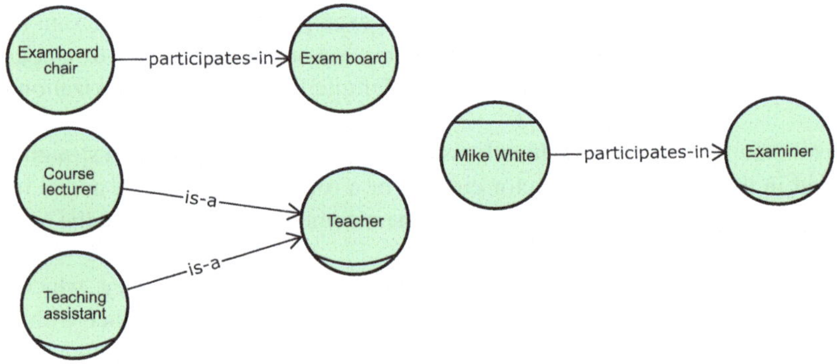

Fig. 4 Examples of actor association links

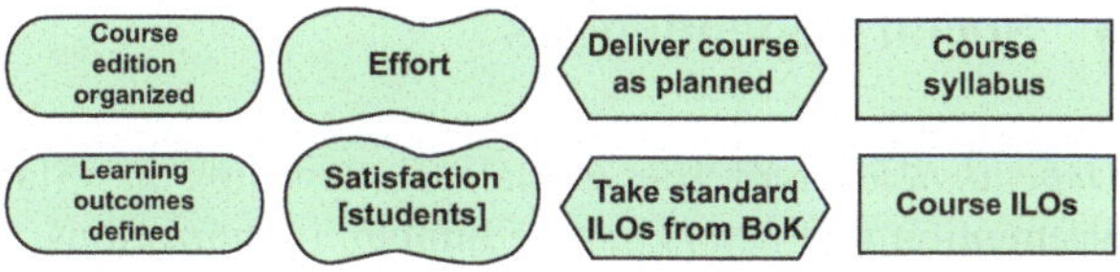

Fig. 5 Examples of intentional elements

5 Intentional Elements

Intentional elements are the things actors want. As such, they model different kinds of requirements and are central to the iStar 2.0 language. An intentional element appearing inside the boundary of an actor denotes something that is desired or wanted by that actor. An intentional element can also appear outside of actor boundaries, as part of a dependency relationship between two actors (see Sect. 6). In this section, we focus on the former case: elements inside actor boundaries. The following elements are included in the language:

- *Goal*: a state of affairs that the actor wants to achieve and that has clear-cut criteria of achievement. For example, in Fig. 5, Course edition organized is a goal because it defines a state without prescribing a specific plan to reach it.
- *Quality*: an attribute for which an actor desires some level of achievement. For example, the entity could be the system under development and a quality its performance; another entity could be the business being analyzed and a quality the yearly profit; in Fig. 5, the quality Satisfaction refers to the entity students. The level of achievement may be defined precisely or kept vague. Qualities can guide the search for ways of achieving goals and also serve as criteria for evaluating alternative ways of achieving goals.[5]
- *Task*: represents actions that an actor wants to be executed, usually with the purpose of achieving some goal. For example, Deliver course as planned is a task because it assumes that a specific course of actions has been defined.
- *Resource*: a physical or informational entity that the actor requires in order to perform a task. For example, the Course syllabus or the Course intended learning outcomes are informational resources in the illustrative example.

Goals are graphically represented as ovals, while qualities are represented as more curved cloud-like shapes. Tasks are represented as hexagons to highlight their more structured definition in terms of a process to be followed. Resources are represented as rectangles. Figure 5 shows examples of the intentional elements.

[5] iStar 2.0 departs from the original goal/softgoal dichotomy, which distinguishes these concepts based on the existence of a clear-cut metric for satisfaction, and from the Non-Functional/Functional Requirement distinction, as the use of this distinction varied in practice. By including qualities, which can be either "soft" or "hard" using *i** terminology, and by including the qualifies relationship between qualities and goals (Sect. 7.4), we clarify the relationships between goals and qualities.

6 Social Dependencies

Dependencies represent social relationships in iStar 2.0. This, along with the assumption that actors can be human, organizations, technical systems (hardware, software), or any combination thereof, makes iStar 2.0 a socio-technical modeling language. A dependency is defined as a relationship with five arguments:

- *depender* is the actor that depends for something (the dependum) to be provided.
- *dependerElmt* is the intentional element within the depender's actor boundary where the dependency starts from, which explains why the dependency exists.
- *dependum* is an intentional element that is the object of the dependency.
- *dependee* is the actor that should provide the dependum.
- *dependeeElmt* is the intentional element that explains how the dependee intends to provide the dependum.

Dependencies (illustrated in Fig. 6) link the dependerElmt within the depender actor to the dependum, outside actor boundaries, to the dependeeElmt within the dependee actor. The link is drawn with a "D" symbol indicating direction, with the D acting as an arrowhead ">," pointing from dependerElmt to dependum to dependeeElmt.

Both the dependerElmt and the dependeeElmt can be omitted. This optionality is used when creating an initial Strategic Dependency view (see Sect. 8), or to support expressing partial knowledge, e.g., when the "why" (dependerElmt) or the "how" (dependeeElmt) of the dependency are unknown. For example, in Fig. 6, the quality dependency for Effective education omits the dependeeElmt. If both are omitted, the dependency links the depender actor to the dependee actor through the dependum.

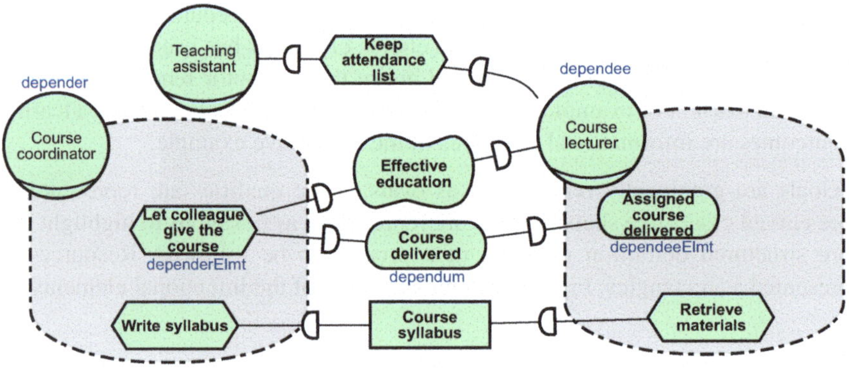

Fig. 6 Examples of dependencies. The textual annotations in blue highlight the arguments of the dependency for goal Course delivered

The type of the dependum specializes the semantics of the relationship:

- Goal: The dependee is expected to achieve the goal and is free to choose how. For example, in Fig. 6, the Course lecturer is free to choose how to achieve the dependum goal Course delivered.
- Quality: The dependee is expected to sufficiently satisfy the quality and is free to choose how.
- Task: The dependee is expected to execute the task in a prescribed way. In Fig. 6, the Teaching assistant is expected to execute the task Keep attendance list, which refers to a specific course of action.
- Resource: The dependee is expected to make the resource available to the depender.

This way, different dependency types indicate different degrees of freedom afforded by the depender to the dependee, with qualities and goals allowing the highest degree of freedom, tasks medium, and resource the lowest.

6.1 Rules and Restrictions

When a depender depends on the dependee for its dependerElmt, the depender cannot (or chooses not to) provide the dependerElmt on its own. Thus, an intentional element that acts as dependerElmt cannot be refined or contributed to.

It is possible that one or more of the dependerElmt, dependum, and dependeeElmt have the same element name. In this case, each of these elements is nevertheless distinct, as they reflect the separate viewpoints of the depender, the relationship between the two actors, and of the dependee, respectively.

Dependency relationships should not share the same dependum, as each dependum is a conceptually different element; in some cases, a dependum in one dependency is achieved, but is not achieved in another dependency, even if the dependums may have the same name. In other words, an actor cannot depend on more than one actor for the same dependum, or two actors cannot depend on the same dependum from an actor.

7 Intentional Element Links

There are four types of links between intentional elements: *refinement*, *NeededBy*, *contribution*, and *qualification*. These are described in the following subsections and are summarized in Table 1.

Table 1 Links between intentional elements: overview

		Arrowhead pointing to			
		Goal	*Quality*	*Task*	*Resource*
Link starts from	*Goal*	Refinement	Contribution	Refinement	n/a
	Quality	Qualification	Contribution	Qualification	Qualification
	Task	Refinement	Contribution	Refinement	n/a
	Resource	n/a	Contribution	NeededBy	n/a

7.1 Refinement

To promote ease of adoption, iStar 2.0 features a generic relationship called *refinement* that links goals and tasks hierarchically. Refinement is an n-ary relationship relating one parent to one or more children. An intentional element can be the parent in at most one refinement relationship.

Two types of refinement exist—and apply to any kind of parent (goal or task)—that define the logical operator that relates the parent with the children:

- *AND*: The fulfillment of all the n children ($n \geq 2$) makes the parent fulfilled.
- *Inclusive OR*: The fulfillment of at least one child makes the parent fulfilled. This relationship allows for a single child.

A parent can only be AND-refined or OR-refined, not both simultaneously. Depending on the connected elements, refinement takes different meanings:

- If the parent is a *goal*:
  - In the case of AND, a *child goal* is a sub-state of affairs that is part of the parent goal, while a *child task* is a sub-task that must be fulfilled
  - In the case of OR, a *child task* is a particular way (a "means") for fulfilling the parent goal (the "end"), while a *child goal* is a sub-goal that can be achieved for fulfilling the parent goal
- If the parent is a *task*:
  - In the case of AND, a *child task* is a sub-task that is identified as part of the parent task, while a *child goal* is a goal that is uncovered by analyzing the parent task
  - In the case of OR, a *child goal* is a goal whose existence is uncovered by analyzing the parent task which may substitute for the original task, while a *child task* is a way to execute the parent task

Refinement relationships do not imply a strictly top-down process; they can be built from the bottom-up or top-down or via a mixed approach.

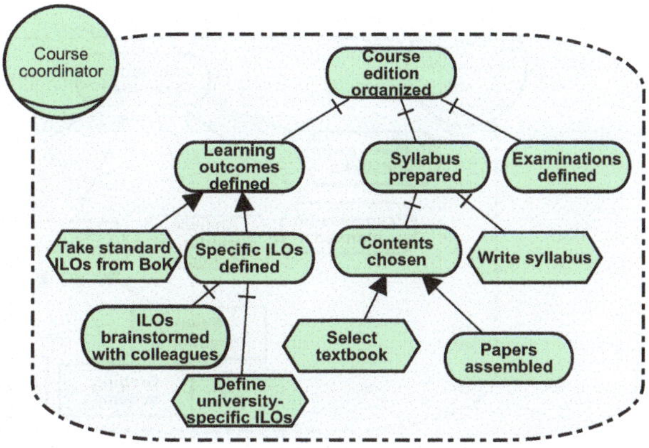

Fig. 7 Examples of refinement links

Graphically,[6] *refinement* is expressed as a set of links directed from the sub-elements to the parent element. We employ a T-shaped arrowhead to denote AND-refinement and a solid arrow directed towards the parent to represent OR-refinement (we use the original *i** symbol).

Figure 7 exemplifies the notation. The refinement of Course edition organized shows a goal decomposed into three sub-goals that are all necessary (*AND-refinement*) to achieve the parent. The refinement of Learning outcomes defined shows alternatives (*OR-refinement*): either the standard learning outcomes are taken from a body of knowledge or specific learning outcomes are defined for that course given at that university. This refinement shows also that the sub-elements can be either tasks or goals, depending on whether a concrete set of actions to execute can be identified.

7.2 *NeededBy*

The *NeededBy* relationship links a task with a resource and it indicates that the actor needs the resource in order to execute the task. This relationship does not specify what is the reason for this need: consumption, reading, modification, creation, etc. Graphically, NeededBy is represented as an arrow with a circle arrowhead directed toward the task, as shown in Fig. 8. In the example, the task Grade exams is linked to three resources by NeededBy links: Exam questions, Grading scheme, and Exam grades. Although this is not represented formally, the first two are used as input, and Exam grades is the task's output.

[6] As mentioned in Sect. 2, an accurate study of the graphical definition of refinement (and other relationships) is left to future versions of the language.

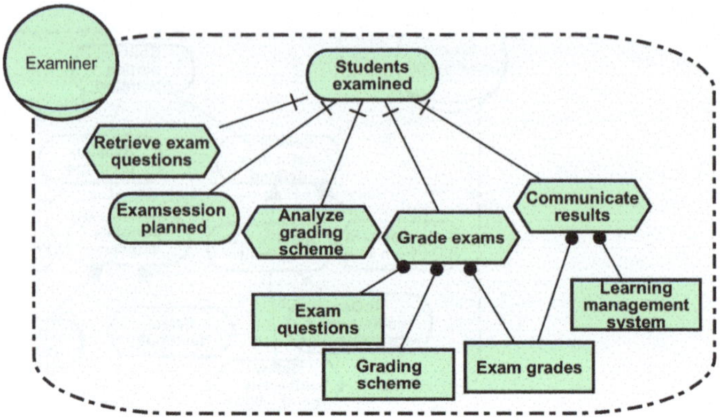

Fig. 8 Examples of the NeededBy relationship

7.3 Contribution

Contribution links represent the effects of intentional elements on qualities and are essential to assist analysts in the decision-making process among alternative goals or tasks. Contribution links lead to the accumulation of evidence for qualities. We talk of qualities being *fulfilled* or *satisfied*, having sufficient positive evidence, or being *denied*, having strong negative evidence.

Contributions are defined as relationships from a source intentional element to a target quality and having one of the following types:

- *Make*: The source provides sufficient positive evidence for the satisfaction of the target.
- *Help*: The source provides weak positive evidence for the satisfaction of the target.
- *Hurt*: The source provides weak evidence against the satisfaction (or for the denial) of the target.
- *Break*: The source provides sufficient evidence against the satisfaction (or for the denial) of the target.

Contributions are represented graphically as solid arrows with a text label that indicates the contribution type. The model in Fig. 9 shows that the two alternatives for fulfilling the goal Contents chosen contribute differently to the quality Suitability for university; the goal Select textbook has a negative (*hurt*) impact on the quality, while Papers assembled has a positive (*help*) impact. The alternatives to fulfill goal Course delivered have an opposite impact on the quality Sense of control: the task Deliver course as planned makes the quality, as the course coordinator would teach the course as they planned; and the task Let colleague give the course breaks the quality.

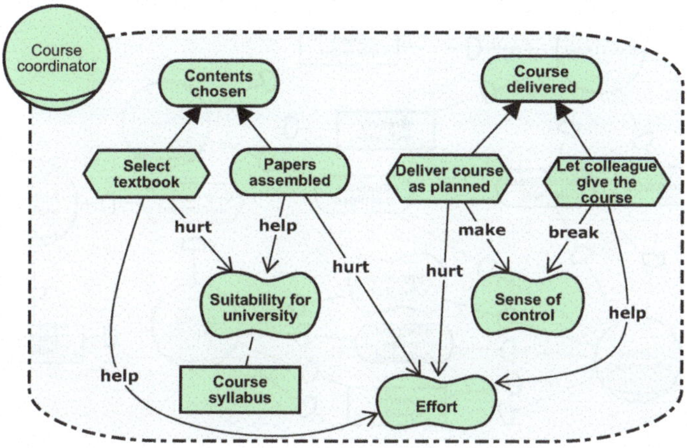

Fig. 9 Example of contribution links

7.4 Qualification

The *qualification* relationship relates a quality to its subject: a task, goal, or resource. Placing a qualification relationship expresses a desired quality over the execution of a task, the achievement of the goal, or the provision of the resource. The qualification relationship is represented graphically via a dotted line connecting the element that is qualified with a quality.

For example, in Fig. 9, the quality "Suitability for university" refers to the resource "Course syllabus," indicating that the Course coordinator cares about a course syllabus that is suitable for a specific university.

Qualities are not necessarily attached to other elements through a qualification link. For example, "Effort" is a standalone quality that does not qualify any other element, and it obviously refers to the effort that the actor itself has to put.

8 Model Views

When using iStar 2.0, the analyst creates a *model*. Such model can be visualized via multiple perspectives or *model views* (see also [4]). We specifically introduce three views that stem from the original *i** proposal and some extensions: the Strategic Rationale view, the Strategic Dependency view, and the Hybrid view.

Strategic Rationale (SR) The SR view shows all of the detail captured in the model, including actors, dependencies, actor association links, and the internal details of each actor. Modelers can view the strategic rationale inside each of the actors in the model. An SR view for our scenario is shown in the online appendix.

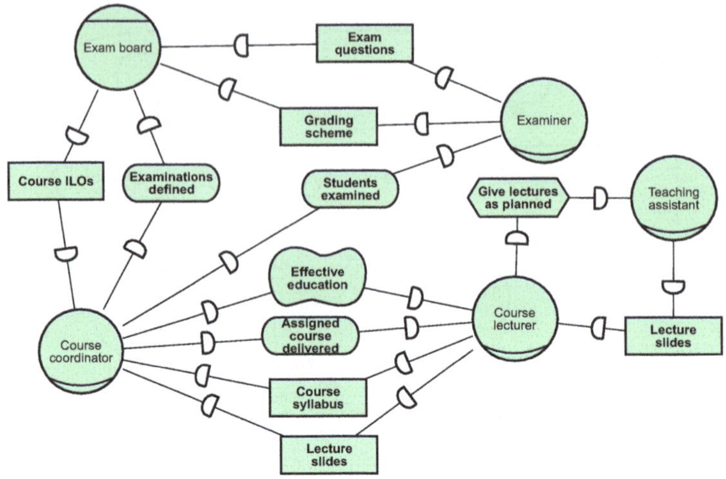

Fig. 10 An SD view of the Course Organization scenario

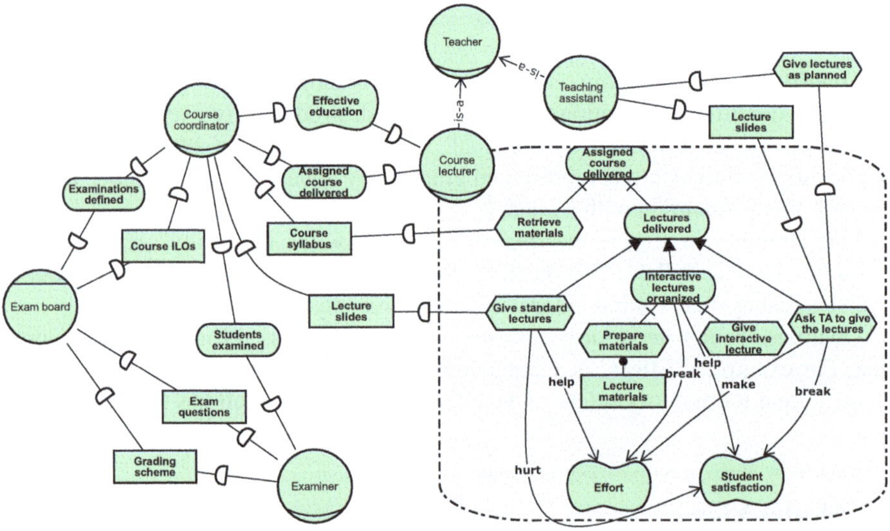

Fig. 11 A Hybrid SD/SR view of the Course Organization scenario

Strategic Dependency (SD) The SD view shows each actor in the model, the actor association links, and the dependency relationships from depender to dependum to dependee. Figure 10 shows an SD view of our illustrative scenario.

Hybrid SD/SR It is often useful to combine SD/SR views where some of the actors are open, but not all, focusing on the strategic rationale of a particular set of actors, and the actor links are hidden. This view is illustrated in Fig. 11 with a focus on the

Course lecturer. Another example, focusing on the Course coordinator, is shown in Fig. 1.

Further useful views can be defined as needed, for example, the *actor view*, showing only actors and actor links, or a *functional view*, hiding all qualities, contribution, and restriction links.

9 Metamodel

The metamodel for iStar 2.0 is shown in Fig. 12. The concepts and relationships in the metamodel have been explained and illustrated in the previous sections.

We describe a number of integrity constraints that explain more detailed constraints on the models that the iStar 2.0 metamodel allows:

- The *is-a* relationship applies only between pairs of roles or pairs of actors.
- There should be no *is-a* cycles.
- There should be no *participates-in* cycles.
- A pair of actors can be linked by at most one actor link: it is not possible to connect two actors via both *is-a* and *participates-in*.

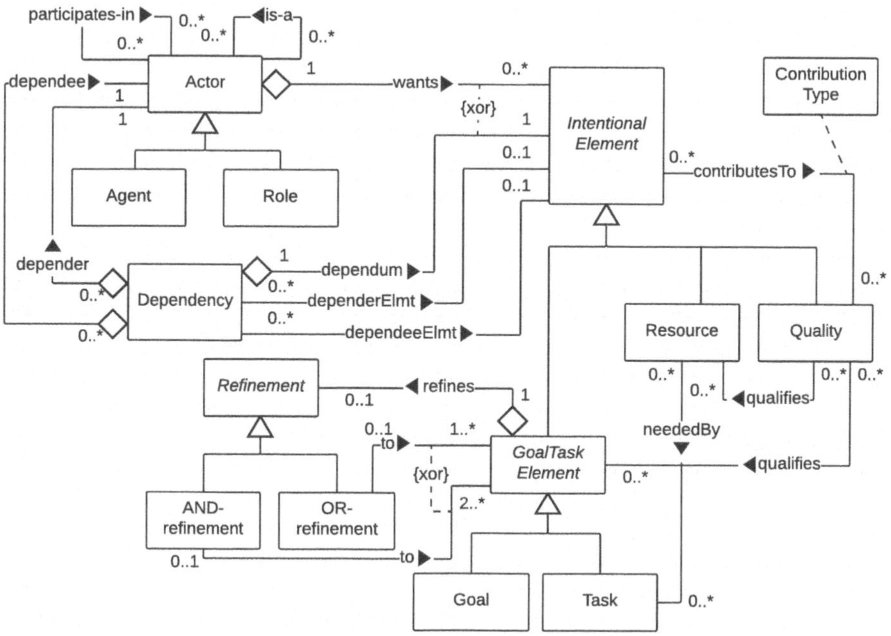

Fig. 12 Metamodel of iStar 2.0

- In a dependency D, if the *dependerElmt* x exists, then the actor that wants x is the same actor that is D's *depender*.
- In a dependency D, if the *dependeeElmt* y exists, then the actor that wants y is the same actor that is D's *dependee*.
- The *depender* and *dependee* of a dependency should be different actors.
- For a dependency, if a *dependerElmt* x exists, then x cannot be refined or contributed to.
- The refinement relationship should not lead to refinement cycles (e.g., G OR-refined to G_1 and G_1 OR-refined to G, G OR-refined to G, etc.).
- The relationships between intentional elements (*contributesTo*, *qualifies*, *NeededBy*, *refines*) apply only to elements that are wanted by the same actor.
- An intentional element and a quality can be linked by either a *contributesTo* relationship or a *qualifies* relationship, but not by both.
- It is not possible for a quality to contribute to itself.

Finally, note that some classes in the metamodel are abstract (*GoalTask Element*, *Intentional Element*, *Refinement*) as they are used to group together (via specialization) concrete classes that share some characteristics. On the other hand, *Actor* is also specialized, but it is a concrete class, thereby denoting that actors can be instantiated without further specialization.

10 Conclusion and Outlook

This chapter presented the results of the iStar standardization process that has led to the definition of the iStar 2.0 language. Supported by the research community of iStar, we promote the adoption of iStar 2.0 for educational and training purposes. This chapter does not conclude the standardization process. Following iterative design principles, we encourage the entire community to assist us in conducting studies about the ease of use, the adequacy for teaching, the expressiveness, the graphical notation, and the automated reasoning techniques that can support iStar 2.0.

References

1. Ayala, C.P., Cares, C., Carvallo, J.P., Grau, G., Haya, M., Salazar, G., Franch, X., Mayol, E., Quer, C.: A comparative analysis of i*-based agent-oriented modeling languages. In: Proceedings of the 17th International Conference on Software Engineering and Knowledge Engineering (SEKE), pp. 43–50 (2005)
2. Cares, C., Franch, X., Perini, A., Susi, A.: Towards interoperability of i* models using iStarML. Comput. Stand. Interfaces **33**(1), 69–79 (2011)
3. Dalpiaz, F., Franch, X., Horkoff, J.: istar 2.0 language guide (2016)
4. Dalpiaz, F., Paja, E., Giorgini, P.: Security Requirements Engineering: Designing Secure Socio-Technical Systems, 1st edn. MIT Press, Cambridge (2016)

5. Dalpiaz, F., Franch, X., Horkoff, J.: iStar 2.0 diagram for a university course organization (2024). https://doi.org/10.5281/zenodo.11281518
6. Franch, X., López, L., Cares, C., Colomer, D.: The *i** framework for goal-oriented modeling. In: Domain-Specific Conceptual Modeling, Concepts, Methods and Tools, pp. 485–506. Springer, Berlin (2016)
7. Horkoff, J., Aydemir, F.B., Cardoso, E., Li, T., Maté, A., Paja, E., Salnitri, M., Piras, L., Mylopoulos, J., Giorgini, P.: Goal-oriented requirements engineering: an extended systematic mapping study. Requir. Eng. **24**, 133–160 (2019)
8. Lucena, M., Santos, E., Silva, C., Alencar, F., Silva, M.J., Castro, J.: Towards a unified metamodel for i*. In: Proceedings of the IEEE International Conference on Research Challenges in Information Science (RCIS), pp. 237–246 (2008)
9. Najera, K., Martínez, A., Perini, A., Estrada, H.: An ontology-based methodology for integrating i* variants. In: Proceedings of the 6th International *i** Workshop, CEUR Workshop Proceedings, vol. 978, pp. 1–6 (2013)
10. Pimentel, J., Castro, J.: pistar tool–a pluggable online tool for goal modeling. In: 2018 IEEE 26th International Requirements Engineering Conference (RE), pp. 498–499. IEEE, Piscataway (2018)
11. Yu, E.S.K.: Modelling strategic relationships for process reengineering. Ph.D. Thesis, University of Toronto (1996)

Towards an iStar 2.0 Extension for Analyzing Goal Variability

Sotirios Liaskos, Shakil M. Khan, and John Mylopoulos

Abstract Goal models of the *i** family have been shown to be suitable for concisely representing and analyzing goal variability. In standard *i**, goal variability emerges due to the presence of OR-refinements, which describe alternative ways by which stakeholder goals can be fulfilled. On closer inspection, however, variability exists in goal models beyond what can be represented by OR-refinements. Firstly, given one set of tasks that fulfill the root goals, there are many alternative orderings by which those tasks can be performed. Secondly, tasks can have many alternative outcomes. In the past, we have proposed various approaches for analyzing these two types of variability, each accompanied by an extension to the *i** notation that allows translation of the visual goal model into a formal specification suitable for automated identification of goal-fulfilling alternatives. In this chapter, we propose a consolidation of these extensions into *iStar T*, a unified extension to the current *iStar 2.0* modeling language. *iStar T* proposes a minimum set of added modeling constructs and a core set of rules that allow translation of models into specifications usable by different reasoning systems. We describe the extensions, and, as examples, we sketch the rules to translate into Hierarchical Task Network and Golog specifications and the kinds of automated analysis that can be done with the result.

S. Liaskos (✉)
School of IT, York University, Toronto, ON, Canada
e-mail: liaskos@yorku.ca

S. M. Khan
University of Regina, Regina, SK, Canada
e-mail: shakil.khan@uregina.ca

J. Mylopoulos
University of Toronto, Toronto, ON, Canada
e-mail: jm@cs.toronto.edu

X. Franch et al. (eds.), *Social Modeling Using the i* Framework*,
https://doi.org/10.1007/978-3-031-72107-6_6

1 Introduction

Since its introduction in the mid-1990s, the *i** modeling language [27] has had a substantial influence in the study of the engineering of software-intensive systems. Its ability to combine modeling of intra-agent intentional structures with interagent social dependency ones in an accessible semi-formal manner has found a large variety of applications in a broad range of areas. It has further been the central reference point of a large and diverse ecosystem of related languages, tools, methods, and analysis techniques. One of the many attractive aspects of *i** and the languages it has inspired is their ability to model *goal variability*, that is, alternative ways by which actor goals can be fulfilled [22]. In *i**, goal variability is modeled both concisely, allowing encoding of large numbers of alternatives within relatively small and readable decomposition structures and in a way that is amenable to useful analysis by allowing characterization of the alternatives subject to criteria.

In this chapter we discuss the notion of goal variability and review the ways by which it occurs in goal models. We then propose *iStar T*, an extension to *i**'s latest standard *iStar 2.0* [6], aimed at facilitating representation of the variability that emerges along temporal and causal dimensions of goal models. The *iStar T* dialect combines and consolidates disparate extensions we have introduced over the past years for different variability modeling and analysis purposes. It introduces a minimum set of core constructs that has proved useful for a variety of variability modeling applications and is amenable to translation into various formal specifications to enable automated reasoning and analysis. As examples, we sketch how *iStar T* can be translated to Hierarchical Task Networks (HTN) [23] and Golog [15] specifications and how the latter can be used for automated reasoning about goal variability. *iStar T* can hence be the basis for developing core modeling and translation tools that can be extended into more specialized languages and toolsets.

We organize the chapter as follows: In Sect. 2 we describe how variability is encoded in *i**-type goal models. In Sect. 3 we present the *iStar T* extension. Then in Sects. 4 and 5, we outline how *iStar T* diagrams can be translated to HTN and Golog specifications and allow for useful automated reasoning. We conclude with pointers to related efforts and discuss opportunities for future work in Sect. 6.

2 Variability in *i** Models

Let us demonstrate how variability emerges in goal models through an example. In Fig. 1, an iStar 2.0 [6] (our reference *i** language specification henceforth) hybrid strategic dependency (SD)-strategic rationale (SR) diagram can be viewed depicting the intentional structure of an interaction between a merchant and a customer. The latter depends on the former to receive a quote for a product of interest and, following order placement and payment completion, to receive the product shipment. The merchant depends on the buyer for receiving order and payment. Both

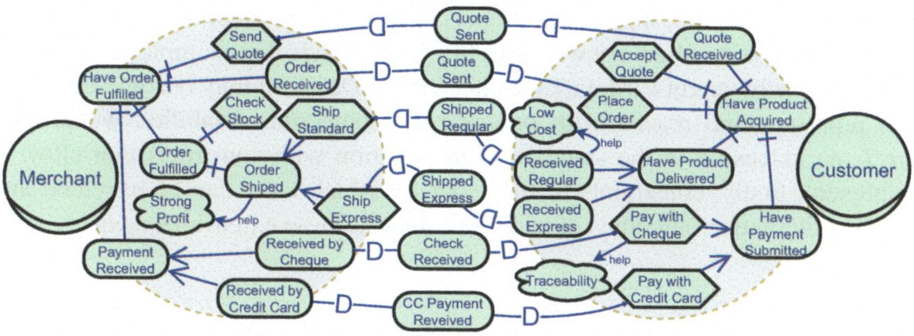

Fig. 1 A merchant-customer iStar 2.0 diagram

actors want to fulfill their top-level goals, *Have Order Fulfilled* and *Have Product Acquired*.

We use the term *goal variability* to express both the notion that there are alternative ways by which such root goals can be fulfilled [22] and to refer to the set of these alternatives. Such variability is primarily represented through OR-refinements of goals and tasks. In the example, OR-refinements are used to represent different speeds by which *Merchant*'s *Order Shipped* can be fulfilled (express and regular), as well as different ways by which the *Customer* can *Have Payment Submitted*.

The meaning of OR-refinement-based variability can vary depending on the content of the participating goals and the aspect in which the refinement children differ. For example, variability in methods of paying for the order can be seen as *instrument* variability, whereas variability in delivery times is *temporal* variability. Additional examples of kinds of variability that an OR-refinement represents include *agentive* (different actors responsible for fulfilling the goal), *locational* (different locations at which a goal can be fulfilled), or *extent* (different degrees by which goal-fulfillment activities can be performed, e.g., intensity, level, amount, etc.). These categories, inspired by case frame literature [8], have been proposed to be used as tools for eliciting OR-refinements [17, 25]. Moreover, the presence of contribution links to quality goals allows representation of the rationale for certain choices among OR-refinement sibling goals or, conversely, guides the choice when a preference of one or more quality goals over others is given [18, 22].

However, variability in *i**-type intentional structures may exist beyond what an OR-refinement can represent. Two additional types of variability that are of interest here are *ordering variability* and *outcome variability*. Ordering variability refers to the multiplicity by which sets of actions to fulfill goals can be ordered. In our example, a product can be shipped before or after a payment has been received. Outcome variability, on the other hand, is based on the acknowledgment that, in reality, tasks do not bring about the same outcome every time they are attempted. Rather, attempt of a task leads to the occurrence of one out of multiple outcomes. For example, *Ship Express* may fail due to a mishap in the shipping process, or either of the outcomes of a task (not seen in the figure) *Choose Payment Option*, e.g., cash or credit card, may occur. Importantly, different outcomes may influence how variability is handled elsewhere in the goal model. For example, if *Customer* chooses to pay by credit card, tasks such as *Apply Discount* may become disabled.

To represent and reason with ordering and outcome variability, we propose *iStar T*, an extension to the standard *iStar* notation with constructs that allow us to represent, firstly, constraints to the order by which tasks can be executed and, secondly, alternative outcomes of tasks. We discuss these extensions next.

3 Elements of *iStar T*

The extensions proposed for *iStar T* allow expressing temporal and conditional relationships between goals and tasks and outcome variability in the latter. An *iStar T* model, such as the one shown in Fig. 2, contains the following added elements: (a) a set D of *domain propositions*, (b) a set $\mathcal{E}$ of *effect elements* (also: *effects*) containing elements or sets of elements from D, (c) a set $\mathcal{P}$ of *effect groups*, each associated with a task $t \in \mathcal{T}$, (d) a set of C of *condition elements* (also: *conditions*), each containing Boolean formulae built with elements from D, and (e) an *initialization element* (also: *initialization*) $\mathcal{I}$ containing a set of elements from D.

In addition, the following link types are introduced. Firstly, *precedence links* and *negative precedence links* can originate from any of goal, task, and condition element and target any of goal, task, and effect. Secondly, *effect links* originate from tasks and target any of a unique effect $e \in \mathcal{E}$ or an effect group $p \in \mathcal{P}$. We next look at each of these additions in more detail.

Domain Propositions, Condition Elements, and Effects The added *domain propositions* are used to represent properties of the domain such as its state as tasks are performed for the fulfillment of actor goals. Examples of such domain propositions include *itemInStock*, *shipmentLost*, and *hasCheckingAccount*. Domain propositions appear in the diagram in three kinds of visual elements: conditions, effects, and initializations. Conditions, represented as rectangles in the diagram, contain arbitrary consistent formulae constructed using domain propositions and common logical connectives: **NOT**, **AND**, and **OR**. Thus:

hasCreditCard **AND** (**NOT** *priceExceedsThreshold* **OR** *thresholdLifted*)

is an example of the content of a condition element. Effects, represented as ovals, contain a list of one or more propositions, e.g., *chequeReceived, accountUpdated*.

Causal Constraints and Non-determinism Tasks and effects are connected with each other using effect links which represent causal constraints. Effect links towards single effects convey that attempt of the task from where the link originates deterministically (i.e., with no uncertainty) makes the propositions listed in the effect true. In Fig. 2, *Customer* task *Pay with Credit Card* points to effect *ccPayReceived*, meaning that attempt of the task makes the proposition in the effect true.

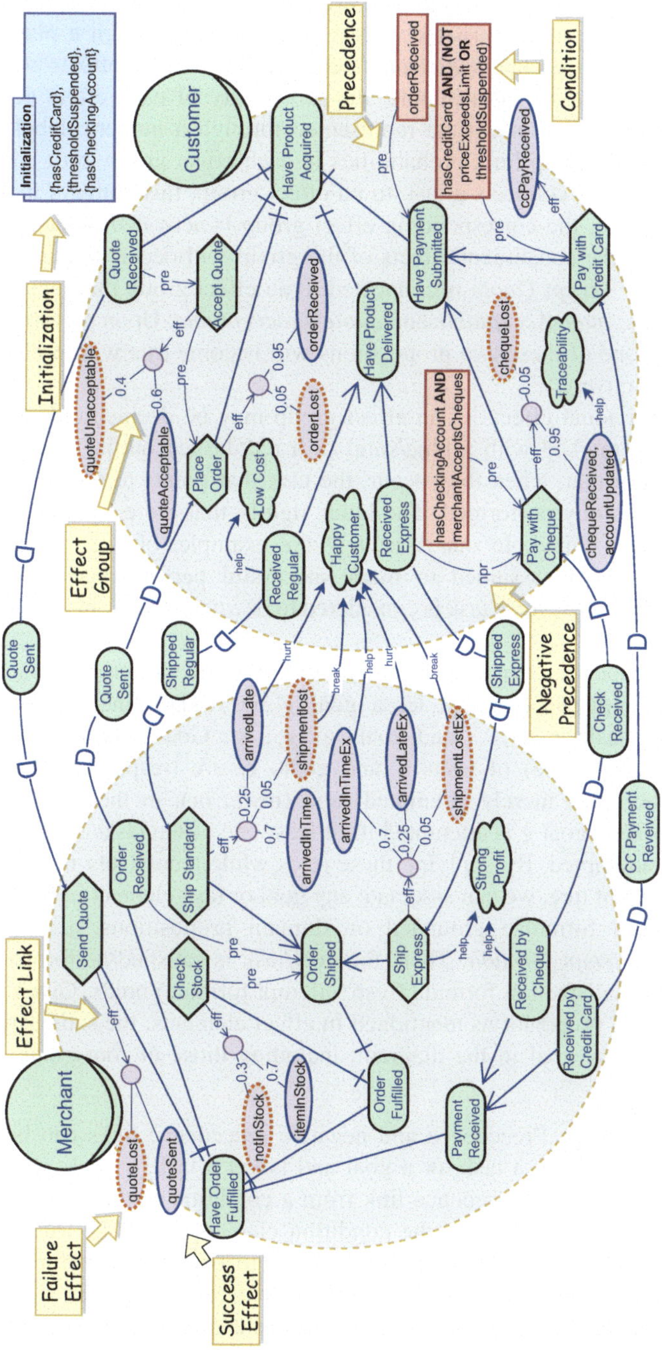

Fig. 2 Extension of the merchant-customer iStar 2.0 model of Fig. 1 using *iStar T* elements

When we want to represent that performance of a task has multiple possible effects, we use effect groups. Effect groups are represented through a filled circular element on which the set of possible effects is connected through a plain effect group line. When the group is *activated*, exactly one of the effects will non-deterministically occur. When available, the probability of each effect occurring upon effect group activation can be represented through a numeric label on the corresponding effect group link; probabilities in each effect group must add up to 1. When an effect link connects a task to an effect group, this conveys that when the task is attempted, the corresponding effect group is activated, which, in turn, means that one of the constituent effects of the group will occur. In our example, the *Customer* task *Accept Quote* is connected to an effect group that includes two possible outcomes: *quoteAcceptable* and *quoteUnacceptable*. Upon performance of the task, exactly one of these two propositions will become true with probabilities 0.6 and 0.4, respectively.

Moreover, individual effects of an effect group may be deemed either *success* or *failure* effects, marked with a blue/solid or a red/dashed outline, respectively. The former signify that, when they occur, the task that points to the effect group is assumed successfully performed. The latter signify that the corresponding task attempt has instead failed. In our *Accept Quote* example, of the two effects it may have, only one is assumed to mark successful performance of the task (*quoteAcceptable*). However, a task is considered to be *attempted*, if any of its effects occurs.

A failed task does not contribute to the fulfillment of its parent goal, though it marks its attempt. Specifically, let a goal g be AND-refined (respectively, OR-refined) into tasks $t_1, t_2, \ldots$ and goals $g_1, g_2, \ldots$. Goal g is satisfied iff all (respectively, at least one) of tasks t_i and goals g_i are (resp., is) successfully performed (rather than merely attempted) and (resp., or), in the case of goals, satisfied. Likewise, a goal g is attempted iff at least one of the tasks t_i and goals g_i is successfully attempted. By applying these rules while recursively traversing the AND/OR refinement tree, we can associate any goal or task element in the diagram with two Boolean formulae grounded on domain propositions, a *satisfaction formula* and an *attempt formula*. Then, the goal/task is satisfied/performed (resp. attempted) iff the satisfaction formula (resp. attempt formula) holds. Given a value configuration of all propositions mentioned in effect elements, the satisfaction and attempt status of any goal in the diagram, including those of root goals, can be decided.

Temporal Constraints Precedence and negative precedence links can be drawn from a condition element, a task, or a goal and target a task, a goal, or an effect within an effect group. A precedence link from a condition element, task, or goal to a task means, respectively, that the condition element has to be true, the task has to be successfully performed, or the goal has to be satisfied before the task can be attempted. A precedence link towards a goal can be seen as a shorthand to drawing separate precedence links from the same origin to each of the tasks in the model that are descendants of the goal. When a precedence link targets an effect within an effect group, the effect cannot be brought about unless the origin is, respectively, true/satisfied/performed. A negative precedence link from a condition element, task, or goal targeting an effect in effect group, a task, or a goal means, respectively, that the targeted effect cannot be brought about, the targeted task cannot be attempted, and none or the leaf-level successor tasks of the goal can be attempted, if, respectively, for the origin possibilities, the condition element is true, the origin task has been successfully performed, or the origin goal has been *attempted* (rather than satisfied).

In Fig. 2, the precedence between goal *Quote Received* and task *Accept Quote* implies that the goal must be deemed satisfied before the task can be attempted. This will be true if Merchant's task *Send Quote* is successfully performed, meaning that the *quoteSent* outcome occurs. If *quoteLost* occurs instead, *Quote Received* is not considered satisfied and, as such, *Accept Quote* cannot be attempted.

Effect Histories and Initializations As actors act in the domain to satisfy their goals, tasks are assumed to be attempted bringing about deterministic or nondeterministic effects, which, in turn, decide if the tasks and their parent goals can be assumed performed and satisfied, enabling or disabling the possibility of attempting other tasks or goals in the next step. An *effect (occurrence) history* is a constraint-satisfying sequence of effects resulting from a corresponding sequence of tasks (the *task history*) from a state in which no task has been attempted. A *goal satisfying history* with respect to a goal is an effect history leading to a state in which the goal has been fulfilled. Such a history describes one way to bind goal variability, where specific OR-refinement alternatives are chosen, a specific execution order is attempted, and specific outcomes have come about.

Further, initializations contain a vocabulary of propositions that must be set to true or false prior to the calculation of histories. Their content is of the form $\{p_1\}$, $\{p_2\}$, ..., where p_i are propositional atoms to be initialized.

Contribution Links In *iStar T* contribution links can be drawn from effects to quality goals, signifying that it is the outcomes of tasks that contribute to qualities, rather than their mere attempt. For example, that *Ship Express* has been attempted does not offer any information with regard to whether quality *Happy Customer* is positively affected. The latter depends on the outcome of the attempt. For example, if the shipment is lost, that has a very negative contribution to the quality goal in question despite the intent. Contributions can be seen as activated and deactivated by task attempts taking place throughout a satisfying history, through enabling propositions contained in the task's effects or arbitrary conditions. Consequently, a goal satisfying history is associated with a trajectory of activations and deactivations of contribution links that target each quality goal.

Structural Restrictions We finally note that a number of structural constraints and scope restrictions are introduced in the current version of *iStar T* to simplify the formalization and analysis process. The most important are (i) that every task must be connected through an effect link to an effect or effect group, (ii) that tasks are not further refined into other tasks or goals, and (iii) that goals must either be refined or delegated; no goal can exist at the leaf level. Thus, meaningful *iStar T* diagrams consist of one or more goal refinement trees, rooted at goals which are progressively refined and/or delegated into lower-level subgoals and eventually tasks, each of which is associated with an effect or an effect group.

4 Formalizing *iStar T*

One of the purposes for defining *iStar T* is to allow automated reasoning about goal variability via translation into suitable formal specification languages. The authors have proposed various ways in the past for performing such translations based on different extensions to i^* catering for different variability analysis purposes [18, 19, 21]. Our goal is to distill *baseline translation rules* which can be extended to fulfill specific needs. The baseline rules depend on the target specification language. In this chapter, we showcase development of rules for two targets: Hierarchical Task Networks (HTN) [23] and Golog [15]. Both target languages have been shown to be useful for a variety of tasks including identification of optimal solutions based on different criteria [18, 21], behavioral customization of software [19], and development of simulations for reinforcement learning [20].

Our presentation is informal and example-based and aimed at showcasing the principles behind the translation rules and their capabilities in terms of the analysis they support. An authoritative report with a formal presentation and analysis of the core translation rules is upcoming. For better comprehension of the presentation that follows, the reader may find useful to refer to the examples of Fig. 3.

4.1 HTN Planning

We start by showing how the extended goal models can be translated to HTN specifications, which in turn can be used to identify goal satisfying histories.

HTN planners receive a *domain specification* and a *problem specification* as input and generate a solution to the latter as output. The domain specification consists of a set of domain predicates $v \in V$ describing properties of objects $b \in B$ that are of interest in the domain, a set of *operators* $o \in O$, representing actions in the domain, and a set of *methods* $\in M$ describing ways by which higher-level planning objectives can be decomposed into lower-level operators or other methods.

Domain predicates, such as `has(customer,quote)`, are used to describe the state of the domain as agents perform actions described by operators. Moreover, *axioms* show that the predicate that is the *head* of the axiom is true if the expression

<table>
<tr><th>iStar T</th><th>HTN</th><th>Golog</th></tr>
<tr><td>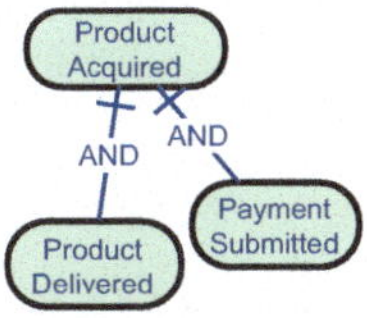
</td><td>(:method productAcquired
()
(:unordered
(productDelivered)
(paymentSubmitted)))
(:- productAcquiredSat
(and (productDeliveredSat)
(paymentSubmittedSat)))
(:- productAcquiredAtt
(or (productDeliveredAtt)
(paymetnSubmittedAtt)))</td><td>proc(productAcquired,
(productDelivered:paymentSubmitted) #
(paymentSubmitted:productDelivered)).

productAcquiredSat(S) :-
productDeliveredSat(S), % and
paymentSubmittedSat(S).

productAcquiredAtt(S) :-
productDeliveredAtt(S); % or
paymentSubmittedAtt(S).</td></tr>
<tr><td>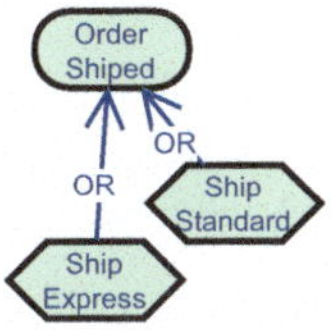
</td><td>(:method orderShipped
()
((shipExpress)))
(:method orderShipped
()
((shipStandard)))
(:- orderShippedSat
(or (shipExpressSat)
(shipStandardSat)))
(:- orderShippedAtt
(or (shipExpressSat)
(shipStandardSat)))</td><td>proc(orderShipped,
shipExpress # shipStandard). % pick

orderShippedSat(S) :-
shipExpressSat(S);
shipStandardSat(S).

orderShippedAtt(S) :-
shipExpressAtt(S);
shipStandardAtt(S).</td></tr>
<tr><td>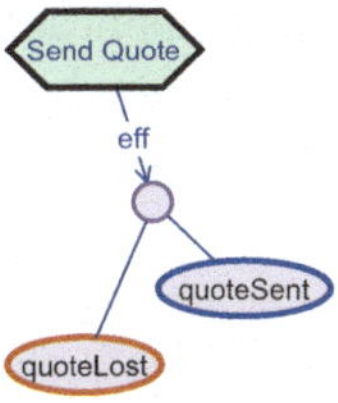
</td><td>(:operator (!quoteSent)
(...) ; precondition
() ; delete list
(quoteSent)) ; add list
(:operator (!quoteLost)
(...)
()
(quoteLost))
(:method sendQuote
()
((!quoteSent)))
(:method sendQuote
()
((!quoteLost)))
(:- sendQuoteSat
((quoteSent)))
(:- sendQuoteAtt
(or (quoteSent)
(quoteLost)))</td><td>proc(sendQuote,
quoteSent # quoteLost).

poss(quoteSent) :- ...
poss(quoteLost) :- ...

quoteSent(do(A,S)) :-
quoteSent(S); A = quoteSent.
quoteLost(do(A,S)) :-
quoteLost(S); A = quoteLost.

sendQuoteSat(S) :-
quoteSent(S).
sendQuoteAtt(S) :-
quoteSent(S);quoteLost(S).</td></tr>
<tr><td>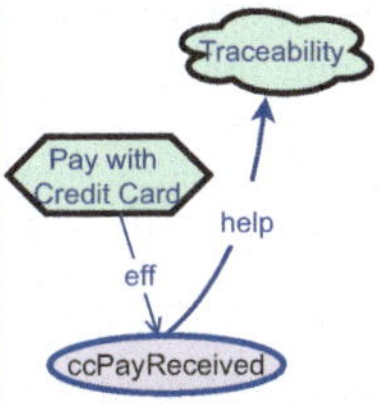
</td><td>(:method paywithCreditCard
()
((!ccPayReveivedNat)
(q_contr traceability plus)))
(:operator (!ccPayReceivedNat)
()
()
(ccPayReceived))
...
(:method
(q_contr ?quality help)
(sat ?goal FS) ; if
((!!fullSat ?goal)) ; tasks
() ; else
((!!partSat ?goal)))</td><td>proc(paywithCreditCard,
ccPayReceived).

poss(ccPayReceived) :- ...

ccPayReceived(do(A,S)) :-
ccPayReceived(S);
A = ccPayReceived.

sat(traceability,part,do(A,S)) :-
sat(traceability,part,S);
A = ccPayReceived;
A = ... % other help contributors</td></tr>
</table>

Fig. 3 Translation rules by example

in the *tail* of the axiom is satisfied. Thus, the following axiom says that 0-ary predicate `orderShipped` is true if any of the propositions in the tail is satisfied:

```
(:- (orderShipped) ; head
    (orderShippedByAir ∨ orderShippedByLand)) ; tail
```

Operators represent the transitioning of the domain from one state to another, through changes in the truth values of domain predicates. Each operator o is associated with an *add list* and a *delete list*, which list predicates that turn true and false, respectively, upon application of the operator. Operators also have a *precondition* formula, constructed with elements from V, which denote that the operator cannot be applied at a given state, unless the precondition is satisfied at that state. The following is an example of an operator:

```
(:operator (!payWithCreditCard) ; Operator name
           (hasCC ∧ (¬priceExceedsLimit ∨ limitSuspended)) ; precondition
           ((paymentPending)) ; Delete list
           ((ccPayReceived))) ; Add list
```

Methods are used to guide the planner into searching for sequences of actions that are plausible in the domain of interest. An example of a method is as follows:

```
(:method (orderfulfilled)      ; method name
        (orderReceived)        ; method precondition
        (:unordered (!checkStock) (orderShipped) )) ; task list
```

In the above, the method `orderfulfilled`, which can be utilized if `orderReceived` is true, shows how the problem of having the order fulfilled decomposes into the application of operator `!checkStock` and application of another method called `orderShipped`, in no specific order. There may be many alternative methods named `orderfulfilled` for the planner to choose from when constructing a plan.

4.1.1 Specification Generation

We now turn to how we translate *iStar T* models into HTN domain specifications.

Goals and Tasks Each goal and task in the goal diagram is, firstly, mapped into two propositions (0-ary predicates) in the HTN domain: one that signifies its successful attainment (*attainment proposition*) and one that signifies its attempt (*attempt proposition*). Secondly, each goal and task is mapped to a method name.

Thirdly, we look at how the goal or task is refined. If a goal is AND-decomposed into *n* other goals and/or tasks (sub-elements), a *refinement method* is introduced, named after the goal being decomposed and containing an unordered list of method or operator names corresponding to all *n* sub-elements. When a goal is OR-decomposed into the *n* sub-elements, *n* refinement methods are introduced instead, each named after the goal being decomposed. The task list of each of the *n* methods contains one method or operator name corresponding to each of the sub-elements of the OR-decomposition. Further, we treat the dependency as a one-subgoal OR-refinement of the depender goal to the dependee element.

When the element is a task, it is associated with an effect or an effect group. The translation then treats this association as an OR-decomposition and introduces as many methods as the effects in the group (one in the case of a deterministic effect), whose name is the method name associated with the task and the action list in each method has the name of the effect operator associated with the effect (more below).

Fourthly, an *attainment axiom* is introduced associating the attainment proposition of the parent goal with the conjunction (AND-decompositions) or disjunction (OR-decompositions) of attainment propositions of the sub-elements. Fifthly, an *attempt axiom* is introduced that associates the attempt proposition of the parent goal with the disjunction of attempt propositions of the sub-elements independent on whether it is an AND- or OR-decomposition.

Effects Each effect element e is translated into a distinct *effect operator*. The add list of the effect operator contains the domain predicates listed in the effect shape and the delete list is empty. Calculation of the precondition of the operator is as follows: Consider first the set A_e of all the goal and task elements that are ancestors to effect element e, i.e., that exist in the path between the effect and the root goal. Consider next the sources of all precedence links that target the elements in A_e. These sources can be goals, tasks, or conditions. Construct then the conjunction ϕ_{pre} of the attainment propositions (goals and tasks) and condition formulae (condition elements) that correspond to these sources. Consider next all the sources of the negative precedence links that target the elements in A_e, which are again goals, tasks, or conditions. Construct the disjunction ϕ_{npr} of the *attempt* propositions (goal and task elements) and condition formulae (condition elements) that correspond to these sources. Assign then $\phi_{pre} \wedge \neg\phi_{npr}$ as the precondition to the effect operator.

Qualities Each quality q is translated into a domain object `q` and two predicates `sat(q,l)` and `den(q,l)`, which carry the level l of satisfaction and denial of quality q, respectively. Consider then a contribution link from effect element e towards a quality q. The effect element is either associated with a task (deterministic case) or is part of an effect group (nondeterministic case). The contribution link is translated into an invocation of a reserved `(quality_contr ?cont ?dest)` method, where `?cont` describes the kind of contribution and `?dest` the destination. This is done by simply adding the method name `quality_contr` in the task list of the method that is associated with the task that brings about the effect. For example, if task t sends an effect link to an effect group e_1, e_2, e_3, and, say, e_2 sends a *helps* contribution link to quality q, then the method that decomposes t into e_2 has a task list that includes both the effect operator for e_2 and method `(quality_contr help q)`.

The `quality_contr` method, together with associated helper reserved operators, is responsible for affecting the `sat(q,l)` and `den(q,l)` predicates based, e.g., on the label of the contribution link and the existing satisfaction and values. The exact structure of these methods and operators depends on the framework adopted for representing and aggregating contribution and satisfaction/denial values. For example, established label propagation rules [12] can be applied for updating the value of `sat(q,l)` and `den(q,l)` every time `quality_contr` is invoked.

4.2 Golog

We now turn to how *iStar T* goal models can be translated to specifications of the Golog family. Golog [15] is a high-level agent programming language based on the situation calculus [16], a language for modeling dynamic domains. Golog has been the basis of many extensions including ConGolog [14] which allows for concurrency, interrupts, and exogenous actions; IndiGolog [7] which allows for interleaved action, sensing, and planning; and DT-Golog [3] that allows for reasoning with probabilistic actions. In addition, simulating dynamic domains encoded in the underlying situation calculus can be used for model-free reinforcement learning [20]. Hence, having a core set of rules for translating *iStar T* models to Golog facilitates accessing diverse analysis, reasoning, and execution tools.

Core concepts of Golog are *fluents*, *actions*, and *situations*. Fluents are used to describe what is true in the domain at a given situation. They are represented through n-ary predicates with a situation term as their last argument, as in `hasRead(quote,customer,s)`. A situation is a first-order term that represents a sequence of actions from an initial situation S_0 where no action has been performed. The function symbol `do(a,s)` is used to denote the situation which results from performing action `a` in situation `s`. Situations emerge from nested application of the function as in $\mathtt{do(a}_n\mathtt{,do(a}_{n-1}\mathtt{,...,do(a}_1\mathtt{,S}_0\mathtt{)...)))}$. Finally, a special predicate `poss(a,s)` is used to state that action `a` is executable in situation `s`.

To describe a domain, a set of axioms are defined over the above constructs. The most important are *action precondition axioms* and *successor state axioms*. The former are defined for each action `a` and describe the conditions under which actions can be performed. For example, the following axiom says that for customer c to pay a merchant m by check in situation s, the former needs to have a checking account, and the latter needs to be accepting of checks in the same situation:

```
poss(payWithCheque(c,m),s) ↔ hasCheckingAccount(c,s) ∧ acceptsCheques(m,s)
```

Successor state axioms are defined for each fluent and describe how the fluent's truth value changes due to the performance of tasks. For example, the fluent `quoteSent(s)` holds in a given situation if it was already true in the previous situation or the latest action has made it true:

```
quoteSent(do(a,s)) ↔ quoteSent(s) ∨ (a = sendQuote)
```

Golog allows the development of high-level programs that describe agent behavior while abiding by the action theory defined by the axioms. Programming constructs of interest are *sequences* and *nondeterministic choices* of actions which are used in *procedures*. Of the following procedures, `orderFulfilled` contains an action sequence in its body comprising of an action and another procedure to be executed in that order, and `orderShipped` is a nondeterministic choice between two actions:

```
proc(orderFulfilled, checkStock : orderShipped)
proc(orderShipped, shipExpress | shipStandard)
```

4.2.1 Specification Generation

We now sketch the rules for translating *iStar T* models into Golog specifications.

Goals and Tasks Each goal and task in the model is, firstly, translated into one attainment fluent and one attempt fluent. Secondly, a Golog procedure named after the element in question is added. If the element is an OR-decomposed goal, or a depender goal, the body of the procedure contains a nondeterministic action choice among a set of procedure names referring to the sub-elements or the one dependee element. If the element is a task, the body contains a nondeterministic choice among the effect actions (more below) that correspond to the one or more effects associated with the task. If the element is an AND-decomposed goal, the procedure body contains a nondeterministic choice among a set of action sequences that constitute all possible permutations of the sub-elements, except for those that are impossible due to temporal constraints among the subgoals.

Effects Each effect is translated into (a) an *effect action*, (b) as many *effect fluents* as the propositions that are contained in the effect. For each of the actions, an action precondition axiom is constructed, exactly as in the case of HTN translation: the sources of precedence (respectively, negative precedence) links targeting every ancestor of the effect are collected and together form a conjunction (resp., disjunction) of the corresponding attainment (resp., attempt) formulae. The conjunction of the two formulae, with the latter (the one collecting constraints from negative precedence links) negated, is then placed as precondition for the introduced action.

Furthermore, each of the introduced fluents $\texttt{effFluent}_i$ relating to the effect corresponds to a successor state axiom of the form:

$$\begin{aligned}\texttt{effFluent}_i\texttt{(do(a,s))} \leftrightarrow{} & \texttt{effFluent}_i\texttt{(s)} \vee \\ & \texttt{(a = effAction}_1\texttt{)} \vee \texttt{(a = effAction}_2\texttt{)} \vee \ldots\end{aligned}$$

where $\texttt{effAction}_i$ are effect actions corresponding to effects that mention $\texttt{effFluent}_i$. Finally, the truth values of attainment and attempt fluents associated with goals and tasks are determined, via appropriate axioms, by AND/OR formulae grounded on effect fluents and reflecting the underlying refinement structure.

Qualities For each quality q, two fluents `sat(q,l,s)` and `den(q,l,s)` are introduced representing the level of satisfaction and denial evidence associated with the quality in situation `s`. For each of these fluents, a number of successor state axioms is constructed showing how different quality satisfaction values are acquired due to the occurrence of effects that have a contribution to the quality. For example, following again the qualitative two-level satisfaction representation system (partially/fully satisfied/denied) [12], the axiom of the form:

$$\begin{aligned}\texttt{sat(q,full,do(a,s))} \leftrightarrow{} & \texttt{sat(q,full,s)} \vee \\ & \texttt{(a = ppEffect}_1\texttt{)} \vee \texttt{(a = ppEffect}_2\texttt{)} \vee \ldots\end{aligned}$$

says that quality `q` is fully satisfied in the next situation if it already were in the previous situation or one of the effects $\texttt{ppEffect}_i$ from where a *make* contribution link originates targeting `q` has occurred.

5 Automated Identification of Solutions

The specifications resulting from the above translations can be used as a basis for automatically generating goal satisfying effect histories (solutions) using the corresponding reasoning tools—HTN planners and Golog interpreters. At least three kinds of solutions can be generated: arbitrary solutions, solutions under given quality constraints, and solutions that optimize a preference specification over qualities.

Arbitrary Solutions The tools are useful for identifying any constraint-satisfying solution when no other desiderata exist. In the HTN case, given the resulting domain specification, a planner is able to search for plans that satisfy a specific problem specification. The latter consists of a list of initially true predicates and a top-level task to be fulfilled. Hence, by instantiating the *iStar T* model's initialization into a set of HTN predicates and assigning a root goal of interest to be the top-level task, we can get the HTN planner to generate plans, each constituent operator of which mapping to an effect in a goal satisfying history. In the presence of effect groups, the planner returns non-deterministically chosen scenarios of execution. In the Golog case, the interpreter is capable of running Golog programs relative to an initial situation, outputting a situation (i.e., a sequence of actions) at which the program terminates. Thus, by setting the fluents corresponding to an instantiation of the *iStar T* model's initialization to hold in the initial situation S_0, we can run the procedure that represents the top-level goal we are interested in generating a solution for. Given the mapping of actions to leaf-level effects, the results represent scenarios of task outcomes.

Solutions Under Constraints We often desire to generate solutions under hard constraints, and, specifically, desired quality satisfaction values. For example, we may be interested in solutions which never receive a negative contribution to quality goal *Safety*, or in which, at the end only, goal *Happy Customer* is fully satisfied. To find such solutions relative to a top-level goal g, in both HTN and Golog cases, we work as follows: Firstly, we create a formula ϕ_q describing all such constraints. Then in the *iStar T* model, we introduce a dummy terminal task t_r and a dummy root goal g_r. Next, we set g and t_r to be AND-refinements of g_r and connect them with a precedence link from g to t_r. We then translate as per the corresponding rules and add ϕ_q as a precondition to t_r. We note that there is more nuance than we can cover here: for example, universal/existential constraints on the entire history (e.g., there does not exist a negative contribution to the *Safety* quality) are addressed differently from those that are posed on aggregates of contributions (e.g., the cumulative contribution to *Low Cost* at the end is above a threshold). A general framework

Fig. 4 Reasoner output format (different solutions)

HTN	*Golog*
1: (!QUOTESENT)	1: s0
2: (!QUOTEACCEPTABLE)	2: quoteSent
3: (!ORDERRECEIVED)	3: quoteAcceptable
4: (!ITEMINSTOCK)	4: orderReceived
5: (!ARRIVEDINTIME)	5: itemInStock
6: (!CHEQUERECEIVED)	6: arrivedLateEx
7: (!FINAL)	7: payWithCreditCard
8: (!SAT HAPPYCUSTOMER PS)	[sat(happyCustomer, pd, ...),
9: (!SAT STRONGPROFIT PS)	sat(strongProfit, ps, ...)]
...	

for quality satisfaction analysis in light of time-ordered contributions to qualities would be a useful future extension of *iStar T*.

Optimal Solutions With the appropriate extensions and revisions, the translation rules can also produce specifications that allow identifying solutions that are optimal with respect to an objective function. It has been shown that the Golog specification can be augmented with a relatively simple reward structures to allow decision theoretic optimization using DT-Golog [21]. Further, the Golog programs are particularly useful for performing simulations of the intentional structure, which can be useful in reinforcement learning applications [20]. Moreover, HTN operators can accept simple cost parameters allowing HTN planners to search for minimum-cost plans. Rules can, hence, be defined that map contributions to qualities to such cost values. A complete treatment of how minimum-cost HTN planning can be used for optimizing quality goal satisfaction desiderata is another promising extension of *iStar T*.

Output Format Sample outputs of the tools can be seen in Fig. 4. The action lists correspond to effect histories in Fig. 2. In the HTN output, impacts to quality goals are displayed as separate trailing actions. In the Golog output, following solution generation, quality satisfaction fluents that are true in the situation that corresponds to the solution are printed. Post-processing procedures can use the quality satisfaction aspect of the output as an input to more advanced satisfaction propagation analysis algorithms [12] and visualizations.

6 Concluding Remarks

A great many extensions to *i** have been introduced to make the language usable for specific purposes [13], and many procedures have also been proposed for automated reasoning about goal models via using established reasoning tools and for different purposes, e.g., SMTs [24] and model checkers [9] to name two. Our proposed extension, *iStar T*, attempts to systematize and consolidate extensions that have been introduced for the purpose of supporting analysis of different kinds of goal variability, including ordering and outcome variability. It further complements similar work on goal model formalization (e.g., [4, 10, 26]) in that the set of extensions it introduces is minimal enough to allow formalization into different formal specification languages. In this chapter we showcased HTN and Golog, but similar procedures for formalizing *iStar T* to other languages appear to be possible. This includes different subsets and versions of PDDL [11] for compliant planners as well as specification languages for model-checking [5]. This allows researchers with different analysis needs to have a common starting point. An additional opportunity for future work is a baseline for advanced reasoning with quality goals, including different kinds of preference specifications and a treatment of satisfaction propagation in quality goal graphs within the context of time-ordered actions.

Further, the visual complexity of *iStar T* is deserving of some investigation. The additional elements required for forming a complete model arguably affect the comprehensibility of the resulting diagram. To address this, interactive model slicing can be investigated whereby parts of the diagram (precedence links, effect groups, etc.) are displayed only on demand. Likewise, the definition of separate viewpoints, such as a temporal and/or a causal one, can be explored for separating concerns, as per common practice—e.g., URN [2] introduces two sub-languages, GRL and UCM, for modeling intentional and causal aspects, respectively. Finally, the introduction and use of a textual syntax, in the spirit of TGRL [1], could prove useful for taming complexity, particularly during model development.

References

1. Abdelzad, V., Amyot, D., Alwidian, S., Lethbridge, T.: A textual syntax with tool support for the goal-oriented requirement language. In: Proceedings of the Eighth International i* Workshop (2015)
2. Amyot, D., Mussbacher, G.: User requirements notation: the first ten years, the next ten years (invited paper). J. Softw. **6**(5), 747–768 (2011)
3. Boutilier, C., Reiter, R., Soutchanski, M., Thrun, S.: Decision-theoretic, high-level agent programming in the situation calculus. In: Proceedings of the 17th Conference on Artificial Intelligence (AAAI-00), pp. 355–362. AAAI Press, Austin (2000)
4. Bryl, V., Massacci, F., Mylopoulos, J., Zannone, N.: Designing security requirements models through planning. In: Proceedings of the 18th International Conference on Advanced Information Systems Engineering (CAiSE'06) (2006). https://doi.org/10.1007/11767138_4
5. Cimatti, A., Clarke, E., Giunchiglia, E., Giunchiglia, F., Pistore, M., Roveri, M., Sebastiani, R., Tacchella, A.: NuSMV 2: An opensource tool for symbolic model checking. In: Proceedings of the International Conference on Computer-Aided Verification (CAV 2002). Copenhagen, Denmark (2002)
6. Dalpiaz, F., Franch, X., Horkoff, J.: iStar 2.0 language guide. Comput. Res. Reposit. (CoRR) **abs/1605.0** (2016). http://arxiv.org/abs/1605.07767
7. De Giacomo, G., Lespérance, Y., Levesque, H.J., Sardina, S.: IndiGolog: A High-Level Programming Language for Embedded Reasoning Agents, pp. 31–72. Boston, MA (2009)
8. Fillmore, C.J.: The case for case. In: Bach, Harms (Ed.) Universals in Linguistic Theory, pp. 1–88. Holt, Rinehart, and Winston, New York (1968)
9. Fuxman, A., Liu, L., Mylopoulos, J., Pistore, M., Roveri, M., Traverso, P.: Specifying and analyzing early requirements in Tropos. Requir. Eng. **9**(2), 132–150 (2004)

10. Gans, G., Jarke, M., Lakemeyer, G., Vits, T.: SNet: A modeling and simulation environment for agent networks based on i* and ConGolog. In: Proceedings of the 14th International Conference on Advanced Information Systems Engineering CAiSE'02, pp. 328–343. Toronto (2002)
11. Ghallab, M., Howe, A., Knoblcok, C., McDermott, D., Ram, A., Veloso, M., Weld, D., Wiklins, D.: PDDL—The planning domain definition language. Technical Report, Yale Center for Computational Vision and Control. Technical Report CVC TR-98-003/DCS TR-1165 (1997)
12. Giorgini, P., Mylopoulos, J., Nicchiarelli, E., Sebastiani, R.: Reasoning with goal models. In: Proceedings of the 21st International Conference on Conceptual Modeling (ER'02), pp. 167–181 (2002)
13. Gonçalves, E., Castro, J., Araújo, J., Heineck, T.: A systematic literature review of iStar extensions. J. Syst. Softw. **137**, 1–33 (2018)
14. Lespérance, Y., Kelly, T.G., Mylopoulos, J., Yu, E.S.K.: Modeling dynamic domains with ConGolog. In: Proceedings of the the 11th International Conference on Advanced Information Systems Engineering (CAiSE'99). Heidelberg (1999)
15. Levesque, H.J., Reiter, R., Lespérance, Y., Lin, F., Scherl, R.B.: GOLOG: A logic programming language for dynamic domains. J. Logic Programm. **31**(1–3), 59–83 (1997)
16. Levesque, H., Pirri, F., Reiter, R.: Foundations for a calculus of situations. Electr. Trans. AI **2**(3–4), 159–178 (1998)
17. Liaskos, S., Lapouchnian, A., Yu, Y., Yu, E., Mylopoulos, J.: On goal-based variability acquisition and analysis. In: Proceedings of the 14th IEEE International Requirements Engineering Conference (RE'06). IEEE Computer Society, Minneapolis (2006)
18. Liaskos, S., McIlraith, S., Sohrabi, S., Mylopoulos, J.: Representing and reasoning about preferences in requirements engineering. Requir. Eng. J. **16**, 227–249 (2011)
19. Liaskos, S., Khan, S.M., Litoiu, M., Jungblut, M.D., Rogozhkin, V., Mylopoulos, J.: Behavioral adaptation of information systems through goal models. Inf. Syst. **37**(8), 767–783 (2012)
20. Liaskos, S., Khan, S.M., Golipour, R., Mylopoulos, J.: Towards goal-based generation of reinforcement learning domain simulations. In: Proceedings of the 15th International i* Workshop. CEUR Workshop Proceedings (2022)
21. Liaskos, S., Khan, S.M., Mylopoulos, J.: Modeling and reasoning about uncertainty in goal models: a decision-theoretic approach. Softw. Syst. Model. **21**, 1–24 (2022)
22. Mylopoulos, J., Chung, L., Liao, S., Wang, H., Yu, E.: Exploring alternatives during requirements analysis. IEEE Softw. **18**(1), 92–96 (2001)
23. Nau, D.S., Au, T.C., Ilghami, O., Kuter, U., Murdock, J.W., Wu, D., Yaman, F.: SHOP2: an HTN planning system. J. Artif. Intell. Res. **20**, 379–404 (2003)
24. Nguyen, C.M., Sebastiani, R., Giorgini, P., Mylopoulos, J.: Multi-objective reasoning with constrained goal models. Requir. Eng. **23**(2), 189–225 (2018)
25. Rolland, C., Souveyet, C., Achour, C.B.: Guiding goal modeling using scenarios. IEEE Trans. Softw. Eng. **24**(12), 1055–1071 (1998)
26. Wang, X., Lespérance, Y.: Agent-oriented requirements engineering using ConGolog and i*. In: Bi-Conference Workshop at Agents 2001 and CAiSE'01 (AOIS-2001) (2001)
27. Yu, E.S.K.: Towards modelling and reasoning support for early-phase requirements engineering. In: Proceedings of the 3rd IEEE International Symposium on Requirements Engineering (RE'97). pp. 226–235. Annapolis (1997)

Goal-Oriented Modeling of Safety-Critical Systems

Moniky Ribeiro, Jaelson Castro, and Maria Lencastre

Abstract Safety requirements are key elements to Critical Systems. However, it is quite challenging for Requirements Engineers to handle them, and often Safety Engineers do not model adequately the safety requirements derived from their safety analysis. In order to allow the early modeling of safety requirements by both Requirements and Safety Engineers, our objective is to define an approach that integrates a well-accepted Goal Oriented Requirements modeling language, that is fit for safety modeling, with a well-known safety analysis technique. The iStar4Safety and Systems Theoretic Process Analysis (STPA) techniques were chosen as the candidate techniques for alignment. By integrating the two techniques, our proposal will enable a more systematic and comprehensive approach to model early safety requirements. It will enhance the identification and analysis of safety-related concerns, facilitate communication among stakeholders, and support the development of safer and more reliable critical systems.

1 Introduction

Safety-Critical Systems (SCSs) can cause severe losses, including human fatalities, economic damage, and environmental harm when specific hazards occur [1]. Ensuring safety throughout the SCS life cycle requires robust methods and processes [2]. Requirements engineering is vital for SCS development, as unclear requirements can jeopardize system quality [3], and effective communication is essential to avoid safety issues from misinterpretations during requirements definition [4].

Goal-oriented languages like iStar, KAOS, and GRL help justify early-stage requirements [5]. iStar [6], widely used in requirements engineering, has many

M. Ribeiro (✉) · J. Castro
Universidade Federal de Pernambuco, Recife, Pernambuco, Brazil
e-mail: smsr@cin.ufpe.br; jbc@cin.ufpe.br

M. Lencastre
Universidade de Pernambuco, Recife, Pernambuco, Brazil
e-mail: mlpm@ecomp.poli.br

X. Franch et al. (eds.), *Social Modeling Using the i* Framework*,
https://doi.org/10.1007/978-3-031-72107-6_7

extensions, including some for safety modeling [7]. However, requirements engineering and safety analysis are often conducted separately, hindering the integration of best practices from both fields [4].

Our work stems from the challenges in expressing safety analysis results through natural language and the inadequacy of common requirements specification languages in addressing SCSs, coupled with the necessity to enhance communication between safety analysts and requirements engineers. Requirements engineers often lack inherent safety expertise, necessitating systematic guidance to incorporate safety requirements from the project's inception. Conversely, safety engineers require modeling techniques to articulate safety requirements, as natural language is prone to ambiguity. Our goal is to devise an approach called RESafety that seamlessly integrates iStar4Safety, a goal-oriented requirements modeling language, tailored for safety modeling, with STPA (Systems Theoretic Process Analysis), a renowned safety analysis technique [8]. This integration aims to streamline early safety requirements modeling systematically and comprehensively.

To demonstrate our approach's efficacy, we apply it to a real-world project involving the development of a low-cost Insulin Infusion Pump System (IIP), a collaborative effort between academia and industry. The IIP serves as a medical device designed to administer rapid-acting insulin doses through a catheter beneath the patient's skin, intended for managing type I diabetes mellitus while maintaining optimal glucose levels in the patient's bloodstream.

The remainder of this chapter is structured as follows: Sect. 2 introduces some background information; Sect. 3 describes related work; Sect. 4 presents our approach for the integration of requirements and safety analysis together with an illustration of its use; Sect. 5 addresses some threats to validity; finally, Sect. 6 presents some final considerations and sketches future work.

2 Background

In this section we provide some introduction to STPA [8] and the iStar4Safety language [9].

2.1 Systems Theoretic Process Analysis (STPA)

The STPA is part of the STAMP (System-Theoretic Accident Model and Processes) model [8]. STPA presents a new way of analyzing safety, as it also considers that accidents can be caused by the interaction between system components, unlike previous techniques that focus solely on individual components.

STPA is based on systems theory, where a system's main properties should be considered emergent properties. Controller modeling abstracts the roles of controlled processes and controllers and their interfaces through a model to achieve a holistic system view. Furthermore, the control model allows the analysis of control actions between components and their respective feedback.

Previous researches [10, 11] show that STPA not only detects known hazard causes identified by methods like FTA and HAZOP but also uncovers novel safety scenarios. In order to carry out a safety analysis with STPA, a set of four steps are required, namely:

1. Define the purpose of the analysis
2. Model the control structure
3. Identify unsafe control actions (UCAs)
4. Identify Loss Scenarios

2.2 *iStar4Safety*

iStar4Safety language is an iStar 2.0 extension, where four new safety elements were added— **Safety Goal**, **Hazard**, **Safety Task**, and **Safety Resource**—and a new link called **obstruct** [9].

The Safety Goal and Hazard elements are specializations of the iStar 2.0 Goal element. **Hazards** can obstruct **Safety Goals**, represented by the new **"obstruct"** link connecting to the constructors. Hazards are conceptualized as a specialization of goals because they can be considered anti-goals, i.e., that are desired not to happen. Hence, hazards should be avoided. Additionally, Safety Goal elements have the **"Accident impact level"**property that can take one of five values according to the worst accident level that will happen if some hazard obstructs a safety goal. This categorization is important, especially when prioritization is a concern.

3 Related Work

Our approach is novel as it relies on goal modeling language (iStar4Safety), using insights brought by the STPA technique defined by Leveson and Thomas [8]. Below, we discuss some related work.

Sharifi et al. [12, 13] propose a FinTech certification methodology combining the GRL goal modeling with UCM process modeling. They begin with stakeholder identification using the onion model, followed by creating a GRL strategic dependency model. This model is expanded with the UCM model to trace functional goals. They then conduct an STPA analysis, using its artifacts to update models and create assurance cases. Unlike Sharifi et al., who use UCM for process modeling, we simplify by using only iStar4Safety and STPA techniques.

The SARSSi* approach outlined in Vilela et al. [14] combines the STPA technique with the iStar goal-oriented requirements modeling technique, generating a preliminary safety analysis. An essential difference is that the former uses iStar in its standard version to model safety elements, while our process relies on iStar4Safety. Moreover, their use of the STPA technique is only sketched.

In Debbech et al. [15], the authors propose GOSMO (Goal-Oriented Safety Management Ontology) for developing safety metrics using the UFO (Unified Foundational Ontology) and the Organization-Based Control Access (Or-BAC) Model. GOSMO reinterprets terminologies based on reference models and standards, focusing on safety measures. Our approach differs by modeling early safety concepts using parts of a previous metamodel [16, 17]. We emphasize modeling initial safety requirements with a lightweight approach, adding minimal new elements to the language. Instead of creating a complex GORE modeling language, we define a subset of safety concepts for the early requirement phase. Future work may develop lightweight and heavyweight versions of the extension or add optional constructors as needed.

It is worth noting Yu's seminal work on goal modeling for security [18], which defines a set of security and privacy-specific analysis mechanisms and integrates them into the usual requirements engineering process. In doing so, they claim that security and privacy requirements could be addressed together with other functional and nonfunctional concerns early on. Yu has also proposed a methodological framework for security requirements elicitation and analysis centered on vulnerabilities [19]. The framework comprises a modeling framework that extends i* with the concept of vulnerability and relations that allow modeling and understanding effects of vulnerabilities on security requirements. Yu's work on security has inspired us to consider goal modeling for safety. We began proposing an extension of iStar that incorporates safety concepts and relations. We now define an approach that integrates safety analysis with goal modeling.

4 Integrating Goal-Oriented Requirements Engineering with Safety Analysis with RESafety

Given the necessity for analysts to elicit and model safety requirements, we aim to present a process facilitating the early definition of safety requirements alongside modeling the other early system requirements.

Therefore, the solution was to develop an approach called **RESafety** that integrates iStar4Safety with STPA. RESafety allows requirements engineers to use tested principles derived from safety analysis community to guide their requirements elicitation and SCSs modeling. Similarly, safety engineers may find ways to state their findings using an extension of a popular GORE language.

Below, we outline a series of steps designed to integrate principles from STPA into iStar4Safety, so both techniques will be method chunks. Consequently, familiarity with safety analysis techniques will not be a prerequisite for the more streamlined modeling of safety and requirements in a broader context.

In Fig. 1, we present the steps of our approach. It was inspired by the STPA analysis technique [8].

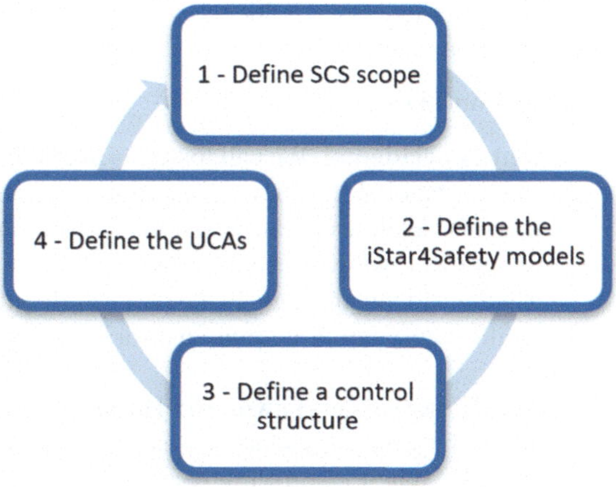

Fig. 1 RESafety iterative process

In the following, we explain all steps. The granularity level of this process's phases depends on the knowledge of the system. Each iteration will contribute to more complete artifacts, so it is therefore an iterative and incremental process. In each step, we offer a practical demonstration of the application of that specific step, using the example of an Insulin Infusion Pump System (IIP), thus aiding in comprehension and facilitating a better grasp of the process.

Step 1: Define Safety-Critical System (SCS) scope

In this initial step, we must establish and/or update the scope of the system we model. The output of this step will be the updated safety analysis and early requirements document. This step sets the stage for subsequent phases where the analysts refine the data, drill down, and interpret it to gain insights and make decisions. Here, we have two possibilities: During the first iteration, new artifacts and definitions will be created or used from, for example, a preceding safety analysis. Furthermore, one may address some items in this step during the first iteration at a very high level or even ignore them because it is the initial modeling iteration. In the subsequent iterations, the analysts can update, change, or insert issues that have yet to be defined early, thanks to the process's iterative and incremental nature. We define below the elements that must be considered. We divide the elements of this step into "General Concerns" and "Safety Concerns," as listed below.

1. **General Concerns**

   - Define the analysis objectives.
   - Problem definition.
   - Gather the resources needed for effective analysis.
   - Define the system, the system boundary, its components, and possible interactions between them.

- Define strategic stakeholders, such as persons or internal and external systems and components.

2. **Safety Concerns**

- **Identify accidents:** We call losses as **accidents**. A loss involves something of value to stakeholders. Several examples of accidents (losses) of various types, including death accident, mission accident, and so on, are reported in [8]. In our approach we will use the **"Ax"** to label accidents. Analysts may identify further accidents through analysis. The reference to individual components or specific causes, such as "human error," must be avoided in accidents definition [8].
- **Identify system-level hazards:** Hazards are system states or set of conditions that in the case of a worst-case environmental condition will lead to accidents [8]. When identifying hazards, the analyst must specify the associated accidents, ensuring traceability between hazards and accidents. Furthermore, suppose the analyst already has UCAs identified from a prior STPA analysis or earlier iterations; verifying whether these UCAs are linked with defined hazards is imperative. Otherwise, analysts must specify a new hazard related to the UCA. This is because UCAs are also the causes of hazards. Avoid referencing individual components in the hazard definition. We can use the **"Hx"** identifier for the hazards, to meet traceability. In [8], the authors refine the H1 hazard into sub-hazards. We believe that sub-hazards could be the refinement of hazards, and the differentiation between them and the causes of the hazards would be the identifiers of the "hazard" type constructors.
- **Identify hazard causes:** Hazard causes are conditions alone or associated with others, sufficient for the related hazard to occur [1, 9, 16]. Causes of hazards differ from hazards because hazards do not refer to isolated components. At this point, analysts must associate UCAs with the hazards they will lead to. You can also choose to insert other causes found by the safety analysis. From the UCAs, functional requirements and safety constraints for the system can be defined. If the cause of hazard is a UCA, we can create the **"UCAx"**; otherwise, we can use the **"HCx"** identifier for the hazard cause, to meet traceability.
- **Identify hazard mitigations:** Hazard mitigation endeavors to either prevent accidents from happening altogether or to minimize their impact if they do occur. System-level constraints define system-level conditions or behaviors that must be achieved to prevent system-level hazards. At the system level, [8] recommends that safety constraints are not solutions related to a particular context or implementation. However, analysts must define safety constraints for the UCAs found. In our approach, safety constraints will be associated with the UCAs that they treat or with hazards found and not associated with UCAs. We can use the **"SCx"** identifier for the system-level safety constraints, or the **"Cx"** tag for constraints specifically related to components or a UCA.

Finally, consider documentation, models, safety analyses, and all pertinent artifacts associated with the system as foundational references to facilitate non-safety and safety requirements elicitation. Such reuse can alleviate the burden of the analysis process.

Step 1: Illustration

We illustrate the process undertaken in the initial iteration, denoted as Step 1.

1. **General Concerns**

   - Define the analysis objectives: This analysis aims to model an IIP through iterative processes, producing updated versions of the system analysis document.
   - Problem definition: The IIP is categorized as a Safety-Critical System, meaning that unforeseen or undesirable behavior could result in accidents leading to financial losses, environmental damage, injuries, or fatalities. Developed to aid in treating type 1 diabetes mellitus, automated IIP offer enhanced treatment flexibility by automating multiple stages of the infusion process, mimicking human physiological responses. These pumps administer both rapid-acting (bolus) and continuous (basal) insulin dosages.
   - Resources needed for effective analysis:
     - Articles [20–24] and books [1, 8]
     - Other ones, like standards and manuals
   - Define the system, the system boundary, its components, and possible interactions between them.
     - System: Insulin Infusion Pump System (IIP).
     - System boundary: We will consider in this analysis the IIP and stakeholders directly involved in the use of the pump.
     - Components:
       - Control buttons/liquid crystal display/audio system/microcontroller/stepper motor/stepper motor driver/mechanical transmission/insulin syringe/infusion set/pump/human controller/patient
       - Interactions between components: to define
   - Strategic stakeholders:
     - Patient/medical support/technical support/manufacturers

2. **Safety Concerns**

   - **Identify accidents:**
     - A1—The patient is injured or killed from overexposure or undertreatment.
     - A2—A nonpatient is injured or killed by IIP.

  - A3—Damage or loss of equipment.
  - A4—Loss of equipment reputation.

- **Identify system-level hazards:**
  - H1—Dose delivered to the patient is wrong in quantity, location, or timing [A1] [A4].
  - H2—A nonpatient is unnecessarily exposed to treatment [A2] [A4].
  - H3—Equipment operated beyond limits [A3] [A4].
- **Identify hazards causes:** For better understanding, consider that analysts identified the hazard causes UCA1 and UCA2 after the initial iteration, aided by the control structure model:
  - UCA1—Do not send command for basal dosage [H1].
  - UCA2—Commands excessive basal dosage [H1].
  - HC1—Broken insulin valve, delivering free flow of insulin [H1].
- **Identify hazard mitigations:** We chose not to model a system-level safety constraint because we decided to handle all child-hazards through controller constraints.
  - C1—Command for basal dosage needs to be sent [UCA1].
  - C2—Commands for basal dosage need to be correct [UCA2].
  - C3—The insulin valve needs regular checks to ensure it's working properly [HC1].

Step 2: Model or update the iStar4Safety models

In this phase, the analyst is tasked with modeling or updating the iStar4Safety Strategic Dependency (SD) and Strategic Rationale (SR) models, considering the inputs from Step 1. If safety concerns were addressed in Step 1, you must incorporate the new information to create/update the models here.

1. **SD Model Create/Update:** Initially, the SD model must be modeled to include/update actors and allow better visualization of their relationships in an abstract way. Results from Step 1 and other iterations should be used here. Please note that the SD model will also reflect the changes made to the SR model.
2. **SR Model Create/Update:** Modelers need to start defining or updating the SR model based on the current information and iteration. Here, we outline the modeling process (adapted from [9]) and specify tags for each element. Elements identified by the analyst in Step 1 will have their own identifiers, along with identification for related elements, making it easier to trace and model at this stage.

   2.1 Create the iStar model of the system without safety elements (non-safety-related part).

2.2 Create a safety goal (ID: SGx). Here, modelers need to carefully pinpoint and depict the key objectives of the involved parties (as discussed in Step 1, *Identifying Accidents*). Then, the analyst should integrate these goals as elements within the iStar4Safety framework. Specifically, the analyst should model the objectives that were identified as accidents in Step 1 as Safety Goal elements.
2.3 Insert all system-level hazards found in Step 1 linked to the accident associated with the safety goal. Associate safety goals and hazards using the **obstruct** link. The analyst should model the hazards as "Hazard" construct with the identifier "Hx."
2.4 Identify all causes for each identified hazard. The causes are related to the UCAs found in Step 4; others may also be found by analysis. The causes of the hazards will be the child-hazards of the hazard. For hazards with associated UCAs, consider which columns of the UCAs table have been filled. The analyst must model the cause of the hazard using the "hazard" construct. The hazard cause identifier will be "UCAx" if it falls into this category, or "HCx" if it is not a UCA.
2.5 Model the mitigation strategy for each leaf hazard—i.e., safety constraints found in Step 1. The elements used for its modeling will be the safety tasks and safety resources. The analyst should model the safety constraint with the safety task element associated with the identifier "SCx" if it is a system-level safety constraint or as "Cx" if it is a controller constraint, a constraint generated for the UCA. Safety Tasks constructors can be used associated with Safety Resources, according to the need.
2.6 Associate the mitigation strategy with an actor which will be responsible for its achievement through dependency links.

Guidelines 1 through 6 can be repeated for successive iterations until all safety requirements are met. More information on how to use iStarSafety and modeling examples can be found at [9, 25].

Step 2: Illustration

Figure 2 represents the SD model based on the control structure depicted in Fig. 4. The IIP functionalities used in this example come from artifacts previously grouped during Step 1. We grouped the stepper motor driver, stepper motor, mechanical transmission, and insulin syringe elements in the "Delivery elements set" actor. Furthermore, control actions external to the system applied to it were associated with the "External environment" actor.

The SR model encompasses all actors and their interrelationships, along with the details of each actor. Due to space constraints, for the purpose of exemplification, we only depict a subset of the original model.

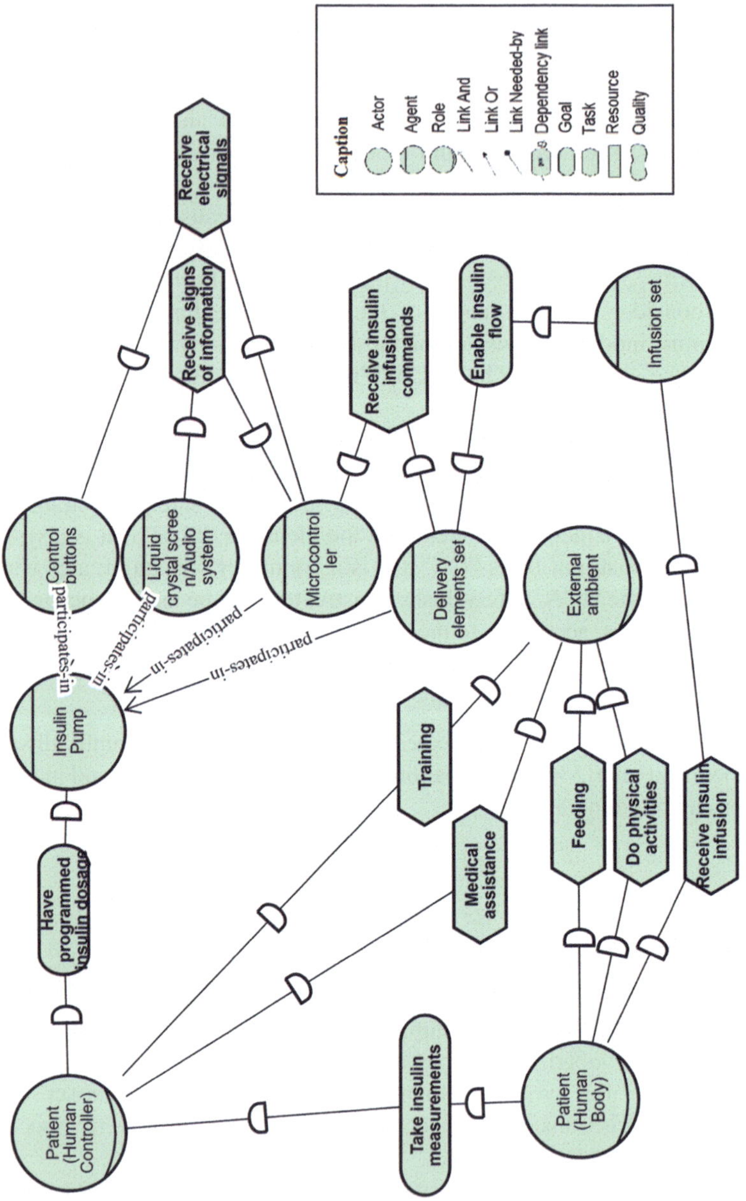

Fig. 2 Insulin Pump SD model

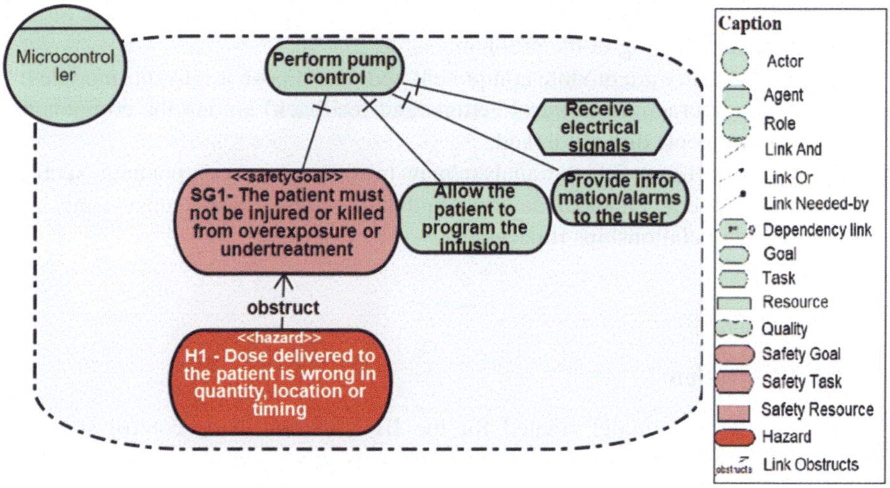

Fig. 3 Excerpt of the first iteration SR model of microcontroller actor

In Fig. 3, the microcontroller actor was chosen to serve as a representative component. Note that **SG1** and **H1**, if we consider the first iteration, were defined in Step 1. The analyst can refine them in future iterations and add causes and safety constraints.

Step 3: Define a control structure for the SCS

To define actors, limits, and functionality, researchers must create/update a control structure representing the exchanges among actors constituting the system. With the data available from the ongoing iteration, it becomes imperative to model/update elements within the control structure. The analyst must then model/update the elements described below, if feasible, considering the current iteration.

- Actors
- Control actions carried out by the actors
- Control actions carried out between actors
- Feedback between actors
- Controller control algorithm
- Controller process model

The inputs for developing the control structure must stem from the outcomes of the preceding phases: the groundwork laid for system modeling (Step 1) and the iStar4Safety SD and SR models (Step 2). The arrangement of elements within the control structure must adhere to the following sequence [8]:

1. Represent the actors of the iStar4Safety models as components of the hierarchical control structure.

2. Decompose the components into their inherent sub-components based on the existing understanding of the problem.
3. Establish the software module component and decompose it into sub-modules.
4. Specify the interactions (control actions and feedback) among the components or sub-components directly linked.
5. [Optional] At this point, the analyst may introduce new components, such as users, hardware/mechanical devices, and hardware/software subsystems, and establish new relationships if necessary.

Step 3: Illustration

Figure 4 shows the model created for the IIP structure. This control structure delineates the flow between components in an IIP. The analyst has the option to reuse an existing control structure from a prior STPA analysis or create one from scratch as needed.

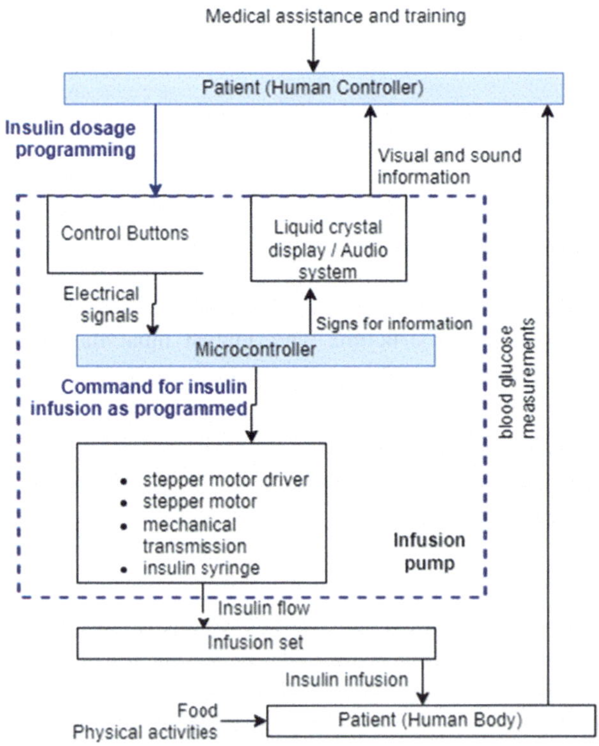

Fig. 4 Insulin infusion pump system controller model

Step 4: Define the UCAs in the control structure

Having the control structure at hand, the requirements engineers must define through analysis which control actions may require attention in terms of safety, then being treated as UCAs [8]:

- Control actions that may be unsafe:
  - Those that, if not carried out, could lead to accidents
  - Those that, if carried out, could lead to accidents
  - Those that, if provided ahead of time or even after time, could lead to accidents
  - And, finally, those that are provided for a long or short time that could lead to accidents

As stated in [8], the delineation of UCAs serves to pinpoint behaviors that analysts must prevent. Each UCA must be linked with one or more hazards at the system level; analysts outline these hazards in Step 1. Consequently, when identifying UCAs, analysts must ascertain their association with specific hazards, thereby ensuring traceability between UCAs and hazards. For UCAs not yet linked to any identified hazard, analysts should contemplate updating the list of hazards, in the next iteration, to incorporate the new hazard revealed through that UCA. RESafety follows an iterative methodology. Hence, analysts will revise the artifacts at each step during subsequent phases, as required.

Step 4: Illustration

When analyzing the control structure presented in Fig. 4 and comparing it with the knowledge of analysts and artifacts, we find that the control action *Command for insulin infusion as programmed* can be unsafe in all four situations described in Step 4.

Thus, we generated Table 1, detailing in which situations this action can be an UCA. Note that due to space constraint, only a subset of the conceivable UCAs was presented.

Table 1 UCAs definition

Control action	Not providing causes of hazard	Providing causes of hazard	Too early, too late, out of order	Stopped too soon, applied too long
Command for insulin infusion as programmed	UCA-1: Do not send command for basal dosage	UCA-2: Commands excessive basal dosage	UCA-3: Commands basal dosage for each hour of the day in the wrong order	UCA-4: Commands extended bolus too short

With the results found in Step 4, return to Step 1, if it is necessary to further refine the models. Figure 5 shows the updated SR model with the causes of hazards and mitigations (safety constraints) found during the current iteration. The analyst will implement this SR model update during Step 2 of the next iteration.

Upon conclusion of Step 4, other iterations can occur (return to Step 1), allowing the analysis to be refined.

5 Threats to Validity

Below, we outline potential threats to the validity of our analysis. While this work provides a partial example of an IIP, our focus is primarily on early safety requirements analysis, where safety requirements are preliminary. The iterative nature of the analysis process will evolve both the analysis and its models. Due to space constraints, only partial models are presented here, yet they encompass critical system characteristics comprehensively. Moreover, our involvement in the modeling process may introduce confirmation bias.

Another threat to the validity of our work is the need for further evaluation of the iStar4Safety language by safety professionals and requirements engineers. Preliminary validation with students suggests potential justified acceptance. Professional evaluation remains pending.

6 Conclusions and Road Map

In this paper, we introduce a novel approach that combines iStar4Safety's goal-oriented modeling language with STPA, facilitating systematic and comprehensive early safety requirements modeling. We have used the iStar4Safety GORE language for modeling safety requirements. Through a structured process comprising four iterative steps, we integrate the chosen iStar4Safety, with STPA, blending actions inspired by STPA. We are following the design science methodology [26] to propose our approach. *RE4Safety* hopes to improve safety concern identification, stakeholder communication, and system reliability. It will enable requirements analysts to address safety issues early using a familiar language, while providing safety engineers with advantages, such as integrating their safety analysis with a requirements modeling technique. To further illustrate its potential, we will define safety requirements for at least another Safety-Critical System. We are currently investigating how concept of Loss Scenarios, present in STPA analysis, could be integrated into our approach. One possibility is to model the Loss Scenarios using process modeling languages like BPMN.

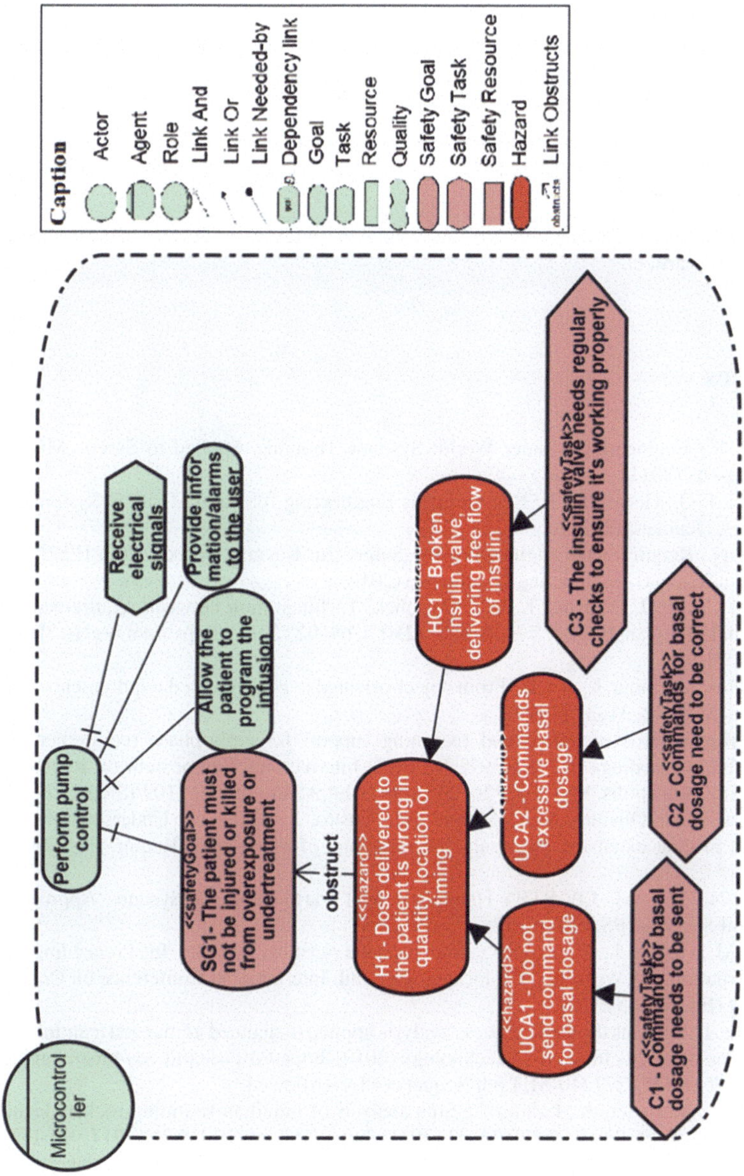

Fig. 5 Excerpt of the SR model of microcontroller actor in second iteration

In future research, we plan to validate our approach using the Technology Transfer framework, which includes Static and Dynamic Validation [27]. We also wish to develop a plug-in for the piStar4Safety tool to support the approach. One useful feature of this tool could be the generation of documentation and reports from iStar4Safety models.

Furthermore, we aim to explore how qualities like security, reliability, and privacy impact the system and interact with safety properties.

Acknowledgments The authors would like to express their gratitude for the financial support provided by CNPq, CAPES, and FACEPE. Their support has been instrumental in the successful completion of this research.

Disclosure of Interests The authors have no competing interests to declare that are relevant to the content of this article.

References

1. Leveson, N.: Engineering a Safer World: Systems Thinking Applied to Safety. MIT Press, Massachusetts (2011)
2. Martins, L.E.G., Gorschek, T.: Requirements Engineering for Safety-Critical Systems. River Publishers, Denmark (2021)
3. Leveson, N.: Requirements engineering and Safety. In: Keynote Speech, 20th IEEE International Requirements Engineering Conference (2012)
4. Vilela, J., Castro, J., Martins, L.E.G., Gorschek, T.: Integration between requirements engineering and safety analysis, J. Syst. Softw. **125**(C), 68–92 (2017). https://doi.org/10.1016/j.jss.2016.11.031
5. Mylopoulos, J., Chung, L., Yu, E.: From object-oriented to goal-oriented requirements analysis. Commun. ACM **42**, 31–37 (1999)
6. Yu, E.S.K.: Towards modeling and reasoning support for early-phase requirements engineering. In: Proceedings of ISRE '97: 3rd IEEE International Symposium on Requirements Engineering, Annapolis, MD , pp. 226–235 (1997). https://doi.org/10.1109/ISRE.1997.566873
7. Gonçalves, E., de Oliveira, M.A., Monteiro, I., Castro, J., Araújo, J.: Understanding what is important in iStar extension proposals: the viewpoint of researchers. Requir. Eng. **24**, 55–84 (2019)
8. Leveson, N., Thomas, J.P: STPA Handbook. MIT Partnership for Systems Approaches to Safety and Security (PSASS) (2018)
9. Ribeiro, M., Castro, J., Pimentel, J.: iStar for safety-critical systems. In: Proceedings of the 12th International i* Workshop Co-located with 38th International Conference on Conceptual Modeling (ER 2019) (2019)
10. Robertson, J.: Systems theoretic process analysis applied to manned unmanned teaming, PHD's Thesis, Massachusetts Institute of Technology (2019). https://dspace.mit.edu/bitstream/handle/1721.1/122516/1121277240-MIT.pdf?sequence=1&isAllowed=y
11. Fugivara, S., Merladet, A., Lahoz, C.: Stpa analysis of brazilian sounding rockets launching operations. Microgr. Sci. Technol. **33**, 43 (2021). https://doi.org/10.1007/s12217-021-09871-x
12. Sharifi, S., McLaughlin, P., Amyot, D., Mylopoulos, J.: Goal modeling for fintech certification. In: Guizzardi, R.S.S., Mussbacher, G. (eds.) Proceedings of the Thirteenth International iStar Workshop Co-located with 28th IEEE International Requirements Engineering Conference (RE 2020). CEUR Workshop Proceedings, CEUR-WS.org, vol. 2641, pp. 73–78 (2020)

13. Sharifi, S., Amyot, D., Mylopoulos, J., McLaughlin, P., Feodoroff, R.: Towards improved certification of complex fintech systems–A requirements-based approach. In: IEEE 30th International Requirements Engineering Conference Workshops (REW). Melbourne (2022)
14. Vilela, J., Silva, C., Castro, J., Martins, L.E.G., Gorschek, T.: Sarssi*: A safety requirements specification method based on STAMP/STPA and i* language. In: Anais do I Brazilian Workshop on Large-scale Critical Systems, SBC, Porto Alegre, RS, Brasil, pp. 17–24 (2019)
15. Debbech, S., Bon, P., Collart-Dutilleul, S.: Conceptual modelling of the dynamic goal-oriented safety management for safety critical systems. In: Proceedings of the 14th International Conference on Software Technologies (ICSOFT 2019). SCITEPRESS—Science and Technology Publications, Lda, Setubal, PRT, pp. 287–297 (2019). https://doi.org/10.5220/0007932502870297
16. Vilela, J., Castro, J., Martins, L.E.G., Gorschek, T., Silva, C: Specifying safety requirements with gore languages. In: Proceedings of the 31st Brazilian Symposium on Software Engineering, pp. 154–163. SBES'17 ACM, New York (2017)
17. Vilela, J., Castro, J., Martins, L.E.G. , Gorschek, T.: Safe-RE: A safety requirements metamodel based on industry safety standards. In: Proceedings of the XXXII Brazilian Symposium on Software Engineering (SBES '18). Association for Computing Machinery, New York, pp. 196–201 (2018). https://doi.org/10.1145/32662373266242
18. Liu, L., Yu, E., Mylopoulos, J.: Security and privacy requirements analysis within a social setting. In: 21st IEEE International Requirements Engineering Conference (RE). Monterey Bay, California, vol. 2003, p. 151 (2013). https://doi.org/10.1109/ICRE.2003.1232746
19. Elahi, G., Yu, E., Zannone, N.: A vulnerability-centric requirements engineering framework: analyzing security attacks, countermeasures, and requirements based on vulnerabilities. Requir. Eng. **15**, 41–62 (2010). https://doi.org/10.1007/s00766-009-0090-z
20. Martinazzo, A.: Gerenciamento de risco de uma bomba de infusão de insulina de baixo custo (in English: Risk management of a low-cost insulin infusion pump), Master's Thesis, Universidade Federal de São Paulo (2022)
21. Martins, L.E.G., Faria, H.D., Vecchete, L., Cunha, T., Oliveira, T.D., Casarini, D.E., Colucci, J.A.: Development of a low-cost insulin infusion pump: Lessons learned from an industry case. In: 2015 IEEE 28th International Symposium on Computer-Based Medical Systems (2015). https://doi.org/10.1109/CBMS.2015.14
22. Zhang, Y., Jetley, R., Jones, P.L., Ray, A.: Generic safety requirements for developing safe insulin pump software. J. Diabetes Sci. Technol. **5**, 1403–1419 (2011). https://doi.org/10.1177/193229681100500612
23. Zhang, Y., Jones, P.L., Jetley, R.: A hazard analysis for a generic insulin infusion pump. J. Diabet. Sci. Technol. **4**(2), 263–283 (2010). PMID: 20307387. https://doi.org/10.1177/193229681000400207
24. Bas, E.: STPA methodology in a socio-technical system of monitoring and tracking diabetes mellitus. Appl. Ergon. **89**, 103190 (2020). ISSN 0003-6870. https://doi.org/10.1016/j.apergo.2020103190
25. Ribeiro, M.: Desenvolvimento de uma extensão da linguagem de modelagem iStar para Sistemas Críticos de Segurança—iStar4Safety. (in English: Development of an extension of the iStar modeling language for Safety Critical Systems—iStar4Safety), Master's Thesis, Universidade Federal de Pernambuco (2019)
26. Wieringa, R.: Relevance and problem choice in design science. In: International Conference on Design Science Research in Information Systems, pp. 61–76 (2010)
27. Gorschek, T., Garre, P., Larsson, S., Wohlin, C.: A model for technology transfer in practice. IEEE Softw. **23**(6), 88–95 (2006)

Social Dependence Relationships and Their Role in Social Modelling Languages

John Mylopoulos, Daniel Amyot, and Amal Ahmed Anda

Abstract Social modelling languages, pioneered by *i**, are intended to model and analyze social settings consisting of actors (human or cyber) and social dependencies between them. The purpose of this chapter is to compare and contrast three variants of social dependence relationships that constitute the conceptual foundation of the *i** requirements modelling language, a business process modelling language (Azzurra), and a legal contract specification language (Symboleo).

1 Introduction

In his PhD thesis [17, 20], Eric Yu proposed *i** as a requirements modelling language founded on the concepts of actor (a role or an agent), goal, task, and social dependence relationships (aka social dependencies) between a depender actor who wants a goal to be satisfied and a task to be performed by a dependee actor.

It turns out that social dependency is a very powerful concept that constitutes the foundation for social modelling and has spawned interesting variants that serve as primitives for new languages, including Azzurra [4], intended for modelling business processes, and Symboleo [8], intended for specifying legal contracts. The purpose of this chapter is to compare and contrast these variants with *i**'s original social dependence relationship and highlight the implications these variations have on the expressiveness and formal reasoning facilities of each modelling language.

The new social modelling languages have been studied over a 12-year period that involved many collaborators beyond the authors.

J. Mylopoulos · D. Amyot (✉) · A. A. Anda
University of Ottawa, Ottawa, ON, Canada
e-mail: jm@cs.toronto.edu; damyot@uottawa.ca; aanda@uottawa.ca
https://sites.google.com/uottawa.ca/csmlab/

X. Franch et al. (eds.), *Social Modeling Using the i* Framework*,
https://doi.org/10.1007/978-3-031-72107-6_8

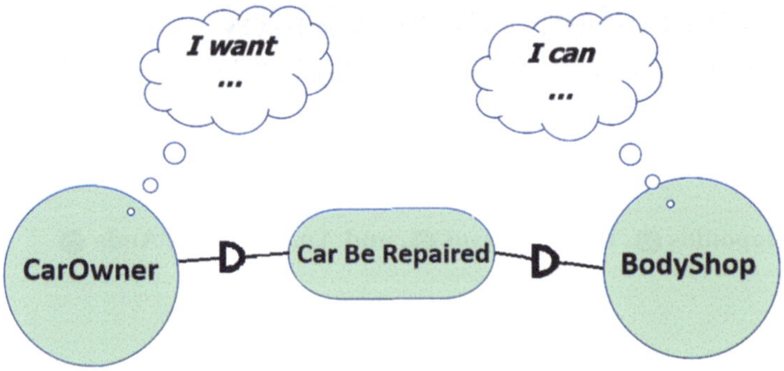

Fig. 1 Example of social dependency in *i**

2 Social Dependencies

As shown in Fig. 1,[1] in a social dependency, the depender wants something, a goal or task, and the dependee is able and willing to deliver. In *i**, this is represented in terms of two actors (respectively, the depender and dependee) and a social dependency involving a dependum goal or task. Moreover, the force of the dependence can vary from weak to strong on either side of the dependence. Consider a car owner's dependence on a body shop to repair her car: it is usually weak on the car owner's side because there are other body shops that can do the job and strong on the body shop's side because that's the mission of a body shop—to deliver body shop services to anyone who asks for them.

Contrast this with one's dependence on a renown surgeon for a rare medical operation. This one is strong on the client's side, because there are no substitute dependees. The force of the dependence on the dependee's side is more important, as she is responsible for delivering the service. That force is defined along two dimensions: ability to deliver the service and degree of commitment to deliver. The dependence on the renown surgeon is strong on ability and medium on commitment, as surgeons will postpone scheduled operations in case of an emergency.

Now, as shown in Fig. 2, consider a beggar who depends on passersby to get some money. This is a social dependence too, and it is weak on both sides: The beggar can switch to another kind of dependence to get money, e.g., work, while the passersby haven't even agreed explicitly to the beggar to deliver the service; they are just willing to do it, occasionally. Here, the dependence is statistical: some passersby give money; others don't. Note that this dependence constitutes a weak form of dependence in the sense that there is no commitment on the part of any one dependee to deliver. This weak variant of social dependence is not compatible with *i**.

[1] Adapted from Eric Yu's lecture notes on *i**.

Fig. 2 A weak dependency

*i** does recognize the importance of the force of a dependence by allowing three possible levels of force: critical, committed, and open [19]. But, as discussed in the sequel, it turns out that in several areas of research, people have opted for defining specializations of social dependence relationships where the strength of dependence is built into their semantics. Commitments, obligations, and powers are three such relationships.

The use of *i** to build requirements models for services goes back to Diana Lau's master's thesis at the University of Toronto, presented in [6] but also in [1, 10]. All three proposals use the Tropos methodology [3] for deriving agent-oriented software implementations from stakeholder requirements. Beyond Tropos, *i** has had many other offshoots, including the Goal-oriented Requirement Language (GRL), part of the User Requirements Notation (URN) standard [2].

3 Commitments (Azzurra)

Originating in the area of multi-agent systems [15], commitments capture a social dependence where there is an explicit speech act executed "Depender: I want X – Dependee: I commit to fulfill X." This kind of dependence has substantially more force than the beggar's dependence on passersby. It means that the server intends to deliver, provided some conditions hold. So, commitments are social dependencies that always arise from intentions, rather than mere practice, and are established through speech acts. More formally, commitments are 4-tuples C(debtor, creditor, antecedent, consequent), where creditor is the depender, while debtor is the dependee. Moreover, the commitment is fulfilled when consequent becomes true, provided the antecedent is true.

Moreover, commitments go through states, such as "created," "active," "suspended," "success," and "failure." Allowable state transitions can be defined by a state diagram, as shown in Fig. 3.[2] Note that commitments constitute a specialization of social dependencies, with better fleshed out semantics, proposed for use in multi-agent systems. They also come with a precise level of force for the debtor/server who intends to fulfill what she committed to, while the creditor/client has the *right* to expect that the commitment will be fulfilled. The passersby

[2] What is shown in Fig. 3 is actually a simplification of a commitment's life cycle in Azzurra.

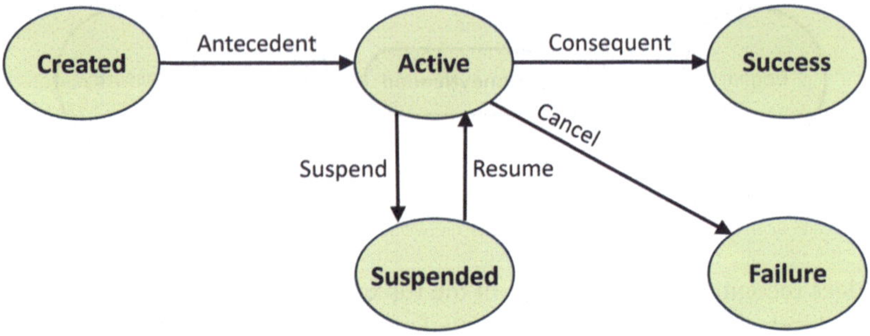

Fig. 3 The life cycle of a commitment

mentioned earlier have no commitment toward the beggar and, in turn, she has no right to expect anything from them.

Azzurra is a conceptual modelling language for business processes. Its main thesis is that business processes being social artifacts need to be defined in social terms, rather than system-oriented ones (e.g., Petri nets, BPMN, and the like). Accordingly, business processes (aka "protocols") are defined in terms of roles and commitments, with constraints attached. Azzurra models can be seen as specifications that describe what a business process is intended to achieve without getting into the details of how to achieve it. Table 1 presents an Azzurra protocol for fracture treatment (adapted from [4]). The protocol includes as parameters a hospital number that serves as key for treatment instances, a patient, and a specialist; it also includes role parameters, such as a radiologist and a surgeon, as shown.

There are nine commitments for this protocol, each using a $< trigger > \rightarrow < commitment >$ format. The first, C1, is triggered when the protocol is instantiated and has as roles the specialist (server) and patient (client), and it is unconditional (antecedent = true) and is fulfilled when the patient is examined, then diagnosed, and then dis-hospitalized. The second commitment C2 is triggered if there is no need for X-rays and fulfilled when a sling is made for the patient. Protocol refinements constrain the agents that participate in a protocol instance. For example, agents may be constrained on how many concurrent commitments they have for a given role, such as a surgeon for treatment protocol instances (max-per-role). Finally, the KB defines some domain axioms, which can be used to reason about propositions that serve as triggers, antecedents, or consequents of commitments.

Azzurra supports two types of reasoning for protocols. ENACTPROTOCOL determines how an event updates the state of a protocol instance and of the commitment instances therein. CHECKCOMPLIANCE checks whether an occurred event violates the specification of a protocol instance. This corresponds to identifying commitments that are not created/fulfilled, unexpected commitment operations, and protocol constraint violations.

In summary, commitments specialize and improve the semantics of social dependence relationships. They also come with a bounded first-order logic for specifying triggers, antecedents, and consequences. Finally, and most importantly,

Table 1 An Azzurra protocol for fracture treatment

protocol Treatment(**key** hospnr, pt : Patient, sp : Specialist) {

ag-variables: rc : RehabCentre, ra : Radiologist, or : Orthopedist, su : Surgeon, nu : Nurse;

commitments:
init → C1 : C(sp, pt, T, Examined · Diagnosed · Dehospd) final
XRayRequested → C3 : C(ra, sp, T, XRayPerformed)
XRayRequested → C4 : C*(sp, ra, XRayPerformed, FractAssessed) FractAssessed →
C5 : C(or, sp, T , ((Fixated ⊕ Plastered) ∨ fulfil(C6) ∨ SlingMade))
FractAssessed →≤2h C6 : C*(su, or, SurgeryRequested, Operated)
Operated [¬ fused] → C7 : C(nu, pt, T, RcChosen(rc))
RcChosen(rc) → C8 : C(rc, pt, T, fulfil-p(RehabGiven,
key=hospnr, pat-id=pt, ref-sp=sp))
MedPrescribed(m) → C9 : C(nu, sp, T, MedApplied(m)) can-deleg-no-resp(C3)
NoXRayNeeded → C2 : C(or, sp, T, SlingMade)
deadline(C2, 2h)

protocol refinements:
role-confl(Radiologist,Orthopedist)

kb:
implies(XRayRequested, Diagnosed)
implies(NoXRayNeeded, Diagnosed)
implies(MedPrescribed(m), Diagnosed)
mutExcl(XRayRequested, NoXRayNeeded)
}

Azzurra is a more appropriate language than *i** for describing social settings, as it commits the dependee to deliver and gives the depender the right to expect satisfaction of the dependum.

4 Obligations and Powers (Symboleo)

Obligations are commitments with legal force. The legal force is defined through powers that a creditor has toward the debtor of an obligation to cancel or suspend an obligation or other power or initiate new obligations or powers. Obligations constitute a specialization of the concept of commitment in that they can be created, cancelled, etc. by someone who has the power to do so. In turn, powers constitute a specialization of obligation in that they can include in their consequent the creation, cancellation, suspension, etc. of other powers or obligations.

Obligations and powers constitute the basic elements of legal contracts. Legal contracts have served as foundation for business transactions worldwide for millennia that go as far back as the Romans. Legal contracts can be thought as process specifications that describe the space of allowable executions that comply with terms and conditions of a legal contract. The presence of powers in legal contracts makes them a much more malleable concept than that of a business process in that they can be reshaped with the introduction/cancellation of obligations while a contract is being executed ("performed" in Jurisprudence/Law).

Symboleo is a formal specification language for legal contracts, intended to formalize requirements for *smart contracts*. These are cyber-physical software systems running on a blockchain platform that partially automate, monitor, and control the execution of a legal contract. Symboleo is founded on an ontology that is centered around the notions of *obligation* and *power* and also includes *role* and *party* (the agent playing a role in a contract), *asset*, *situation*, and *event*. Situations occur over time, e.g., the situation of commuting to work. Events, on the other hand, happen instantaneously, e.g., arrivedAtWork.

The specification language adopts many elements from Azzurra. Obligations and powers use the same 4-tuple format as commitments. Their antecedents, consequents, and triggers are expressed in terms of events happening in a certain order and satisfying constraints. For example, for a sale contract, the consequent of a delivery obligation may be "Sale item delivered to the delivery address by delivery date."

Listing .1 presents a Symboleo specification for a contract (adapted from [14]). As shown, a Symboleo specification begins with the definition of domain concepts as classes that specialize concepts in the Symboleo ontology.

For example, PerishableGood specializes Asset and has additional attributes describing quantity and quality. Instances of this class include perishable goods (e.g., meat) involved in a sales transaction. The domain model for a contract is followed by declarations of variables that take as values instances of a domain class. Pre-/post-conditions have the same semantics as in program specifications.

The core of a contract specification consists of its obligations and powers. In our example, there are two main obligations: the seller must deliver the goods to the buyer's delivery address by the delivery date (delivery), while the buyer must pay on time the sale amount (payment). The contract also includes several powers, including one that states that if the buyer violates the payment obligation, the seller has the power to terminate the contract (terminateContract). Note that the creditor of a power may choose to not exercise it.

Legal contracts can be logically very complex with many features that go well beyond those of business processes. For instance, even though obligations are meant to be fulfilled, there can also be other obligations or powers that define terms and conditions if they are *not* fulfilled, in the form of penalties, the right of the creditor to cancel, and more. Moreover, some obligations may apply after the successful termination of a contract (and are accordingly called *surviving obligations*). A confidentiality obligation for a sale transaction for a period of 6 months after a contract terminates is an example of a surviving obligation. Contracts may spawn

```
Domain meatSaleDomain // the Domain section of the contract
  // participant models are defined using the Role type
  Seller isA Role with returnAddress: String, name: String;
  Buyer isA Role with warehouse: String;
  Currency isAn Enumeration(CAD, USD, EUR);
  MeatQuality isAn Enumeration(PRIME, AAA, AA, A);
  // the good to be delivered is defined as an Asset
  PerishableGood isAn Asset with quantity: Number, quality: MeatQuality;
  Meat isA PerishableGood;
  // the event delivered happens when the goods are delivered
  Delivered isAn Event with item: Meat, deliveryAddress: String, delDueDate: Date;
  // the event paid happens when amount due is paid
  Paid isAn Event with amount: Number, currency: Currency, from: Buyer, to: Seller, payDueDate: Date;
  // the event paidLate happens when the penalty is paid
  PaidLate isAn Event with amount: Number, currency: Currency, from: Buyer, to: Seller;
endDomain
Contract MeatSale (buyer: Buyer, // the contract body starts here
  seller: Seller,
  qnt: Number,
  qlt: MeatQuality,
  amt: Number,
  curr: Currency,
  payDueDate: Date,
  delAdd: String,
  effDate: Date,
  delDueDateDays: Number,
  interestRate: Number) // parameters of the contract are passed here
Declarations
  // variables of the contract are initiated in this section
  goods: Meat with quantity := qnt, quality := qlt;
  delivered: Delivered with item := goods,
    deliveryAddress := delAdd,
    delDueDate := Date.add(effDate, delDueDateDays, days);
  paidLate: PaidLate with amount := (1 + interestRate / 100) * amt,
    currency := curr,
    from := buyer,
    to := seller;
  paid: Paid with amount := amt,
    currency := curr,
    from := buyer,
    to := seller,
    payDueDate := payDueDate;
Preconditions // safety conditions of the contract are specified below
  IsOwner(goods, seller);
Postconditions // safety conditions of the contract
  IsOwner(goods, buyer) and not(IsOwner(goods, seller));
Obligations
  delivery: // this obligation requires seller to deliver before the due date
    Obligation(seller, buyer, true, WhappensBefore(delivered, delivered.delDueDate));
  // the payment obligation requires buyer to pay before the specified due date
  payment: Obligation(buyer, seller, true, WhappensBefore(paid, paid.payDueDate));
  latePayment: Happens(Violated(obligations.payment)) ->
    Obligation(buyer, seller, true, Happens(paidLate));
Powers
  // if payment obligation is violated then seller can suspend the delivery obligation
  suspendDelivery: Happens(Violated(obligations.payment)) ->
    Power(seller, buyer, true, Suspended(obligations.delivery));
  // if penalty is paid then buyer can resume the delivery obligation
  resumeDelivery: HappensWithin(paidLate, Suspension(obligations.delivery)) ->
    Power(buyer, seller, true, Resumed(obligations.delivery));
  // if delivery is violated then buyer can terminate the contract
  terminateContract: Happens(Violated(obligations.delivery)) ->
    Power(buyer, seller, true, Terminated(self));
Constraints
  not(IsEqual(buyer, seller));
endContract
```

Listing .1 Symboleo specification for a Meat Sale contract from [12]

subcontracts that may be established while a contract is executing. For example, when a developer undertakes a large project in the construction industry, she may not have lined up all the subcontractors and their respective subcontracts. Symboleo specifications can be validated to ensure that they are consistent with the expectations of contracting parties by a tool named SYMBOLEOPC [9] that uses the nuXmv model checker to prove properties about a specification. For the Meat Sale contract, for example, the buyer may want to ensure that there is no successfully terminated execution of the contract where she pays for the meat but the meat is not delivered. Unfortunately, such an execution is possible for the Meat Sale specification because payment obligation is not constrained by delivery. This problem can be fixed by changing the antecedent of the payment obligation from true to happens(delivered, _), which means that payment can only happen after delivery of the meat.

All commercial services are defined in terms of legal contracts and they do include both obligations and powers for contracting parties. But note that not all services need to have an associated legal contract, for example, volunteer services.

5 Discussion

*i** has pioneered and shown the path forward for social modelling and requirements modelling languages. Moreover, the core concept it is based on is that of *social dependency*. However, that concept is semantically unexplored in *i**, leading to weak forms of reasoning with *i** models, as discussed by Yu [18].

Azzurra [4] adopts a semantically refined extension of social dependency, that of *commitment*, and supports some forms of reasoning based on a Prolog inference engine. Symboleo takes things further by adopting the notions of *obligation* and *power* from the Jurisprudence/Law domain and offers full reasoning support in the form of a reasoning tool, SYMBOLEOPC, based on a state-of-the-art model checker, nuXmv. SYMBOLEOPC has been experimentally evaluated and found to scale well with modest-size legal contract specifications [9]. In addition, another tool named SYMBOLEO2SC generates executable smart contract code in JavaScript for the Hyperledger Fabric platform [13]. The resulting smart contract monitors the execution of the original legal contract and flags any violation of the terms and conditions captured by the specification.

6 Conclusions

Social models consisting of actors and social dependencies are useful for capturing requirements for social systems that include software, business processes, and business transactions. We trace the evolution of the concept of social dependence to commitments and then to obligations and powers, focusing on changes in semantics, the languages where these relationships inhere, and the application domains, i.e., the types of artifacts we are defining requirements for.

Of course, the exploration of alternative forms of social dependency is far from complete. One direction that would be interesting to explore concerns *probabilistic* dependencies, where a dependence is fulfilled some of the time, as with the beggar example. Such a dependency relationship would be interesting for analyzing, for example, player interdependencies and strategies for a robotic soccer game [5].

Another direction worth pursuing is the concept of *organizational authority*, where the depender is obliged to accept tasks assigned to them by their boss [11].

Postscript

An earlier version of this work has appeared in [7]. The authors of Azzurra and Symboleo benefited immensely in their research from the notion of social dependency proposed in Eric Yu's thesis and are still exploring its variants and their applications, 31 years after the first paper on *i**, presented at the *First International Conference on Requirements Engineering* [16] (1993), and 29 years after the publication of his thesis [20] (1995). Thank you Eric!

Acknowledgments This work was partially funded by an NSERC Discovery Grant titled *From Legal Contracts to Smart Contract* and by the ORF-RE project *CyPreSS: Software Techniques for the Engineering of Cyber-Physical Systems*.

Competing Interests J. Mylopoulos and D. Amyot are supported by their respective NSERC Discovery Grants.

References

1. Aiello, M., Giorgini, P.: Applying the Tropos methodology for analysing web services requirements and reasoning about qualities of services. University of Trento (2004). http://eprints.biblio.unitn.it/563/
2. Amyot, D., Mussbacher, G. (2011). User requirements notation: the first ten years, the next ten years. J. Softw. **6**(5), 747–768 (2011). https://www.jsoftware.us/vol6/jsw0605-1.pdf
3. Bresciani, P., Perini, A., Giorgini, P., Giunchiglia, F., Mylopoulos, J.: Tropos: an agent-oriented software development methodology. Auton. Agents Multi-Agent Syst. **8**, 203–236 (2004). https://doi.org/10.1023/B:AGNT.0000018806.20944.ef
4. Dalpiaz,F., Cardoso, E., Canobbio, G., Giorgini, P., Mylopoulos, J.: Social specifications of business processes with Azzurra. In: 2015 IEEE 9th International Conference on Research Challenges in Information Science (RCIS), pp. 7–18. IEEE, Piscataway (2015). https://doi.org/10.1109/RCIS.2015.7128859
5. Ferrein, A., Lakemeyer, G.: Logic-based robot control in highly dynamic domains. Rob. Auton. Syst. **56**(11), 980–991 (2008). https://doi.org/10.1016/j.robot.2008.08.010. Semantic Knowledge in Robotics
6. Lau, D., Mylopoulos, J.: Designing web services with Tropos. In: Proceedings. IEEE International Conference on Web Services, 2004, pp. 306–313. IEEE, Piscataway (2004). https://doi.org/10.1109/ICWS.2004.1314752
7. Mylopoulos, J., Amyot, D., Logrippo, L., Parvizimosaed, A., Sharifi, S.: Social dependence relationships in requirements engineering. In: Thirteenth International iStar Workshop (iStar 2020), pp. 55–60. CEUR Vol-2641 (2020). https://ceur-ws.org/Vol-2641/paper_10.pdf

8. Parvizimosaed, A., Sharifi, S., Amyot, D., Logrippo, L., Roveri, M., Rasti, A., Roudak, A., Mylopoulos, J.: Specification and analysis of legal contracts with Symboleo. Softw. Syst. Modell. **21**(6), 2395–2427 (2022). https://doi.org/10.1007/s10270-022-01053-6
9. Parvizimosaed, A., Roveri, M., Rasti, A., Anda, A.A., Alfuhaid, S., Amyot, D., Logrippo, L., Mylopoulos, J.: SYMBOLEOPC: checking properties of legal contracts. Softw. Syst. Modell. (2024). https://doi.org/10.1007/s10270-024-01180-2
10. Penserini, L., Perini, A., Susi, A., Mylopoulos, J.: From stakeholder needs to service requirements. In: 2006 Service-Oriented Computing: Consequences for Engineering Requirements (SOCCER'06), pp. 8–8. IEEE, Piscataway (2006). https://doi.org/10.1109/SOCCER.2006.4
11. Presthus, R.V.. Authority in organizations. In: Democracy, Bureaucracy, and the Study of Administration, pp. 454–463. Routledge, Milton Park (2018). https://doi.org/10.4324/9780429501036-30
12. Rasti, A.: From Symboleo to smart contracts : A code generator. Master's Thesis, University of Ottawa (2022). https://doi.org/10.20381/ruor-28394
13. Rasti, A., Anda, A.A., Alfuhaid, S., Parvizimosaed, A., Amyot, D., Roveri, M., Logrippo, L., Mylopoulos, J.: Automated generation of smart contract code from legal contract specifications with SYMBOLEO2SC. Softw. Syst. Modell. (2024). https://doi.org/10.1007/s10270-024-01187-9
14. Sharifi, S., Parvizimosaed, A., Amyot, D., Logrippo, L., Mylopoulos, J.: Symboleo: Towards a specification language for legal contracts. In: 2020 IEEE 28th International Requirements Engineering Conference (RE), pp. 364–369. IEEE (2020). https://doi.org/10.1109/RE48521.2020.00049
15. Singh, M.P.: An ontology for commitments in multiagent systems. Artif. Intell. Law **7**, 97–113 (1999). https://doi.org/10.1023/A:1008319631231
16. Yu, E.: Modeling organizations for information systems requirements engineering. In: [1993] Proceedings of the IEEE International Symposium on Requirements Engineering, pp. 34–41 (1993). https://doi.org/10.1109/ISRE.1993.324839
17. Yu, E.S.-K.: Modelling Strategic Relationships for Process Reengineering. PhD Thesis, University of Toronto (1995). https://www.cs.utoronto.ca/pub/eric/DKBS-TR-94-6.pdf
18. Yu, E.: Towards modelling and reasoning support for early-phase requirements engineering. In: Proceedings of ISRE '97: 3rd IEEE International Symposium on Requirements Engineering, pp. 226–235 (1997). https://doi.org/10.1109/ISRE.1997.566873
19. Yu, E.S.K., Mylopoulos, J.: From E-R to "A-R"—Modelling strategic actor relationships for business process reengineering. In: Entity-Relationship Approach (ER'94), pp. 548–565 (1994). https://doi.org/10.1007/3-540-58786-1_101
20. Yu, E., Giorgini, P., Maiden, N.A., Mylopoulos, J.: *Social Modeling for Requirements Engineering*, Chapter Social Modeling for Requirements Engineering: An Introduction, pp. 3–10. MIT Press, Cambridge (2011). https://doi.org/10.7551/mitpress/7549.003.0004

Part IV
Applications

Influence Maps: Exploring the Dependencies Between "Soft" and "Hard" Requirements

Alistair Sutcliffe

Abstract Soft requirements such as values, motivations, emotions and beliefs have been proposed as significant phenomena which should be considered during the requirements process. However, it is not clear how such phenomena might augment current goal modelling in *i** beyond supporting or hindering relationships in goal modelling or representing weak dependencies between actors and soft goals. This chapter explores this question through a case study of technology-enhanced home-based support for senior citizens. *i** models are elaborated with values and other soft requirements to evaluate the effectiveness of problem representation for understanding the complexities of requirements for senior health care, and exploring how other knowledge representations might help the analysis process by setting the context for prioritizing goals and hence functional requirements and specification of agents' capabilities, as well as evaluating trade-offs between conflicting goals.

1 Introduction

In this chapter, I will explore potential extensions to the *i** modelling language to cover socio-political and other people-oriented issues such as values and emotions, which may influence system-level requirements (i.e. not only software requirements by also organizational and operational support). While *i** has accommodated many of these issues as "soft goals," two questions arise: (1) whether the semantics of *i** should be extended to include values, motivations and emotions as explicit concepts specializing soft goals and (2) what additional knowledge might be imported from psychology to help requirements engineers define and model these concepts. Soft requirements (SR) are related to non-functional requirements (NFRs) [1, 2] and soft goals [3] in RE but have a wider connotation including the "socio" part of socio-technical systems where user resistance can lead to systems being

A. Sutcliffe (✉)
University of Manchester, Manchester, UK
e-mail: alistair.sutcliffe@manchester.ac.uk

X. Franch et al. (eds.), *Social Modeling Using the i* Framework*,
https://doi.org/10.1007/978-3-031-72107-6_9

resented or rejected [4–6]. In many public-facing systems, use is discretionary, and success depends on requirements matching users' interests, for example, in healthcare, e-government, e-commerce, social media and games. The success of these systems depends not only on "hard" functional requirements (FRs) but also "soft" requirements [7] such as training, help and persuading people that the benefits of using an application outweigh the costs, hence ensuring adoption and continued use.

Software engineering manifestos have drawn attention to values and related phenomena [8, 9], although there is little evidence about how values relate to requirements and how they actually influence users' goals and decisions to accept IT products. Values have also attracted considerable attention in AI as a consequence of bias in classifiers and ethical issues in robotics [10, 11]. Values may emerge from ethnographic analysis [12, 13]; however, interpreting their design implications relies on the intuition and experience of the analyst. Value-sensitive design (VSD: [14]) proposed scenario-based probing of values in the requirements phase to sensitize designs to stakeholder values. In information systems, SR-related concepts have been the focus of technology adoption research over many years [15, 16], which aimed to analyze and eventually predict the critical success factors that influence people to use rather than reject a system. Value-based requirements engineering (VBRE) [17] combined a scenario-based analysis with a taxonomy of values and motivations as an elicitation guide, supplemented with hints on potential design implications. In spite of these initiatives, the state of the art has not progressed beyond case study exemplars investigating value implications in a small number of domain/application contexts [18, 19].

To help requirements engineers elicit and discover the implications of soft and emergent requirements, this chapter addresses three research questions:

1. What are the additional concepts which should be added to *i** to incorporate psychological knowledge for modelling?
2. How should knowledge from psychology be represented and utilized in the RE analysis process?
3. What are the implications of psychological knowledge for socio-technical systems requirements beyond traditional functional and non-functional requirements?

The research approach is a case study "gedanken" experiment, in which new modelling concepts and knowledge representations are proposed and then applied to requirements analysis, leading to reflection on the experience and future research directions in "soft requirements engineering."

In the following sections, experience of previous work on the influence of values and other psychological concepts in human computer interaction (HCI), software and requirements engineering is reviewed. The third section proposes extensions to *i** for modelling values and other psychological concepts both as modelling semantics and as a framework for applying psychological knowledge. The fourth section introduces the case study domain of home-based assistive technology for senior users. The case study applies the *i** modelling proposals to explore stakeholder trade-off analysis and specification of soft requirements. The final section concludes with a brief discussion of future research directions.

2 Previous Work

2.1 Integrating Psychology in HCI

The HCI community (see ACM CHI conferences) attempted to apply knowledge from psychology and social science to develop a theory underpinning the discipline that might predict user behavior when interacting with systems and thereby inform design choices [20]. After 2000, the HCI community moved away from cognitive psychology toward inspiration from the design discipline and sociology (ethnography) to solve the user interface (UI) design problem, with limited success [21]. Early HCI research was inspired by psychological theory as simplified models of human cognition, notably the model Human Processor [22], Interactive Cognitive Sub-systems [23] and the GOMS (goals, operators, methods) modelling language [24]. More complex cognitive theories such as ACT-R [25, 26] and EPIC were implemented as computational architectures to predict human behavior; however, the generality of these theories was limited by the task context and user interface assumptions built into computational simulations. Predictions were too context-limited for effective support of the design process.

Wider-ranging theoretical frameworks, such as CASA (computer as a social actor) [27], have been used to inform UI design choices for multimedia and avatars and underpinned the important discipline of persuasive technology [28]. Needs [29], which describe goals as more general persistent intent, have been applied to user experience research, investigating user preferences [30]. Theories of motivation [31, 32] and emotions [33] have been applied in games [34] and more generally in user-centered design methods [35, 36]. Value taxonomies [37, 38], which describe long-lasting and general attitudes, underpinned value sensitive design [14] as frameworks guiding a scenario-based user-centered design process.

The legacy of HCI's attempts at theory integration was a range of "bridging models" and knowledge representation formats, e.g. design rationale, claims, principles, heuristics and guidelines [39–41] which may be useful for RE. Heuristics and principles encapsulate general knowledge in the form of high-level design goals such as predictability (system operations should be predictable from UI commands), while guidelines record more specific knowledge pertinent to a design issue or UI features such as menus and icons [20, 40]. Claims or psychological design rationale [39, 42] integrate a problem or design issue with solution options and criteria for evaluating the trade-offs of each option. Patterns incorporate rationale and claims into a richer representation with principles, examples, scenarios and design trade-off descriptions in application contexts [43].

2.2 Application of Psychology in RE and SE

Mougouei et al. [8] and Whittle et al. [9] have drawn attention to values and related phenomena, with some evidence about how values influence users' goals and decisions to accept IT products in specific domain/application contexts. Value-based requirements engineering [17] described a scenario-based analysis with a taxonomy of values and motivations as an elicitation guide, supplemented with hints on potential design implications. The Schwartz value taxonomy [38] was applied in a case study deconstructing the European data privacy regulations (GDPR) [18] showing the dependencies between values such as privacy, trust, transparency, accuracy and legality. Zdravkovic et al. [19] surveyed values in distance-education applications, reporting that universalism (ethics), benevolence, self-determination (play), achievement and stimulation (play-fun) were important influences. Value-related social and political issues have been applied to analysis in terms of cultural attributes such as power distance and individualism [44]. Apart from isolated examples (e.g. [45]), few reports of value-based cultural implications have emerged.

Maslow's [32] motivation framework formed part of the VBRE method [17], with heuristics guiding analysts toward requirements implications in user-focused applications as well as hints for motivation in project teams. Callele et al. [46, 47] pioneered the use of emotion for eliciting requirements in games, while Ramos and Berry [48] drew attention to the importance of emotion in socio-technical systems with reference to the role of emotional reaction in system failure due to stakeholder rejection. A more detailed taxonomy of social and political RE issues with guidelines for recognizing affective reactions among stakeholders was proposed by Ramos et al. [6], who applied their approach to analyzing requirements for ERP applications. Personality taxonomies have not been explicitly applied in software development, although personality in terms of individual users was a component of the PCRE [49] method, which did indicate possible influences of personality and motivations on personal goals in user-oriented applications.

3 *i** Models and Influence Maps

Previous recommendations [17] provided generic psychological knowledge as hints and aide memoire for eliciting requirements and elaborating socio-emotional issues, generally expressed as soft goals or non-functional requirements. The first proposal is a modest extension of *i** soft goals with sub-types to represent values and motivations, represented via "contributes" links to soft goals and goals by providing theory-based information to enhance interpretation. Value and motivation theories are presented as simple taxonomies with descriptions and guidelines for interpretation of possible requirements implications, following Thew and Sutcliffe [17], which provides supplementary materials to inform *i** dependency analysis in the form of value/motivation tables, which explain the value, with synonyms and heuristics that indicate possible requirements implications.

The second proposal is process guidance for value/motivation-enhanced *i**dependency analysis on influences to guide inter-stakeholder negotiations and design trade-off analysis. Values-motivation (VM) analysis may facilitate unpacking of soft goals into functional requirements with guidance that indicates dependencies between actors and values as well as representing the requirements trade-off space of design options to resolve possible inter-stakeholder conflicts. Values are implicit in *i** as soft goals; however, this paper argues for the promotion of values are a distinct ontological concept within *i** linking the concept to a taxonomy of values drawn from the psychological literature.

VM-*i** "influence maps" have a further purpose in suggesting specification of soft requirements in socio-technical systems, i.e. requirements which are delivered not as software but as user operating procedures, training materials, configuration options, user guides and manuals [7]. Influence maps are an approach to extend *i** with additional concepts augmented by taxonomies of values drawn from psychology to aid requirements analysis.

4 Case Study: Home-Based Assistive Technology for Senior Citizens

4.1 Survey of Requirements Issues

A preliminary literature survey of home-based assistive technology captured requirements issues in this domain. The survey was not systematic or exhaustive since the aim was to produce sufficient input for the case study rather than survey the domain in detail. The choice of the assistive technology domain was motivated by the many SR issues [7], which arise in person-oriented systems as well as the ethical and safety issues implicit in home-based assistive technology.

Assistive technology studies for seniors and assistive ambient living (AAL) involves smart home technologies, which range from general lifestyle support (assistive daily living, ADL) to more targeted support for specific pathologies, of which dementia has attracted most attention [50, 51]. High-level requirements range from support needs for physical assistance with mobility and specific actions and cognitive/perceptual help with poor eyesight and hearing to more targeted support for cognitive decline and dementia, e.g. reminders, prompts, task-related help (shopping, cooking, finances); chronic disease management (diabetes, heart COPD); physiological monitors for heart rate, blood pressure, blood sugars, body temperature and mobility; and taking medications [52–54]. Another area of support is falls prevention and general safety with technology for motion detection, device controls (cookers), behavior analysis and alerts to contact carers and medical staff; mitigation of loneliness by providing communication with other seniors, friends, family or carers; as well as memory enhancement by photo diaries and audio and video social enhancement including chatbots [55, 56].

A range of cognitive and social issues have been reported: such as motivations to improve the quality of life, utility and usability of technology, fears over privacy, personal data and self (being spied on), intrusiveness, convenience (or the converse, disturbance), fit with lifestyle and daily routines, comfort-helpfulness, controllability, security (being hacked) and physical threats from others and technology. Other problems include reliability, trust and cost of the technology [53]. A recent study of soft issues in the AAL domain [57] proposed "emotional goals" as key stakeholder concerns, such as reassurance, independence, being in control, safety, integration in lifestyle, comfort, empowerment and privacy/security.

4.2 *Analysis of Assistive Technology Requirements*

4.2.1 Strategic Dependencies and Actor Viewpoints

Two areas, falls prevention and chronic condition management, are analyzed as they share many features while representing the wide-ranging challenges in home-based assistive technology. The *i** model of this domain (see Fig. 1) shows

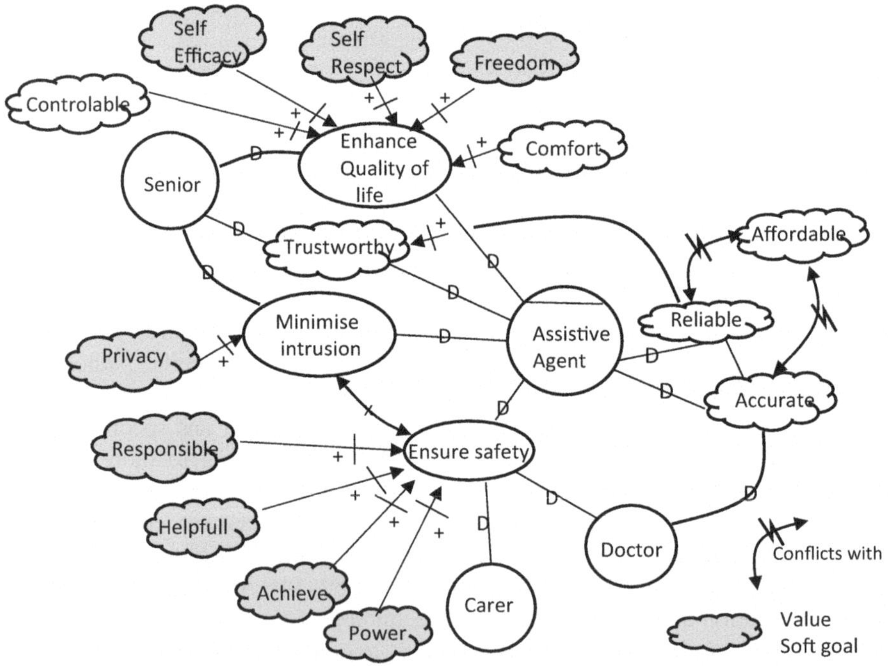

Fig. 1 *i** SD model of the assistive agent senior home-care domain

the dependencies between the assistive technology agent and three stakeholder actors, the senior, carer and doctors/medical professionals, with hard and soft goals dependencies. Three goals, enhance quality of life, minimize intrusion and ensure safety, as well as five soft goals, are motivated by the literature review presented in Sect. 4.1.

The senior actor depends on the assistive agent to enhance their quality of life by improving self-confidence and safety; however, seniors also want the technology to be non-intrusive and not to invade their privacy. The value and motivation tables in Appendix A are applied to review the initial soft goals from each actor's viewpoint. This suggests further value/motivation soft goals, which complement the issues noted in Sect. 4.1, such as self-respect, self-efficacy (empowerment) and freedom, which relate to independence and reassurance, as well as contributing to the quality-of-life goal. Values are modelled as influences on goals and soft goals via "contributes" relationships where they describe possible human actors' views on goal-agent dependencies. Values may be more closely associated with particular actors via goal dependencies; for example, the senior actor's values of self-respect, self-esteem and freedom contribute to the quality of life that the technology may afford. Ownership of values by actors is depicted implicitly by proximity rather than by explicit dependency relationships. Values such as achievement and power contribute to the ensure-safety goal with dependencies from the carer and doctor actors to the assistive technology agent. These values were not apparent from the previous literature review, which has focused on senior/patient concerns; however, carer and doctor depend on the assistive agent to achieve their safety goals, while responsibility and helpfulness represent their altruistic and professional motivations to care for the elderly. Several values contribute to the senior's quality-of-life goal, such as self-respect and freedom through increased confidence and self-efficacy as the older person is empowered to lead a more normal life. Minimizing intrusiveness is related to the privacy value, while reliability contributes towards the trustworthiness of the technology. The next step is to estimate the strength and valency of the values and motivations for each stakeholder's viewpoint on a 7-point scale, where $0 =$ not relevant, $1 =$ very minor importance and $7 =$ extremely important, as illustrated in Table 1. These estimates would be elicited in a workshop with the stakeholders using questions on the importance of each value for achieving goals such as quality of life, intrusiveness and safety. The influences of all soft goals, values and the goals relative to the aims of the overall system are considered for each actor.

High scores which are not shared by all stakeholders may indicate possible conflicts, e.g. the importance of achievement and power for doctors and carers reflects their desire for a safe and effective system, as well as their altruistic motivations of responsibility and helpfulness. However, these concerns may not be so important for senior users whose priorities are quality of life and minimizing intrusion, with contributing values of self-respect, self-efficacy and freedom. Intrusiveness and privacy are concerns not shared by doctors and carers whose focus is on safety and effectiveness of the system. The scores indicate two possible conflicts, represented with the (x) symbol in Fig. 1: (1) between the achievement/safety

Table 1 Stakeholder values

Stakeholder actors				
Value/soft goal	Senior user	Carer	Doctor	Notes
Power	0	1	5	Value
Achievement	0	5	6	"
Responsibility	0	5	6	"
Helpful	0	6	5	"
Freedom	2	1	0	"
Comfort	4	1	0	Soft goal
Self-respect	5	0	0	Value
Self-efficacy	6	0	0	"
Quality of life	6	4	2	Goal
Safety	5	5	5	Goal
Minimal intrusion	7	0	0	Goal
Privacy	6	2	0	Soft goal
Trust	4	4	0	"
Controllable	4	0	6	"
Reliable	3	3	6	"
Accurate	0	0	5	"
Affordable	0	0	1	"

Importance rating: 0 = non-important/not relevant, 1 = very low importance, 3 = somewhat important, 7 = extremely important

concerns of doctors and carers and privacy/intrusiveness for seniors, which is apparent from the quality-of-life values scores of doctors compared to seniors, and (2) the cost-affordability versus reliability and accuracy conflict, where higher scores on these soft goals are doctor/carer concerns. However, the low importance of affordability by doctors, seniors and carers suggests they are not paying for the system, and hence there is a missing actor, the medical commissioning authority (e.g. the National Health Service in the UK) who will be party to this conflict. The scores in Table 2 are illustrative examples; in reality, scores may differ according to stakeholder viewpoints. For example, the importance of quality-of-life values may differ between professional carers and family or friends, who will have more emotional attachment to the senior user. Similarly, the doctor's scores may reflect professional attitudes that rate the effectiveness of the system and control to prevent falls (power) as more important than social responsibility.

This analysis illustrates possible inter-stakeholder value and motivational conflicts for discussion, as well as stimulating ideas for unpacking how requirements might be specified to support the soft-goal values/motivation of each stakeholder. The SD analysis identifies potential inter-stakeholder conflicts which are investigated in more detail in the following strategic rationale analysis, which decomposes the single assistive technology agent into separate agents for falls monitoring and chronic care management.

Table 2 Values trade-off analysis of monitoring/detection technology options (see Fig. 2)

	Design options: falls prevention			
Impact trade-off criteria	Video analysis	Audio analysis	Movement track	Location detection
Reliability	1	2	2	1
Accuracy	3	1	2	−1
Cost	−3	1	1	1
Minimize intrusion/privacy	−3	−2	−2	0
Quality of life	3	1	2	1
Safety	3	1	2	1
Overall score	1	3	7	3

Scored on +3 = very strong and positive contribution, 0 = neutral, −3 very strong and negative

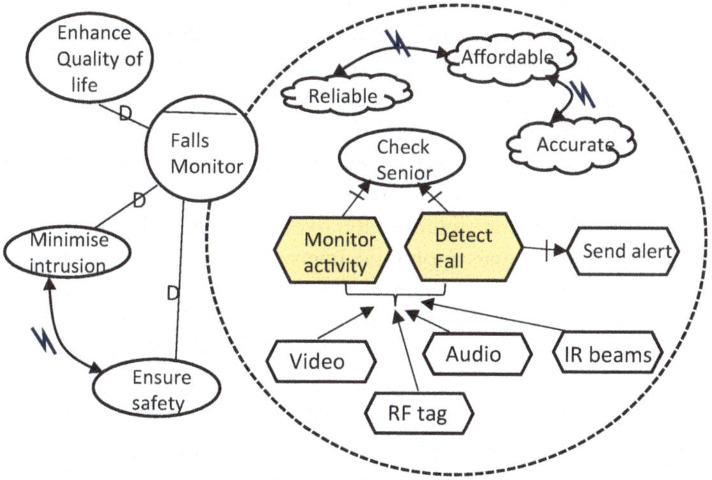

Fig. 2 SR model of the falls monitor sub-system, showing only technology-oriented goals and soft goals

4.2.2 Strategic Rationale: Values and Design Trade-Offs

Fall Monitor Agent

At the SD level, the conflicts between the senior user carer, and doctor stakeholders concerned privacy and the desire for the technology to be non intrusive, with trade-offs between comfort, safety and system effectiveness.

Some technical solutions may be more reliable overall in monitoring and controlling seniors’ behavior but at the cost of more intrusion. The SR model of the falls monitor sub-system is decomposed into goals for monitoring user activity, detecting falls and then signalling an alarm and request for help only if a fall is detected (see Fig. 2). Monitor activity and detect fall tasks could be implemented by different technologies, which may increase the reliability and accuracy of the system but also incur additional cost and hence affordability. Analysis focuses on implementation trade-offs between four technology options for monitoring and analyzing user behavior, illustrated in Table 2. The evaluation criteria are the system goals and technology-oriented soft goals of accuracy, reliability and affordability. Dependencies between the actors and system goals, quality of life, safety and intrusiveness capture the two conflicts identified at the SD level, i.e. reliability, accuracy and affordability and safety versus intrusiveness, where improved safety may come at a penalty of invading the senior's privacy. Each option is assessed on a bipolar scale to record the strength and valency of the impact on each criterion, where a score of +3 indicate a very strong and positive contribution of the criterion, 0 is neutral and −3 for a very strong but negative effect.

The scores in Table 2 are illustrative, but in practice, scores would be debated and agreed in workshops with all stakeholders and requirements engineers who could explain the functionality and provide opinions on how each option might impact privacy, reliability, etc. Accuracy depends on detecting and analyzing falls events while not signalling false alarms. Accuracy is the true/false positive/negative matrix, while reliability is evaluated by the failure rate and potential errors for each technology. Each monitoring modality will capture more or less information for analyzing the senior's movement and detecting exceptions which indicate potential falls. Fidelity of detection contributes to the overall safety and quality of life, which is contrasted with intrusiveness/potential invasion of privacy and the cost of the solution.

Video is tacitly intrusive since the senior's behavior is being recorded, raising data privacy concerns. As falls are generally rare events, this poses a problem for training an AI image-recognition system which may have an impact on reliability and accuracy, since falls movements may be atypical and difficult to recognize. The AI video solution would also be expensive as an emerging novel technology; however, it could score well on safety as behavior analysis could give carers detailed information about the user's location and incident on which to act. Audio (speech and sound analysis) may be more reliable and cheaper as training should be simpler with off-the-shelf automated speech recognition (ASR) software; however, it will provide less information on the senior's state, and it still invades the senior's privacy. Movement tracking by RF tags and wireless detection is an established reliable technology, reasonably accurate and has lower cost with less privacy intrusion. However, it may provide less information on the senior's state and hence be less safe. Finally, location detection by instrumenting the senior's home with infrared beams may be less intrusive; however, the reliability of movement analysis and provision of information on the senior's state could be poor.

Cross-referencing the technology options with the actors' values in Table 1, seniors prioritize quality of life and minimizing intrusion and may therefore favor less reliable but also less intrusive options, such as RF-tag movement tracking. In contrast, doctors prioritize safety and system performance, suggesting a possible preference for the video option. To support requirements negotiation, technology option scores could be prepared for each actor (carers, seniors, doctors) with arguments for and against different design options. Scores for each stakeholder may be compared in a workshop discussion, possibly leading to change in the favored solution. For example, tracking by RF tags may not be optimal if seniors consider wearing tags to be too intrusive. An additional technique is to evaluate the relative importance of each criterion with a weighted decision table where scores are multiplied by critically factors (i.e. reliability, 0.2; accuracy, 0.2; cost 0.1; etc. with a sum of 1.0) and the table recalculated following House of Quality decision exploration techniques [58].

Chronic Condition Management Agent

Many seniors have long-term health conditions which require monitoring of behavior or physiological signs that may indicate changes in their condition requiring intervention of healthcare professionals. Chronic health problems frequently necessitate taking medication on a scheduled basis, which, generally, is the responsibility of the individual patient. The SR model of the chronic care management agent is illustrated in Fig. 3. The agent's goal to care for the senior is decomposed into sub-goals for managing treatment and checking the senior patient. The latter goal will share tasks with the check activity in the falls monitor agent, although other physiological variables (e.g. blood pressure, respiratory oxygen) may also need to the monitored. The previous analysis for monitoring technology options, illustrated in Table 2, would be applied to this agent.

The manage treatment goal is decomposed into three tasks: reminding the senior to take their medication, automatically dispensing medicine/pills and then checking

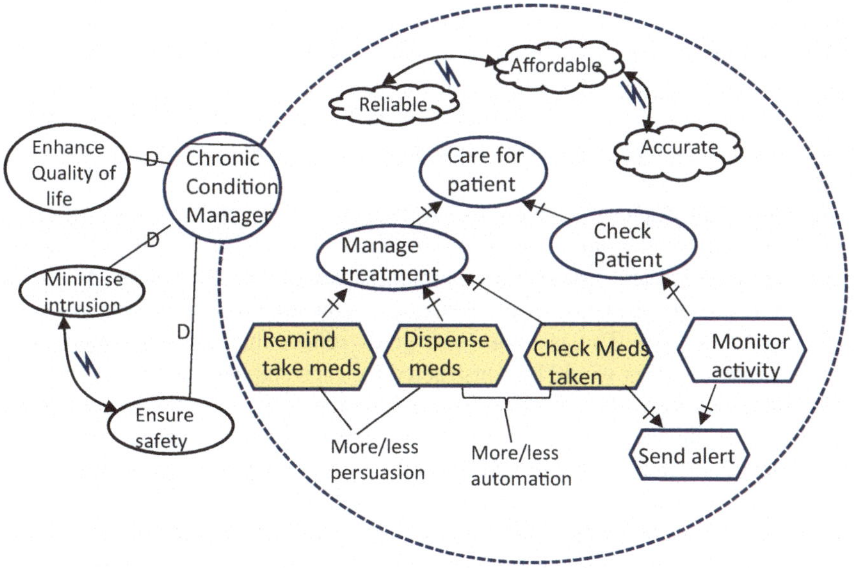

Fig. 3 SR model of the chronic condition manager agent

that the medication has been taken. These impose additional requirements on the monitor activity task, which would be explored in the further analysis that complements the technology options trade-offs, as described for the fall monitor agent.

Analysis in this section investigates the conflict between safety and minimize-intrusion goals by contrasting two technology solutions, one reflecting the desire for the technology to be non-intrusive and therefore more comfortable and the other being safer and more reliable at the cost of more intrusive monitoring and control of seniors' behavior. These are simplified into two alternative views which summarize the degree of automation for stakeholder negotiation. As before, these views would be presented in a co-design workshop where the requirements engineer explains the options and facilitates a debate among the stakeholders. Option 1 for enhanced automation implements auto-dispensing the medications with control systems to ensure the medication is taken. This is accompanied by enhanced persuasion for the remind-to-take medication task, which cannot be turned off by the senior user, with alerts being automatically sent to carers if medication is not taken and the system emits annoying audio/visual reminders until the medication is taken. Option 2, in contrast, has minimal persuasion and less automation, leaving the responsibility for taking medication with the senior. Option 1 with enhanced automation will clearly be more intrusive but may also be safer and meets doctors' priorities to achieve control. The alternative minimal option trusts seniors to follow their medication schedule with light-touch monitoring and alerting only in emergencies. This option is less intrusive but may impair safety: actor- values/goals relationships inform the choice between more automation with increased reliability and safety against less automation, contributing more strongly to quality of life, minimizing intrusion and privacy.

Table 3 contrasts the two solution scenarios with the stakeholder values. The importance and valency of each option are rated as before in a workshop with the stakeholders to elicit the importance of each value as well as quality of life, intrusiveness and safety goals and the impact of each option as a positive or negative influence.

The carer and doctor's viewpoints are represented in the first four value/soft goals, followed by the three main system goals for safety, quality of life and intrusiveness, which are scored from the main stakeholder's viewpoint. The senior actor is more closely associated with intrusiveness and quality of life, whereas safety is a doctor/carer goal. The last four soft goals reflect the senior's viewpoint. In practice, separate tables would be constructed for each stakeholder and then merged into a consensus view. For the senior user, privacy and safety are important soft goals; however, the technology should also be non-intrusive to enhance privacy and comfort, leading to a better quality of life reflected in self-efficacy. For the carer and doctor, values of power and achievement are more important to deliver a safe caring service, as well as being helpful and responsible reflecting altruistic motivation. Option 1 for full automation and more persuasion supports their safety goal and values. This analysis presents possible inter-stakeholder value and motivational

Table 3 Value/soft goal evaluation for automation options trade-off

Value/soft goal	Enhanced automation/persuasion	Minimal automation/persuasion	Focal actor
Power	3	1	Doctor
Achievement	3	−3	Doctor/carer
Responsibility	0	1	Doctor/carer
Helpful	3	−1	Doctor/carer
Quality of life	−3	2	Senior
Safety	3	0	All
Intrusion/privacy	−3	3	Senior
Freedom	−2	2	Senior
Comfort	−2	3	Senior
Self-respect	−3	3	Senior
Self-efficacy	−3	3	Senior

Impact rating +3 = very positive contribution, −3 = very negative impact, 0 = neutral/not relevant. The focal actor column links the technology options shown in Fig. 3 to the actors at the SD level in Fig. 1

conflicts for negotiation as well as making explicit the dependencies between design options and actors' soft-goal values.

Another impact of values and soft goals concerns "soft requirements" [7], i.e. operating procedures, training, user guides, installation guides, etc. Explanation and introduction of the systems to seniors should emphasize the benefits which accord with their values, e.g. how the system will improve their quality of life and confidence (self-efficacy/self-respect) as well as providing reassurance about personal safety. Their concerns over intrusiveness and privacy need to be addressed with explanation about personal data security and the responsibilities of system owners to improve trust. If more controlling functional requirements are deemed appropriate for the medication management goal, then options to override persuasion should be investigated. The value analysis in Tables 2 and 3 should be reviewed when preparing user guides and briefing sessions before the system is introduced. For the carer and doctor roles, soft requirements need to focus on safety and achievement concerns with operating procedure to interpret alerts and monitoring information. Value conflicts may also inform explanations of other stakeholders' viewpoints, for example, the intrusiveness/privacy/trust concerns of seniors. Value conflict analysis informs not only trade-offs at design time, as illustrated above, but inter-stakeholder conversations at runtime, so they can appreciate each others' viewpoints, when dealing with operational problems.

5 Discussion and Conclusions

Analysis of the senior home care domain demonstrated that values may make an important contribution through elaborating analysis with soft goals in *i** models. The case study also revealed a tension between modelling value relationships and dependencies with actors at the system level and more detailed analysis of values owned by each individual actor, as a "viewpoint" analysis. Although the system level view in Fig. 1 illustrates the potential for value conflicts between the senior, carer and doctor actors, clash between the individual actor's values only become apparent in the tabular analysis that highlights potential problems with intrusiveness and persuasion goals.

The addition of psychological knowledge to RE modelling was modest with values [37] being added via contributory relationships to goals and soft goals. In contrast to actor-goals and soft goal dependencies in a specific domain, values are taken from a generic taxonomy; hence, *i** models were constructed to show generic values as concepts that extend understanding of actors' goals and motivations. The extension of *i** models with influence/impact tables supports requirements negotiation where the viewpoints of each actor are represented to facilitate discussion. In the case study, trade-offs were investigated for monitoring and persuasive technology options, which were compared from the perspective of actors' goals, soft goals and values to represent the space of design alternatives. The senior citizen's priorities for quality of life and minimizing intrusiveness were contrasted with the carer's and doctor's interests in safety and efficiency goals, where values augmented understanding of each actor's priorities. This focus continues the debate on the interleaving of requirements and design [59]; however, it also points towards a new direction in RE research to consider how "soft requirements," such as actor values and motivations, can contribute towards design decisions to optimize choice for stakeholders.

The use of value taxonomies and tabular representation of importance-impact rankings was loosely based on design rationale [39, 60] where different design options are compared against trade-off criteria, usually soft goals. The graphical format of design rationale becomes intractable once the number of design options and criteria increase, hence the preference for tables to support requirements negotiation as shared artefacts, e.g. tables in spreadsheet format could be used to investigate different prioritizations in "what if" mode by comparing alternative designs and decision criteria using ranking and weightings. Further research on combining *i** models with other representations is necessary to extend requirements analysis from model inspection to more systematic approaches. Other theories and knowledge from psychology could be introduced in a similar manner, e.g. motivational theory in persuasive technology. However, use of psychology will be limited by complexity of theory and how much time can be devoted to training requirements engineers to understand complex, unfamiliar concepts. Simple forms of importing psychology with easy-to-digest informal theories may be the way forward, where description of concepts and categories can be supplemented with guidelines and heuristics for their application. This approach has been applied in RE for emotions [48] and values/motivations [17] and could extend the *i** modelling language with new concepts and relationships.

References

1. Chung, L.B., Nixon, B., Yu, E., Mylopoulos, J.: Non-functional Requirements in Software Engineering. Kluwer Academic Publishing, Amsterdam (2000)
2. Glinz, M.: On non-functional requirements. In: Proceedings 15th IEEE International Requirements Engineering Conference, pp. 21–26 (2007)
3. Yu, E., Giorgini, P., Maiden, N.A.M., Mylopoulos, J.: Social modeling for requirements engineering: an introduction. In: Yu, E.S.K., Giorgini, P., Maiden, N.A.M., Mylopoulos, J. (eds.) Social Modeling for Requirements Engineering, pp. 3–10. MIT Press, Cambridge (2011)
4. Bergman, M., King, J.L., Lyytinen, K.: Large-scale requirements analysis revisited: the need for understanding the political ecology of requirements engineering. Requir. Eng. **7**, 152–171 (2002)
5. Finkelstein, A.C.W., Dowell, J.A.: Comedy of errors: the London ambulance service case study. In: Proceedings 8th International Workshop on Software Specification and Design, pp. 2–4 (1996)
6. Ramos, I., Berry, D.M., Carvalho, J.: The role of emotion values and beliefs in the construction of innovative work realities. In: Proceedings Soft-Ware 2002: Computing in an Imperfect World, pp. 300–314. Springer, Berlin (2002)
7. Sutcliffe, A.G., Sawyer, P., Bencomo, N.: The implications of 'soft' requirements. In: IEEE 30th International Requirements Engineering Conference, pp. 178–188. IEEE (2022)
8. Mougouei, D., Perera, H., Hussain, W., Shams, R., Whittle, J.: Operationalizing human values in software: a research roadmap. In: Proceedings of 26th ACM Joint Meeting on European Software Engineering Conference, pp. 780–784 (2002)
9. Whittle, J., Ferrario, M.A., Simm, W., Hussain, W.A.: Case for human values in software engineering. IEEE Softw. **38**(1), 106–113 (2019)
10. Bellamy, R.K.E., Dey, K., Hind, M., Hoffman, S.C., et al.: Think your artificial intelligence software is fair? Think again. IEEE Softw. **36**, 76–80 (2017)
11. Paiva, A., Leite, I., Boukricha, H., Wachsmuth, I.: Empathy in virtual agents and robots: a survey. TiiS. **73**, 1–40 (2017)
12. Jirotka, M., Procter, R., et al.: Collaboration and trust in healthcare innovation: the eDiaMoND case study. J. Comput. Supp. Coop. Work. **14**(4), 369–398 (2005)
13. Sommerville, I.T., Rodden, P., Sawyer, P., et al.: Integrating ethnography into the requirements engineering process. In: Proceedings IEEE Symposium on Requirements Engineering (1993)
14. Friedman, B.: Value-sensitive design. In: Schular, D. (ed.) Liberating Voices: a Pattern Language for Communication Revolution, pp. 366–368. MIT Press, Cambridge (2008)
15. Marangunić, N., Granić, A.: Technology acceptance model: a literature review from 1986 to 2013. Univ. Access Inf. Soc. **14**, 81–95 (2015)
16. Venkatesh, V., Bala, H.: Technology acceptance model 3 and a research agenda on interventions. Decis. Sci. **392**, 273–315 (2008)
17. Thew, S., Sutcliffe, A.G.: Value based requirements engineering: method and experience. Requir. Eng. **234**, 443–464 (2018)
18. Perera, H., Hussain, W., Mougouei, D., Shams, R.A., et al.: Towards integrating human values into software: mapping principles and rights of GDPR to values. In: IEEE 27th International Requirements Engineering Conference, pp. 404–409 (2019)
19. Zdravkovic, J., Svee, E.O., Giannoulis, C.: Capturing consumer preferences as requirements for software product lines. Requir. Eng. **201**, 71–90 (2015)
20. Lim, K.Y., Long, J.L.: The MUSE Method for Usability Engineering. Cambridge University Press, Cambridge (1994)
21. Rogers, Y.: HCI Theory: Classical, Modern and Contemporary. Springer Nature (2022)
22. Card, S.K., Moran, T.P., Newell, A.: The Psychology of Human Computer Interaction. Lawrence Erlbaum Associates, Hillsdale (1983)
23. Barnard, P., May, J.: Representing cognitive activity in complex tasks. Hum. Comput. Interact. **14**(1–2), 93–158 (1999)

24. John, B.E., Kieras, D.E.: Using GOMS for user interface design and evaluation: which technique? ACM Trans. Comput. Hum. Interact. **3**(4), 287–319 (1996)
25. Anderson, J.R., Lebiere, C.: The Atomic Components of Thought. Lawrence Erlbaum Associates, Mahwah (1998)
26. Langley, P., Laird, J.E., Rogers, S.: Cognitive architectures: research issues and challenges. Cogn. Syst. Res. **10**(2), 141–160 (2009)
27. Reeves, B., Nass, C.: The Media Equation: How People Treat Computers, Television and New Media Like Real People and Places. CLSI/Cambridge University Press, Stanford/Cambridge (1996)
28. Fogg, B.J.: Persuasive Technology: Using Computers to Change What We Think and Do. Morgan Kaufmann, San Francisco (2003)
29. Sheldon, K.M., Gunz, A.: Psychological needs as basic motives not just experiential requirements. J. Pers. **77**(5), 1467–1492 (2009)
30. Hassenzahl, M., Diefenbach, S., Göritz, A.S.: Needs affect and interactive products: facets of user experience. Interact. Comput. **22**(5), 353–362 (2010)
31. Deci, E.L., Ryan, R.M.: Self-determination theory. Handb. Theor. Soc. Psychol. **1**(20), 416–436 (2012)
32. Maslow, A.H., Frager, R., McReynolds, C., Cox, R., Fadiman, J.: Motivation and Personality. Addison Wesley-Longman, New York (1987)
33. Ortony, A., Clore, G.L., Collins, A.: The Cognitive Structure of Emotions. Cambridge University Press, Cambridge (1988)
34. Johnson, D., Wiles, J.: Effective affective user interface design in games. Ergonomics. **46**, 1332–1345 (2003)
35. Klein, J., Moon, Y., Picard, R.W.: This computer responds to user frustration: theory design and results. Interact. Comput. **14**, 199–140 (2002)
36. Sutcliffe, A.G.: Designing user interfaces in emotionally-sensitive applications. In: Proceedings of Human Computer Interaction INTERACT, pp. 404–422. Springer Verlag, Berlin (2017)
37. Cheng, A.S., Fleischmann, K.R.: Developing a meta-inventory of human values. In: Proceedings of the ASIST Annual Meeting (2010)
38. Schwartz, S.H.: A theory of cultural values and some implications for work. Appl. Psychol. **48**, 23–47 (1999)
39. Carroll, J.M., Rosson, M.B.: Getting around the task-artifact framework: how to make claims and design by scenario. ACM Trans. Inf. Syst. **10**(2), 181–212 (1992)
40. International Standards Organisation: ISO 9241 Ergonomics of Human Computer Interaction Multi Part Standard 100 200 Series. ISO, Geneva (2019)
41. Sutcliffe, A.G.: On the effective use and reuse of HCI knowledge. ACM Trans. Comput. Hum. Interact. **7**(2), 197–221 (2000)
42. Carroll, J.M., Singley, M.K., Rosson, M.B.: Integrating theory development with design evaluation. Behav. Inf. Technol. **11**, 247–255 (1992)
43. Dearden, A., Finlay, J.: Pattern languages in HCI: a critical review. Hum. Comput. Interact. **21**(1), 49–102 (2006)
44. Viega, J., Kohno, T., Potter, B.: Trust (and mistrust) in secure applications. Commun. ACM. **44**, 31–36 (2001)
45. Krumbholz, M., Maiden, N.A.M., Wangler, B., Bergman, L.: How culture might impact on the implementation of Enterprise resource planning packages. In: Advanced Information Systems Engineering, pp. 279–293. Springer, Berlin (2000)
46. Callele, D., Neufeld, E., Schneider, K.: Emotional requirements in video games. In: 14th IEEE International Requirements Engineering Conference (RE'06), pp. 299–302. IEEE (2006)
47. Callele, D., Neufeld, E., Schneider, K.: Augmenting emotional requirements with emotion markers and emotion prototypes. In: 17th IEEE International Requirements Engineering Conference, pp. 373–374. IEEE (2009)
48. Ramos, I., Berry, D.M.: Is emotion relevant to requirements engineering? Requir. Eng. **10**, 238–242 (2005)

49. Sutcliffe, A.G., Fickas, S., Sohlberg, M.: Personal and contextual requirements engineering. In: Proceedings 13th IEEE International Conference on Requirements Engineering, pp. 19–28. IEEE Computer Society Press, Los Alamitos (2005)
50. Brims, L., Oliver, K.: Effectiveness of assistive technology in improving the safety of people with dementia: a systematic review and meta-analysis. Aging Mental Health. **23**(8), 942–951 (2019)
51. Yusif, S., Soar, J., Hafeez-Baig, A.: Older people assistive technologies and the barriers to adoption: a systematic review. Int. J. Med. Inform. **94**, 112–116 (2016)
52. Demiris, G., Hensel, B.K.: Technologies for an aging society: a systematic review of smart home applications. Yearb. Med. Inform. **17**(1), 33–40 (2008)
53. Liu, L., Stroulia, E., Nikolaidis, I., Miguel-Cruz, A., Rincon, A.R.: Smart homes and home health monitoring technologies for older adults: a systematic review. Int. J. Med. Inform. **91**, 44–59 (2016)
54. Turjamaa, R., Pehkonen, A., Kangasniemi, M.: How smart homes are used to support older people: an integrative review. Int. J. Older People Nursing. **14**(4), e12260 (2019)
55. Marikyan, D., Papagiannidis, S., Alamanos, E.: A systematic review of the smart home literature: a user perspective. Technol. Forecast. Soc. Chang. **138**, 139–154 (2019)
56. Zhu, J., Shi, K., Yang, C., et al.: Ethical issues of smart home-based elderly care: a scoping review. J. Nurs. Manag. **30**(8), 3686–3699 (2022)
57. Curumsing, M.K., Fernando, N., Abdelrazek, M., Vasa, R., Mouzakis, K., Grundy, J.: Emotion-oriented requirements engineering: a case study in developing a smart home system for the elderly. J. Syst. Softw. **147**, 215–229 (2019)
58. Hauser, J.R., Clausing, D.: The House of Quality. Harvard Business Review (1988)
59. Nuseibeh, B.: Weaving together requirements and architectures. IEEE Comput. **34**(3), 115–119 (2001)
60. Sutcliffe, A.G.: A technique combination approach to requirements engineering. In: Proceedings: ISRE '97: 3rd IEEE International Symposium on Requirements Engineering, pp. 65–74. IEEE Computer Society Press, Los Alamitos (1997)

Data Analytics from a Social Perspective

Ana Lavalle, Alejandro Reina-Reina, Alejandro Maté, and Juan Trujillo

Abstract Traditional data analytics projects focus on the structure and organization of the data. They take a data-first approach where the main objective is to integrate enterprise and external data transforming them into a valuable asset to be exploited by the organization. In this process, decision-makers often take a passive role. They provide an initial draft of the high-level goals and then accept or reject the results of the project. Compared to this approach, in this chapter, we present how the social perspective of the decision-makers can improve the project results by taking a user-first point of view. In our proposal, decision-makers take an active role in the development process, refining their high-level goals into specific requirements and analysis, without requiring in-depth domain knowledge of the underlying techniques nor the underneath data. As a result, critical decisions are made at an earlier stage in the process, leading to time and cost savings. Furthermore, end-user applications are enhanced, promoting greater intuitiveness and streamlining the decision-making process. Finally, we have checked our proposal in a real-world project showing the benefits of having an integrated view of different stakeholders in the same modeling approach, thereby taking better informed decisions.

1 Introduction

In recent years, there has been an exponential increase in data volume generated, with organizations managing extensive information concerning customers, employees, and various other aspects of their operations. This ongoing trend is projected to intensify further [12], and organizations are faced with the challenge of dealing with numerous diverse sources that require special mechanisms to store, process, and analyze to provide information [11, 24].

A. Lavalle (✉) · A. Reina-Reina · A. Maté · J. Trujillo
Lucentia Research Group - Department of Software and Computing Systems, University of Alicante Carretera San Vicente del Raspeig s/n, San Vicente del Raspeig, Spain
e-mail: alavalle@dlsi.ua.es; alejandro.reina@ua.es; amate@dlsi.ua.es; jtrujillo@dlsi.ua.es

X. Franch et al. (eds.), *Social Modeling Using the i* Framework*,
https://doi.org/10.1007/978-3-031-72107-6_10

Consequently, an increasing number of companies are directing their investments toward Big Data Analytics (BDA) to extract valuable insights crucial to decision-making processes that can confer a competitive advantage [3]. However, authors in [20] reported, after analyzing 300 projects, 55% of BDA projects conclude in failure, with many others failing to achieve their stated objectives. Similarly, in their comprehensive literature review, Reggio et al. [25] identified that the primary factors contributing to project failure include ambiguously defined objectives and insufficient collaboration among data scientists, business personnel, and IT professionals, which are pointed out as highly relevant and increasingly crucial over time. In [5, 6], the critical role of a close collaboration between data scientists and decision-makers is emphasized, with the aim of converting data analysis into actionable insights that confer benefits upon organizations.

As BDA systems grow in complexity, the need for sophisticated analytical systems becomes increasingly important. These include Data Warehouses (DW), customized visualizations, and artificial intelligence systems aligned with corporate strategic objectives. Developing such systems is essential for extracting meaningful value from data. In this context, models that reflect the specific characteristics of these systems are crucial [28]. Additionally, adopting a social perspective in requirements modeling, as suggested by the iStar (henceforth referred *i**) framework, can provide deeper insights into dependencies and better align BDA projects with corporate strategic objectives [10]. This perspective not only helps identify interdependencies among actors within the data ecosystem but also promotes effective collaboration among stakeholders, crucial for the success of complex BDA projects.

Therefore, in this chapter, we present a framework based on *i** for improving the dependency identification and business needs, especially within the domains of BDA projects where DW, Visualizations, and Machine Learning (ML) play integral roles. In particular, this proposal integrates three *i** extensions tailored for DW [23], Visualizations [22], and ML [1]. To the best of our knowledge, up to now these (and other similar proposals) have been traditionally considered in an isolated manner, thereby leading us to different unconnected data analysis modeling approaches.

The presented framework (i) allows to design DW aligned with the different goals specified by decision-makers, thereby ensuring a coherent integration with specific business needs; (ii) helps users to better understand data and its underlying patterns, making it possible to find which is the most suitable manner to visually represent their data; and (iii) enables to capture critical ML requirements for the success of ML systems and suggest which ML models are most appropriate for that context.

Moreover, it ensures that data collection and analysis efforts are directly aligned to the strategic goals of the decision-maker, helping to understand why and what those artifacts are for and how they are aligned to the business goals. This also allows them to prioritize efforts on those artifacts associated with the highest priority goals and which will have the greatest impact.

The rest of the chapter is structured as follows: Sect. 2 summarizes the related work in this area. Section 3 presents our framework based on *i** to approach data analytics from a social perspective. Section 4 describes the application of our proposal over a running example. Finally, Sect. 5 summarizes the conclusions and our future work.

2 Related Work

In the contemporary business landscape, advanced decision-making across strategic, operational, and tactical dimensions is imperative to sustain competitiveness within the market [8]. Over the last decade, significant technological advancements, such as ML or BDA, have reshaped organizational paradigms, emphasizing the criticality of analyzing extensive data from diverse sources to extract actionable insights [18, 24]. The increasing complexity of information systems underlines the importance of effectively harnessing data for the strategic positioning and competitive advantage of organizations. Within this context, models that accurately reflect the specific characteristics of these systems are of paramount importance [28].

Some proposals emphasize the importance of understanding and aligning the objectives of a DW project with the needs and goals of its stakeholders [13]. Authors in [23] extend the *i** framework to help capture and represent the relationships and dependencies between different organizational goals and requirements. By enhancing goal-oriented analysis, the method aims to bridge the gap between high-level organizational goals and the technical details of DW design. Moreover, precursor proposals as GRAnD [14] have coexisted with *i** for DW. This approach advocates for a systematic consideration of the strategic objectives of an organization, translating these goals into specific requirements for the DW. By integrating goal-oriented analysis with the technical aspects of DW design, the framework aims to create more relevant and efficient DW solutions.

These proposals, while comprehensive for the development of DW, do not establish mechanisms for the collaboration of diverse stakeholders from different areas and cannot align with and prioritize information goals. Furthermore, they fall short of addressing the full spectrum of complexities inherent in today's BDA projects. They do not have specific elements to cover aspects such as Visualizations or ML models.

From the Visualization point of view, choosing the most suitable type is a challenging task. Often, decision-makers lack expertise in data visualization and may be uncertain about the specific information they need to extract from data or the most suitable type of visualization to use [16]. This uncertainty can lead to misinterpretations and incorrect results, which can result in missed opportunities and substantial losses [2]. In this sense, techniques are proposed to automatically generate visualizations or dashboards such as [9, 26, 27]. However, all of them rely on the user to choose the type of visualization to use. An *i**-based methodology has been introduced [22] that guides nonexpert users, providing a bridge to the gap between user requirements and visual analytics.

Different proposals have also contributed to the development of ML systems by proposing methodologies and frameworks. For instance, in [7], authors provide support for ML system development through checklists, but these overlook requirements engineering challenges. Elsewhere [19], researchers have attempted to integrate Goal-Oriented Requirements Engineering with ML, albeit focusing on functional requirements. Conversely, authors in [4, 17] concentrate on nonfunctional requirements in the ML domain. A similar effort [1] offers a comprehensive proposal that addresses both functional requirements and nonfunctional requirements, while the potential inclusion of aspects related to deep learning could be considered. It offers a holistic perspective on the development of ML systems.

Therefore, within the literature, we find proposals that emphasize the use of goals while overlooking the social perspective, with weaknesses such as the lack of knowledge of the actors involved or the dependencies and associations among them. We also find proposals that focus on goals but overlook aspects related to Visualizations or ML models.

Moreover, although the proposals based on the *i** framework for DW [23], Visualizations [22], and ML [1] are interesting and complete in themselves, they lack a focus from a social perspective. It would be of great interest to consider more actively and primarily the actors of the system and their goals. This would allow for a better understanding of their interests and the dependencies established between them.

Hence, our approach is designed to create DW aligned with the goals outlined by decision-makers, ensuring their alignment with business requirements. Additionally, it aids users in gaining a deeper comprehension of their data and their underlying patterns, thus facilitating the identification of the most effective methods for visual representation of data. Furthermore, our approach is able to identify the crucial ML requirements essential for the successful implantation of ML systems and to recommend the most suitable ML models for the given requirements.

In this sense, our proposal not only addresses and integrates different areas including DW, Visualization, and ML but also adopts a social perspective that enables the identification of involved stakeholders, their dependencies, and/or associations among them.

3 *i** Framework for Data Analytics from a Social Perspective

With the aim of enhancing requirements modeling in complex BDA projects and aligning dependencies with business needs and stakeholders, we have integrated the *i** extension tailored for DW [23], Visualizations [22], and ML [1].

More specifically, Maté et al. [23] introduce a requirement model based on the *i** framework for decomposing business processes into specific goals. This model also defines *Contexts* and *Measures*, crucial for the development of DW, aligning them with the different goals, thereby ensuring a coherent integration with specific business needs. Lavalle et al. [22] further extend the *i** framework for data visualizations in order to help users better understand data and its underlying patterns, thereby enriching the framework's capabilities to address diverse analytical needs. Lastly, Barrera et al. [1] have extended the *i** framework to focus on capturing ML requirements, encompassing both *functional* and *nonfunctional aspects*. This includes the selection of the most suitable algorithm according to the requirements, as well as defining acceptance thresholds to determine the success of the project and ensure compliance with the goals that are crucial for the success of ML endeavors.

It should be noted that by leveraging the properties of the metamodel, it is possible to connect a *Visualization* or a *MLTask* to an *InformationGoal*. As a consequence, by integrating these extensions, our proposal aims to provide a comprehensive framework based on *i** for improving dependency identification and business needs, especially within the domains of BDA projects where DW, visualizations, and ML play integral roles. The result of integrating these proposals is represented in Fig. 1.

We start from the company's strategic plan. This strategic plan is represented by the *i** extension for DW [23]. This structure follows a refinement process in which, starting from a *BusinessProcess*, the higher-level goals (*StrategicGoals*) are detailed in *DecisionGoals* and *InformationGoals*.

Once the basis of the goal tree is defined, an analysis of how these goals are going to be achieved is performed. This process includes (i) execution of implicit queries from the *InformationRequirements* [23], (ii) *Visualizations* to help to better understand data and their underlying patterns [22], or (iii) defining and implementing ML models *(MLTask)* [1], which allow to classify, group, or predict future values among other applications.

In [23] queries are directly translated into *Measures* and *Contexts*, which are used to answer the user or structure the information. The *InformationRequirements* element implicitly uses *Contexts* and *Measures* through the relationship represented between the elements *Resource* and *Task*.

For each *InformationGoal* there may be one *Visualization* that will be specified by following the *i** extension for Visualizations [22]. For this purpose, the following concepts are used: The *AnalysisType* allows decision-makers to specify which type of analysis they wish to perform. A *Visualization* is characterized by one or more *VisualizationGoals* which describe which aspects of the data the visualization is trying to reflect, and one or more kinds of *InteractionType* that decision-makers will need to have with the visualization. In addition, a *Visualization* makes use of one or more *DatasourceResource* elements to obtain the necessary data from the datasource.

An *InformationGoal* can also be pursued through an *MLTask* following the *i** extension for ML [1]. More specifically, starting from an *InformationGoal*, the abstract class *MLGoal* will result in a specific *ClassificationGoal*, *RegressionGoal*, or *ClusteringGoal*, along with its associated *Indicator* that specifies the degree of compliance of a particular *MLGoal* to be achieved by the *MLTask*.

The *MLTask* encompasses common attributes shared by all ML tasks, facilitating the specification of evaluation aspects such as validation and test procedures, alongside task-specific attributes pertaining to *ClassificationGoal*, *RegressionGoal*, or *ClusteringGoal*, as well as an enumeration of algorithms that allow achieving the specific goal. The *MLTask* is also related to the elements *Source* and *Dataset*, which

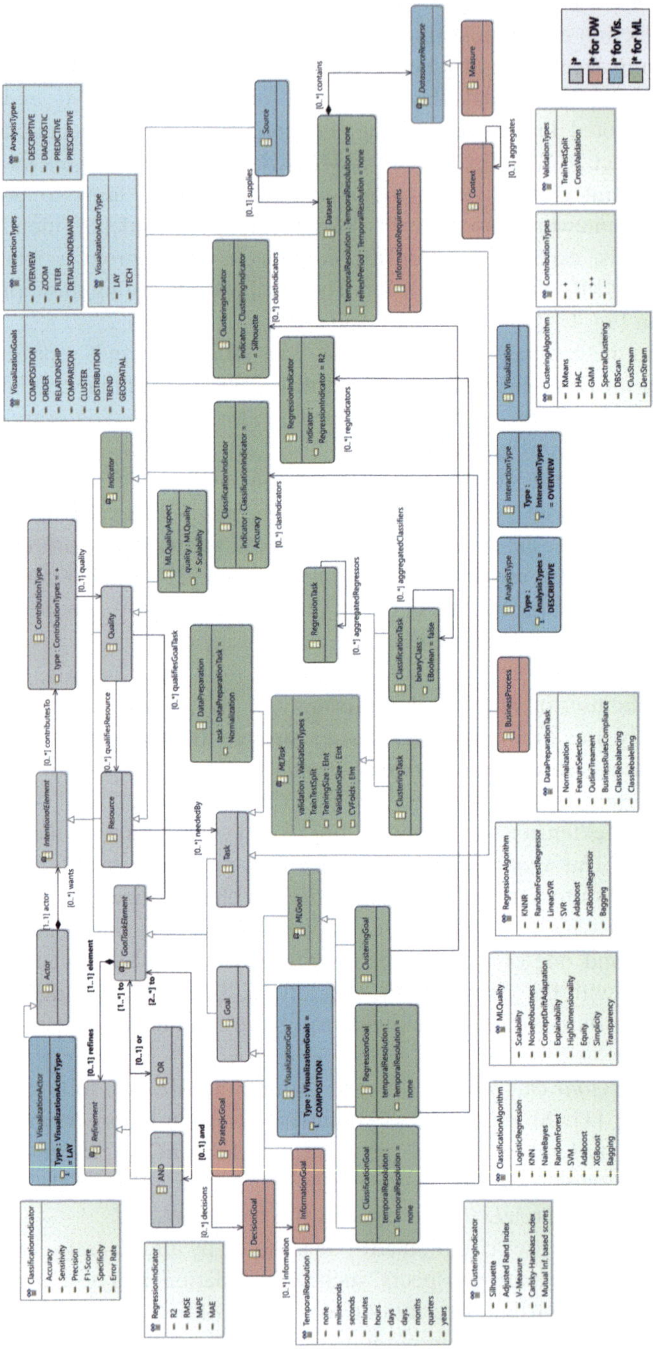

Fig. 1 *i** framework metamodel

specify the sources from which the data will be obtained, as well as other aspects such as the temporal resolution at which the different sources will be integrated to form the dataset used by the *MLTask*.

Finally, the *i** extension allows for defining and enumerating additional preprocessing operations that can be performed in ML, according to project and algorithm needs, by the *DataPreparationTask*. These operations may include specific tasks such as *NormalizationTask* or *OutliersTreatmentTask*. Additionally, it allows for specifying *MLQualityAspects*, which define the various ML qualities that the model must fulfill to select the most suitable ML model.

Therefore, this complete metamodel (Fig. 1) allows to align the business needs with the artifacts that are being created (DW structures, Visualizations, and ML models), helping to understand why and what those artifacts are for and how they are aligned with the business goals. This also allows to prioritize efforts on those artifacts associated with the highest priority goals and which will have the greatest impact.

4 Running Example

The illustrative example focuses on an analytical project within a hotel management context, aimed at strategically increasing revenue. This model captures and aligns requirements from key stakeholders: decision-makers, data scientists, and ML experts, facilitating a comprehensive approach to hotel management. This comprehensive approach ensures all critical perspectives are considered, facilitating the development of solutions that meet the project's objectives effectively. By integrating the diverse requirements and expectations of each role, the model aims to streamline project execution, enhance collaboration, and ensure the final outcome addresses the needs and goals of all parties involved.

After applying our proposal, we have obtained the model detailed in Fig. 2. In the following, we will detail how each *i** extension contributes to the running example.

4.1 Actors' Dependencies

Firstly, Fig. 3 represents the dependencies between actors. These dependencies may arise from the assignment of responsibilities to carry out the required tasks to achieve a goal. There may also be dependencies reflected by the fact that one actor delegates the performance of a task or resource to another actor.

We have exemplified the dependencies generated in the section of the tree hanging from the decision goal *(D)* "Maximize occupancy." In this case, the actors involved are the Decision Maker (Hotelier), the ML Expert, and the Data Scientist. The information goal *(I)* "Analyze the evolution of occupation" is delegated to both actors (ML Expert and Data Scientist); therefore, both will perform tasks related to

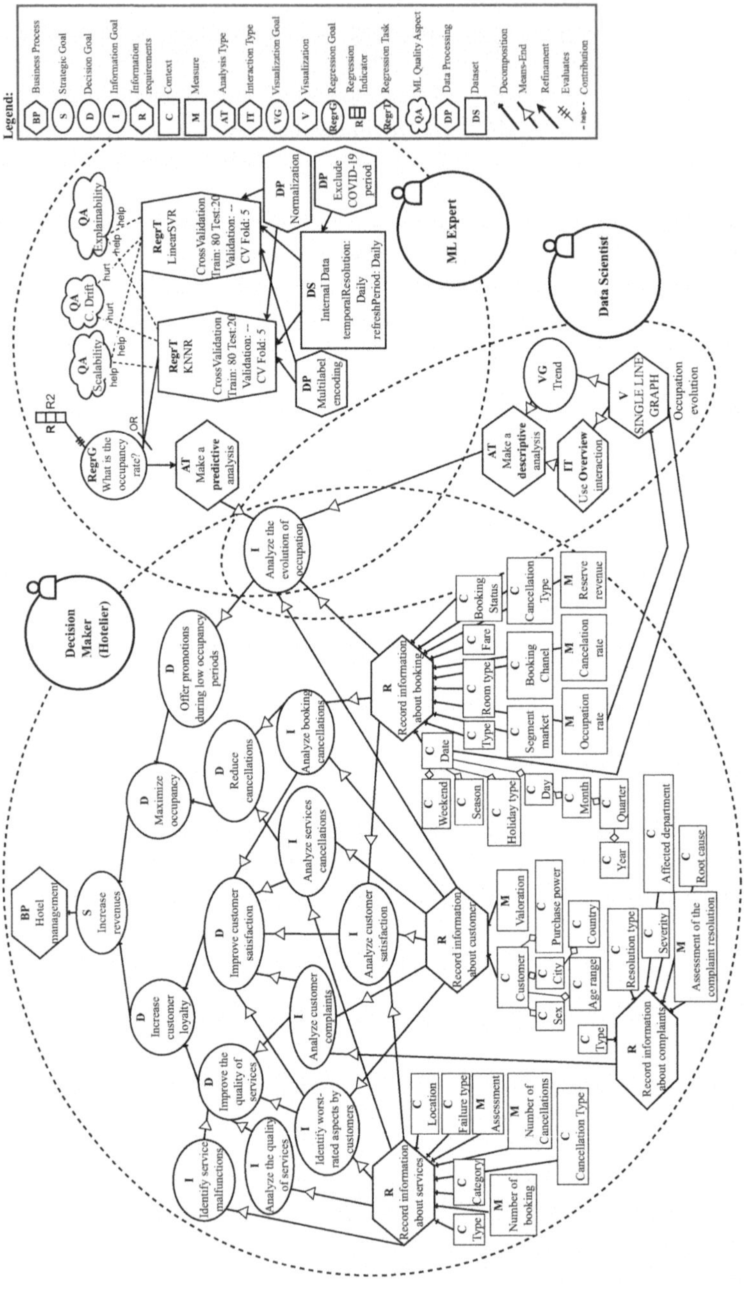

Fig. 2 Application of our *i** framework to the running example

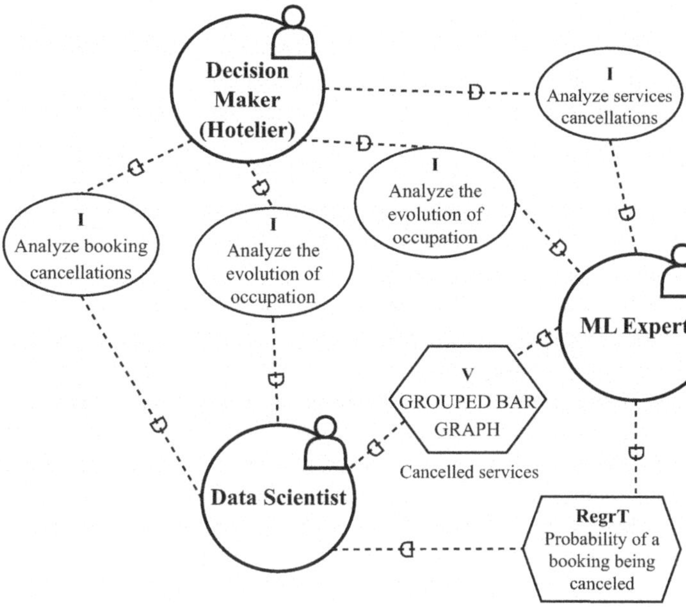

Fig. 3 An example of dependencies between actors

their area in order to address the goal. Regarding the information goal *(I)* "Analyze services cancellations," it is delegated to the ML Expert; however, to achieve this goal, the ML expert needs a specific Visualization. This task is delegated to the Data Scientist. Finally, in the case of the information goal *(I)* "Analyze booking cancellations," it is delegated to the Data Scientist, and for its achievement, an ML task is needed. Therefore, the task of developing an ML model that calculates the probability of a booking being canceled is delegated to the ML Expert.

Furthermore, other types of analysis could be defined or required for the rest of the information goals *(I)*. Due to a lack of visual capacity, in the following sections, we will exemplify only the integration of the proposals and the interconnection between the different actors regarding the *(I)* "Analyze the evolution of occupation."

4.2 Data Warehouses

Regarding Fig. 2, the decision-maker focuses on the hotel management business process *(BP)* where the strategic goal *(S)* is to increase hotel revenues, through decisions such as increasing customer loyalty *(D)* by improving service quality *(D)* and improving the customer satisfaction *(D)*. Moreover, it seeks to maximize the occupancy *(D)* through promoting special offers during low-demand periods *(D)* and reducing cancellations *(D)*. It outlines information needs or information goals alongside tasks for analyzing customer feedback and service data.

Afterward, information goals *(I)* are transformed into information requirements *(R)* and contextualized within specific analysis contexts to drive decision-making processes. This transformation process involves identifying critical data points and metrics that are essential for achieving the strategic goals outlined by the decision-maker. For instance, an information goal *(I)* might be to "Analyze customer satisfaction," which would lead to information requirements *(R)* such as "Record information about customer," "Record information about services," and "Record information about booking." These requirements are then placed within analysis contexts (room type, booking channel, nationality of customers) and measures (assessment), to identify customer behavior or preferences for targeted marketing campaigns and personalized service offerings. This method ensures that data collection and analysis efforts are directly aligned with the strategic goals of the hotel management, facilitating informed decision-making through a structured approach and identifying dependencies such as analyzing complaints that could improve customer ratings as well as the quality of services.

4.3 Visualizations

The use of visual elements may be necessary to achieve information goals *(I)*; in this running example, we have exemplified one of these cases. In order to determine which is the most appropriate visual element, the decision-maker collaborates closely with the Data Scientist to carefully define the visualization context. This context involves detailed information on the specific goals, the target audience, and the nature of the data to be presented. By establishing a clear understanding of these factors, we can determine which visualization type will most effectively convey the desired message and insights to the audience.

In this case, we want to address the information goal *(I)* "Analyze the evolution of occupation." For this purpose, it is decided to carry out a descriptive analysis type *(AT)* as it seeks to answer the question: What has happened?

In order to specify the aspects of the data the visualization is trying to reflect *(VG)* and how users would like to interact with the visualization *(IT)*, a set of guidelines are available in [21]. In this case, following the guidelines, "Trend" has been selected as visualization goal (*VG*) and "Overview" as interaction type *(IT)*. Finally, data that will be used to populate the visualization is defined as context *(C)* "Date" and measure *(M)* "Occupation rate."

Having the visualization context identified, it is used as an input to the suitability function presented in [15] that assesses to which extent (fit, acceptable, discouraged, unfit) each visualization type is suitable for that specific visualization context. According to the suitability scores, the most suitable visualization for the case at hand is a "Single Line Graph," where "Date" will be represented on the x-axis and "Occupation rate" on the y-axis.

4.4 Machine Learning

The definition of information goals *(I)* is insufficient for defining achievable objectives in the field of artificial intelligence. In this sense, it is necessary to decompose an information objective into specific goals, such as classification (*ClassG*), regression (*RegrG*), or clustering (*ClustG*), and to identify precisely what one aims to predict. Additionally, for the accurate evaluation of ML models, it is essential to establish specific metrics within the domain of knowledge that determine whether the objective has been met or not.

In the illustrative example, predicting the occupancy rate has been identified as crucial for forecasting future occupancy and tailoring offers to the hotel's demand. Given that the goal is to forecast the occupancy ratio of the hotel, we establish a regression goal *RegrG* to be measured using the coefficient of determination R2, from which corresponding regression tasks *(RegrT)* will stem, enabling us to achieve the goal. More specifically, the framework allows us to identify the required functional and nonfunctional quality aspects *(QA)*, such as scalability, concept drift, and explainability, and to identify, through a formula defined in [1], the ML models that meet or align with the identified requirements. Specifically, we can see how "KNNR" and "LinearSVR" will be the ML models used to achieve the goal by regression task *(RegrT)*.

Finally, other data preparation tasks *(DP)* are defined, such as normalizing variables through numerical variable "normalization" or "multilabel encoding" for categorical variables, as well as other aspects related to the algorithms, such as the size of the test set (Test:20), the iterations of k-fold cross-validation (CV Fold: 5), or the update periods of the data (refreshPeriod: Daily). Additionally, the framework enables us to identify other relevant considerations through data preparation tasks (DP), such as excluding periods of anomalous hotel occupancy data. In this case, this involves the exclusion of data from the "COVID-19 period", which does not reflect typical conditions.

5 Conclusions and Future Work

This study focuses on enhancing data analytics projects by integrating a social perspective, emphasizing the active involvement of decision-makers throughout the project to refine goals into specific requirements. This approach not only ensures that critical decisions are made early, leading to cost and time savings, but also enhances end-user applications by promoting greater intuitiveness and streamlining the decision-making process. The proposed framework demonstrates the benefits of an integrated view among various stakeholders, leading to more informed decisions without requiring in-depth domain knowledge of the underlying techniques or data.

In conclusion, adopting a user-first perspective in data analytics projects, as exemplified in this work, represents a significant shift from traditional data-driven approaches. By actively involving decision-makers and focusing on the social aspects of data analytics, projects can achieve better alignment with organizational goals, improve stakeholder collaboration, and ultimately enhance project outcomes. Moreover, through the integration of three extensions based on the *i** framework (DW, Visualizations, and ML), this study not only enhances the efficacy and applicability of the proposed approach but also enables the comprehensive addressing of the complexity inherent in modern big data projects. The real-world application of this integrated approach underscores its practical value, offering a promising direction for future research and implementation in the field of data analytics.

Acknowledgments This work has been co-funded by the AETHER-UA project (PID2020-112540RB-C43), a smart data holistic approach for context-aware data analytics: smarter ML for business modelling and analytics, funded by the Spanish Ministry of Science and Innovation, and the BALLADEER (PROMETEO/2021/088) project, a big data analytical platform for the diagnosis and treatment of attention deficit hyperactivity disorder (ADHD) featuring extended reality, funded by the Conselleria de Innovación, Universidades, Ciencia y Sociedad Digital (Generalitat Valenciana).

Competing Interests The authors have no conflicts of interest to declare that are relevant to the content of this chapter.

References

1. Barrera, J.M., Reina-Reina, A., Lavalle, A., Maté, A., Trujillo, J.: An extension of istar for machine learning requirements by following the prise methodology. Comput. Stand. Inter. **88**, 103806 (2024). https://doi.org/10.1016/j.csi.2023.103806
2. Bresciani, S., Eppler, M.J.: The pitfalls of visual representations: A review and classification of common errors made while designing and interpreting visualizations. Sage Open **5**(4) (2015). https://doi.org/10.1177/2158244015611451
3. Constantiou, I.D., Kallinikos, J.: New games, new rules: big data and the changing context of strategy. J. Inf. Technol. **30**, 44–57 (2015). https://doi.org/10.1057/jit.2014.17
4. Cysneiros, L.M., do Prado Leite, J.C.S.: Non-functional requirements orienting the development of socially responsible software. In: Nurcan, S., Reinhartz-Berger, I., Soffer, P., Zdravkovic, J. (eds.) Enterprise, Business-Process and Information Systems Modeling, pp. 335–342. Springer International Publishing, Cham (2020)
5. Davenport, T.H.: How strategists use "big data" to support internal business decisions, discovery and production. Strat Leader. **42**, 45–50 (7 2014). https://doi.org/10.1108/SL-05-2014-0034
6. Davenport, T.H., Patil, D.: Is data scientist still the sexiest job of the 21st century. Harvard Busin. Rev. **15** (2022)
7. de Souza Nascimento, E., Ahmed, I., Oliveira, E., Palheta, M.P., Steinmacher, I., Conte, T.: Understanding development process of machine learning systems: Challenges and solutions. In: 2019 ACM/IEEE International Symposium on Empirical Software Engineering and

Measurement (ESEM), pp. 1–6. IEEE, Piscataway (2019). https://doi.org/10.1109/ESEM.2019.8870157
8. Dubey, R., Gunasekaran, A., Childe, S.J., Bryde, D.J., Giannakis, M., Foropon, C., Roubaud, D., Hazen, B.T.: Big data analytics and artificial intelligence pathway to operational performance under the effects of entrepreneurial orientation and environmental dynamism: a study of manufacturing organisations. Int. J. Prod. Econ. **226**, 107599 (2020). https://doi.org/10.1016/j.ijpe.2019.107599
9. Ehsan, H., Sharaf, M.A., Chrysanthis, P.K.: Efficient recommendation of aggregate data visualizations. IEEE Trans. Knowl. Data Eng. **30**(2), 263–277 (2018). https://doi.org/10.1109/TKDE.2017.2765634
10. Eric, S.: Social Modeling for Requirements Engineering. MIT Press, Cambridge (2011)
11. Fan, J., Han, F., Liu, H.: Challenges of big data analysis. Natl. Sci. Rev. **1**, 293–314 (2014). https://doi.org/10.1093/nsr/nwt032
12. Gantz, J., Reinsel, D.: The digital universe in 2020: Big data, bigger digital shadows, and biggest growth in the far east. IDC iView: IDC Analy. Fut. **2007**(2012), 1–16 (2012)
13. Giorgini, P., Rizzi, S., Garzetti, M.: Goal-oriented requirement analysis for data warehouse design. In: Proceedings of the 8th ACM International Workshop on Data Warehousing and OLAP, pp. 47–56 (2005)
14. Giorgini, P., Rizzi, S., Garzetti, M.: Grand: a goal-oriented approach to requirement analysis in data warehouses. Decis. Supp. Syst. **45**(1), 4–21 (2008)
15. Golfarelli, M., Rizzi, S.: A model-driven approach to automate data visualization in big data analytics. Inf. Visualiz. **19**(1), 24–47 (2020). https://doi.org/10.1177/1473871619858933
16. Gray, C.C., Teahan, W.J., Perkins, D.: Understanding our analytics: a visualization survey. J. Learn. Analy. (2017), https://research.shadowraider.com/jspui/handle/1471/19
17. Horkoff, J.: Non-functional requirements for machine learning: Challenges and new directions. In: 2019 IEEE 27th International Requirements Engineering Conference (RE), pp. 386–391. IEEE, Piscataway (2019). https://doi.org/10.1109/RE.2019.00050
18. Hujran, O., Alarabiat, A., Al-Adwan, A.S., Al-Debei, M.: Digitally transforming electronic governments into smart governments: smartgov, an extended maturity model. Informat. Develop. **39**, 811–834 (2023). https://doi.org/10.1177/02666669211054188
19. Ishikawa, F., Matsuno, Y.: Evidence-driven requirements engineering for uncertainty of machine learning-based systems. In: 2020 IEEE 28th International Requirements Engineering Conference (RE), pp. 346–351. IEEE, Piscataway (2020). https://doi.org/10.1109/RE48521.2020.00046
20. Kelly, J., Kaskade, J.: Cios & big data what your it team wants you to know (2013)
21. Lavalle, A., Maté, A., Trujillo, J., Rizzi, S.: Visualization requirements for business intelligence analytics: A goal-based, iterative framework. In: 2019 IEEE 27th International Requirements Engineering Conference (RE), pp. 109–119. IEEE, Piscataway (2019)
22. Lavalle, A., Maté, A., Trujillo, J., Teruel, M.A., Rizzi, S.: A methodology to automatically translate user requirements into visualizations: experimental validation. Informat. Softw. Technol. **136**, 106592 (2021). https://doi.org/10.1016/j.infsof.2021.106592
23. Maté, A., Trujillo, J., Franch, X.: Adding semantic modules to improve goal-oriented analysis of data warehouses using i-star. J. Syst. Softw. **88**, 102–111 (2 2014). https://doi.org/10.1016/j.jss.2013.10.011
24. Naeem, M., Jamal, T., Diaz-Martinez, J., Butt, S.A., Montesano, N., Tariq, M.I., De-la Hoz-Franco, E., De-La-Hoz-Valdiris, E.: Trends and future perspective challenges in big data. In: Advances in Intelligent Data Analysis and Applications: Proceeding of the Sixth Euro-China Conference on Intelligent Data Analysis and Applications, 15–18 October 2019, Arad, Romania, pp. 309–325. Springer, Berlin (2022)
25. Reggio, G., Astesiano, E.: Big-data/analytics projects failure: A literature review. In: 2020 46th Euromicro Conference on Software Engineering and Advanced Applications (SEAA), pp. 246–255. IEEE, Piscataway (8 2020). https://doi.org/10.1109/SEAA51224.2020.00050
26. Santos, H., Dantas, V., Furtado, V., Pinheiro, P., McGuinness, D.L.: From data to city indicators: A knowledge graph for supporting automatic generation of dashboards. In: The

Semantic Web—14th International Conference, ESWC, pp. 94–108. Springer, Berlin (2017). https://doi.org/10.1007/978-3-319-58451-5_7
27. Vázquez-Ingelmo, A., García-Peñalvo, F.J., Therón, R.: Application of domain engineering to generate customized information dashboards. In: Learning and Collaboration Technologies. Learning and Teaching—5th International Conference, LCT, pp. 518–529. Springer, Berlin (2018). https://doi.org/10.1007/978-3-319-91152-6_40
28. Yu, E.S.: Social modeling and i. In: Conceptual modeling: Foundations and applications: Essays in Honor of John Mylopoulos, pp. 99–121 (2009)

50 Shades of Governance: Using Conceptual Modeling to Set Up Structures Ensuring Digital-Business Alignment

Yves Wautelet and Manuel Kolp

Abstract Within the current technological landscape, novel domains are constantly appearing and act as game changers for organizations. Cloud, data, IT security, and sustainability are domains wherein a clear strategic road map needs to be specified; these can indeed be genuine sources of competitive advantage. This paper explores the application of an *i**-centric framework to achieve digital-business alignment. It follows a design science approach to create an artifact supporting the alignment process; to this end, an enhancement of the Model-Driven IT Governance (MoDrIGo) framework to encompass multiple digital governance domains is made and called MoDrigiGo. With the use of *i**, the latter introduces governance structures and immediately relates them to the functional execution of business IT services, facilitating a nuanced examination of the alignment of new IT developments with digital strategies. This approach addresses the challenges of coordinating various digital domains both in terms of building adequate governance structures and setting up operational tasks effectively supporting the realization of domain-specific strategic objectives. An illustrative example involving the study of the support for the cloud and data strategies within the deployment of a telemedicine service in a hospital is provided.

1 Introduction

For over half a century, conceptual modeling has played a significant role in the development of information systems. The approach involves creating abstract representations of complex organizational environments, user requirements, system features, databases, software architectures, etc. These models, composed of various

---

Y. Wautelet (✉)
KULeuven, Leuven, Belgium
e-mail: yves.wautelet@kuleuven.be

M. Kolp
UCLouvain, Ottignies-Louvain-la-Neuve, Belgium
e-mail: manuel.kolp@uclouvain.be

X. Franch et al. (eds.), *Social Modeling Using the i* Framework*,
https://doi.org/10.1007/978-3-031-72107-6_11

elements, serve as tools for stakeholders to conceptualize, record, and refine the systems they want to build. The technique can also be used for strategy formulation and dissemination so in the domain of governance. Goal-Oriented Requirements Engineering (GORE) proposes the description of an organizational context by mapping out the goals that actors aim to achieve, both individually and collectively. In GORE, the concept of goal is primarily engaged to encapsulate stakeholder needs, illustrating how these requisites can be met or addressed in a proposed socio-technical system.

In contemporary business landscapes, the paradigm of aligning IT with business strategies has undergone a profound transformation. Traditionally, the focus was primarily on achieving so-called Business and IT Alignment (BITA), whereby IT initiatives were tailored to support the core objectives of the organization. However, in the era of digital transformation, this alignment has expanded into a more intricate and multifaceted framework. Digital-business alignment (DBA), as customarily defined here, is *the alignment of strategic considerations spanning the business and evolving digital environments with tactical and operational digital initiatives driven by business needs, encompassing areas such as cloud, IT security, data, the digital transformation itself, artificial intelligence (AI), sustainability, Internet of Things (IoT), and others*. This evolution recognizes that digital governance is no longer confined to a monolithic IT strategy but rather extends into diverse domains, each necessitating a tailored governance and a genuine approach of strategic considerations. In the current digital transformation-driven environment, we thus argue that the alignment focus needs to be shifted from BITA to DBA. This new paradigm seeks harmony between digital domains, business strategies, and stakeholders' needs.

Digital governance refers to the set of policies, procedures, and practices guiding and overseeing the management, use, and protection of digital assets, data, and resources within an organization or digital ecosystem. It plays the central role in this expanded alignment framework, ensuring accountability, compliance, and effective decision-making for the digital domain. As discussed, the intricate web of digital domains encompasses various facets (cloud, data, AI, etc.); each of these domains represents a distinct sphere of influence within the broader digital ecosystem, demanding specialized approaches to ensure optimal performance and compliance. Consequently, the challenge lies in formulating a cohesive solution that effectively expresses the required governance structures and the strategic objectives related to each of these diverse domains. In this context, this paper seeks to propose a comprehensive framework for articulating and managing stakeholders involved in the governance process as well as strategic objectives across these multifaceted digital domains, thereby facilitating a more holistic and integrated approach to enterprise technology alignment in the digital era.

This paper will investigate the following main research question: *how can an i*-centric framework support DBA within the multifaceted nature of digital governance?* This question is explored through the lens of the *Design Science Research* (*DSR*) paradigm, which is particularly suited to the development and empirical evaluation of innovative artifacts. The produced DSR artifact is a refined version of the Model-Driven IT Governance (MoDrIGo) framework [7], known for leveraging the Non-Functional Requirements (NFR) framework [5] and the *i** framework [26] to model organizational structures, processes, and strategies; it will be called *Model Driven digital Governance* (*MoDrigiGo*) and is first presented in this paper. Traditionally utilized to align IT capabilities with business strategies, the MoDrIGo framework's adaptation seeks to extend its application toward facilitating DBA. This adaptation is aimed to address the complexities inherent to digital governance. MoDrigiGo is presented through a refined meta-model, a streamlined application procedure, and a full (meta-level) *i**-based modeling process.

2 Background

Wautelet [19] presents MoDrIGo, a framework using models to determine the alignment of to-be-developed business IT services [20] with the business and IT strategies. To this end, it evaluates how specific internal tasks support or hamper the realization of strategic objectives. Business IT services play a central role in bridging governance with management operations. Unlike methodologies that encompass the entirety of an organization's functionalities, MoDrIGo adopts a more fragmented and detailed approach to dissect and evaluate organizational processes. The framework utilizes *i** modeling [27] for depicting organizational constructs of business IT services and details their strategic alignment (by detailing how operational activities contribute positively or negatively to achieving strategic objectives); the latter can also be rolled up using the NFR framework [5]. While *i** and the NFR framework do share several overlapping concepts, employing both in tandem as done in MoDrIGo offers unique advantages that neither could achieve alone. The *i** framework excels in modeling the relationships and dependencies among various actors within an organization, providing a strategic view of goals, tasks, and resources. This facilitates understanding the intentional relationships and dependencies critical for goal achievement. On the other hand, the NFR framework is specifically designed to handle non-functional requirements (and we use it in MoDrIGo to represent strategic objectives). The latter spans across multiple functional areas and is, in our case, able to furnish a more aggregated and synthetic view of business IT services' impact on strategic objectives of any nature. MoDrIGo has been extended for a better support of agility in governance-level decision-making in [17]; the latter version is called StratAMoDrIGo. The basis for MoDrigiGo however lies in MoDrIGo and not in the extended StratAMoDrIGo version. MoDrIGo and StratAMoDrIGo have been validated on the case study of a Belgian hospital; for the latter version, expert opinions can also be found in [18].

The *i Framework** In *i** (which stands for "distributed intentionality"), stakeholders are represented as (social) actors who depend on each other for goals to be achieved, tasks to be performed, and resources to be furnished [26]. Figure 1 distinguishes the *i** elements and their graphical representation used in the diagrams of the paper. The framework and its applications are described in detail in [26]; it includes the following:

- The Strategic Dependency (SD) model describes a network of dependency relationships among various actors in an organizational context. Actors are usually identified within the context of the model. This model shows who an actor is and who depends on the work of an actor. An SD consists of a set of nodes and links connecting actors. Nodes represent actors and each link represents a dependency between two actors. The depending actor is called *Depender* and the actor who is depended upon is called the *Dependee*.
- The Strategic Rationale (SR) model provides an intentional description of processes in terms of process elements and the rationale behind them. While the SD model maintains a level of abstraction by modeling only the external relationships among actors, the SR model forgoes that abstraction in order to allow a deeper understanding on strategic actors' reasoning about processes to be explicitly expressed. The SR model describes the intentional relationships that are "internal" to actors, such as means-ends relationships that relate process elements, providing explicit representation of "why" and "how" and alternatives. Using knowledge represented in and organized by these modeling concepts, process alternatives can be systematically generated and explored to help actors finding new process designs that better address their interests, needs, and concerns. The SR model is a graph, with several types of nodes and links that work together to provide a representational structure for expressing the rationale behind processes.

The NFR Framework In synergy with the MoDrIGo framework, our methodology incorporates the NFR framework for articulating the strategic objectives of a particular domain. In other words, the NFR framework is applied to create a strategic model. Also, NFR is used to synthetically visualize the impact of a particular business IT service (depicted at this level as an operationalization) for which an adoption decision needs to be taken onto studied digital domains' objectives.

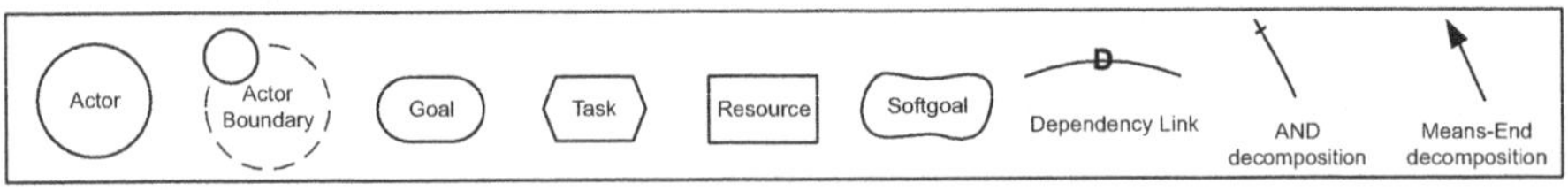

Fig. 1 *i** elements and their graphical representation

3 A Design Cycle Research Approach

This study is conducted under the auspices of the DSR paradigm, as described by Hevner et al. [7]. The essence of this approach does not lie in the quest for an abstract truth but in the creation of an artifact aimed at addressing a pragmatic challenge identified in real-world contexts. DSR prescribes the structuring around and execution of distinct research cycles. This section shows the application of these cycles within our research for building an inclusive digital governance modeling framework.

Relevance Cycle The relevance cycle initiates our research by pinpointing a specific problem within a domain that is then addressed through the creation and application of a targeted design artifact [7]. In the context of this paper, the identified problem is the absence of a structured approach to establish and align governance structures within emerging areas of digital governance, particularly with respect to the integration and alignment of new software developments. We are thus seeking for a genuine solution to ensure DBA that would be based on conceptual models.

Rigor Cycle The rigor cycle focuses on using the right theories and methods to create artifacts that help to expand knowledge in a particular domain [7]. For this cycle of our research, we draw upon the MoDrIGo framework as our foundational methodology. MoDrIGo itself employs the NFR framework to delineate strategic objectives. This allows for a systematic and hierarchical representation of these objectives, ensuring they are clearly defined and aligned with broader organizational goals. Concurrently, the *i** framework is applied to document and link the strategic objectives with the tactical and operational levels to capture and model the complex interdependencies of stakeholders. The strategic and tactical representations facilitated by the integration and traceability between NFR and *i**, respectively, are not arbitrary choices; they have been rigorously tested and validated across a multitude of cases in diverse settings. These rigorous grounds and the widespread acceptance of these frameworks in the academic and professional communities ensure the credibility of our approach. By building on this solid foundation of established frameworks, we ensure that our research is conducted with a high degree of precision and academic rigor, contributing meaningful and well-grounded insights to the field of digital governance.

Design Cycle The design cycle concentrates onto the meticulous construction of the artifact that is the main contribution of the research [7]. Within this paper, we distinguish a unique first design cycle where we sculpt a methodology—MoDrigiGo—represented by an augmented meta-model derived from the one of MoDrIGo. Also, we distinguish a streamlined procedure for its deployment as well as an exposition of the roles involved in its application and their dependencies; the latter is visually presented using a (meta-level) *i** SR diagram. This methodology is universally applicable across emerging digital domains that need to be considered at a strategic level to align adequately with deployed IT solutions (i.e., DBA), thereby effectively leveraging the business opportunities and addressing the threats they may present. Our approach is exemplified through a case study of a hospital faced with the strategic decision-making process regarding the implementation of a telemedicine IT service, encompassing both its cloud deployment model and data strategy. The example is inspired by the case found in [23] but cannot here be considered as a full case study. Full validation is left for future work and would complement this first design cycle.

4 The MoDrigiGo Framework as a DSR Artifact

This section presents MoDrigiGo, the main contribution of the paper. The method is presented through a meta-model, a procedure that applies conceptual modeling for the establishment and analysis of digital governance structures within an organization and an application procedure relating the modeling approach itself formalized with *i**.

4.1 Refined Meta-Model for Digital Governance

The meta-model presented in Fig. 2 enhances the one from the MoDrIGo framework presented in [19], introducing elements that address the specifics of digital governance (the classes and links in bold are the ones that have been added to specifically tackle MoDrigiGo). The refinement is highlighted by the addition of two novel classes, `Digital_Domain_Objective` and `Governed_Digital_Domain`, which underscore our commitment to capturing the essence of digital strategy along with governance organizational structures.

4.1.1 Digital_Domain_Objective

The `Digital_Domain_Objective` class extends the scope of strategic objectives for the inclusion of digital strategies and embeds a `type` attribute. This attribute classifies the objective based on its digital domain, such as cloud computing, data management, digital transformation, or sustainability efforts. Digital strategic objectives further classified and refined in more specific domains are required to be identified and made explicit so that business IT services are not only technically proficient but also strategically aligned with the digital ambitions of the organization (i.e., to ensure DBA).

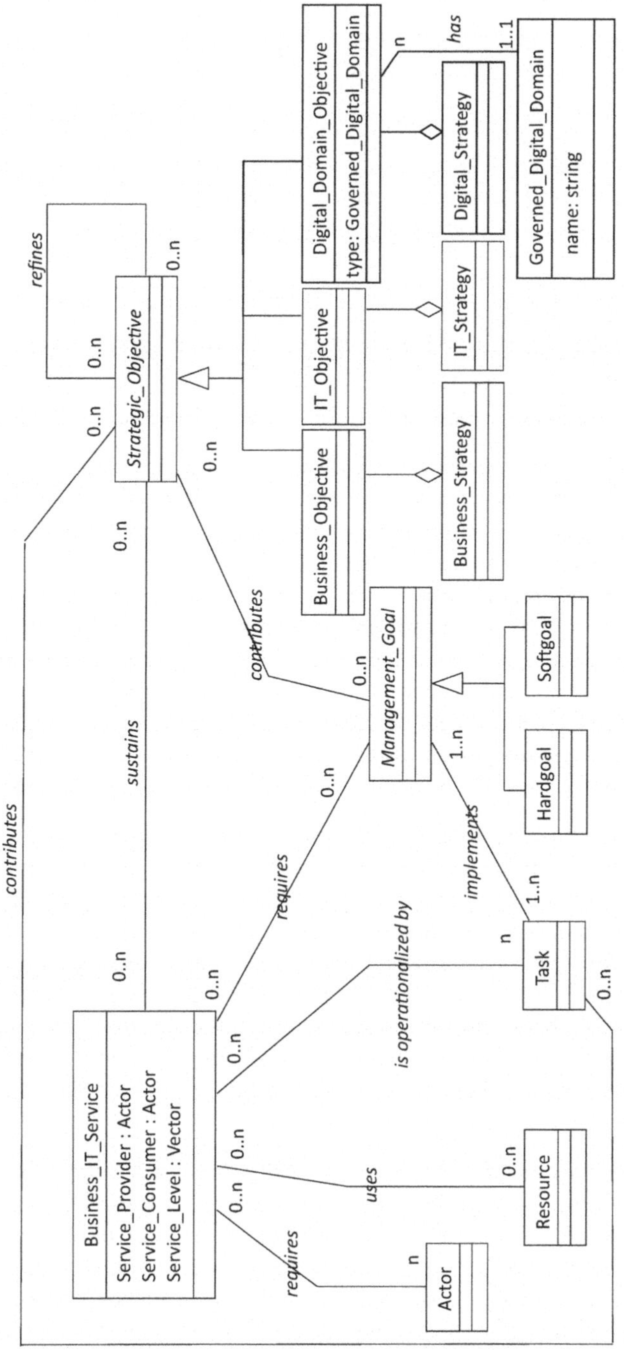

Fig. 2 Meta-model

4.1.2 Governed_Digital_Domain

The Governed_Digital_Domain class encapsulates the specific sectors of the digital landscape that an organization aims to oversee (e.g., cloud, data, digital transformation, sustainability, etc.). Defined by a unique name, each instance embodies a component of the overarching digital strategy, encompassing a segment of the digital governance. The interplay between Digital_Domain_Objective and Governed_Digital_Domain is central to the enhanced meta-model, forging a link between high-level digital strategy and its tangible governance.

4.2 Digital Governance Modeling Streamlined Procedure

This section depicts a streamlined procedure for the application of MoDrigiGo.

Step 1: Initial Business Process Description Our approach starts with a detailed representation of a business process using the *i** framework, adopting the MoDrIGo framework's service-driven modeling approach. Here, each business IT service envisioned for development and deployment is encapsulated within an *i** SR diagram. The process description, rooted in the execution of an IT service and its supporting tasks, sets a foundation for the analytical integration of digital governance considerations. The choice of *i** is particularly relevant because it highlights the involved actors, their goals, tasks, and interdependencies. In later stages of the described procedure, this framework will ensure the integration and traceability of strategic objectives while providing a comprehensive understanding of stakeholder interactions, without focusing on the sequence of task execution.

Step 2: Digital-Domain-Specific Governance Structure Identification and Integration Next, we identify and integrate pertinent governance structures tied to a chosen digital domain, deliberately deferring the consideration of the domain's strategic objectives. These structures, which could range from the *IT Services Department* to the *Digital Governance Board*, are juxtaposed within the *i** SR diagram—developed in Step 1—that articulates core processes. This crucial step reveals the interplay between organizational structures and the governance of the digital domain, relative to the business IT service deployment. For guidance on setting up such governance boards, one may notably refer to established literature, such as Weill and Ross's foundational work [24].

Step 3: Digital-Domain-Specific Strategic Objectives Identification, Integration, and Alignment We then proceed to the meticulous formulation and organization of strategic objectives within an NFR diagram specific to the digital domain in focus. These objectives are subsequently integrated as softgoals within the *i** diagram from Step 2, enabling an analysis of the concordance between business IT service processes and governance structures with the established digital-domain-specific strategic objectives. Concretely, the *i** tasks internal to the diagram's actors are integral part to both the IT service process and the governance architecture. These are scrutinized to evaluate their support in fulfilling the strategic objectives, thus facilitating an evaluation of DBA.

Step 4: Iterative Analysis for Additional Digital Domain(s) Adopting an iterative approach, our methodology circles back to the integration of governance structures and strategic objective alignment for additional digital domains (so back to Step 2 for a new domain). Through this incremental process, we ensure the creation of a comprehensive representation that is responsive to the multifaceted needs of all governed digital domains.

Step 5: Full Assessment of the Models and Decision Taking The final step involves a comprehensive assessment of the established models in light of the organization's strategic direction and operational capabilities. This evaluation is an active decision-making phase where the efficacy, feasibility, and impact of the proposed digital governance structures are appraised together with the overall digital alignment. This examination extends beyond mere functional fit; it incorporates considerations of regulatory compliance, security, user adoption, and return on investment. In pursuit of DBA, a consolidated NFR diagram can be constructed to encompass all strategic objectives from any considered digital domains and roll up the support of a specific business IT service visualized as an operationalization. The Digital Governance Board is the architect of decision-making at this stage, integrating insights from both the *i** and (consolidated) NFR diagrams to make well-informed choices about the business IT services' development, adoption, and deployment.

4.3 Digital Governance Modeling Process Involved Actors

In order to build the organizational models used for DBA, a multitude of specialized roles collaborate, each contributing unique expertise and perspective. The modeling process to sustain the digital governance is depicted as an *i** diagram in Fig. 3; the approach of showing software or modeling development processes with *i** has been taken a few times in literature and is formalized in [22]. The use of *i** here allows for agility and flexibility in the modeling process execution, rather than being directive or sequential in the execution of tasks. Due to a lack of space, we do not fully document the roles here, but it can be found in the online appendix.[1]

[1] The online appendix is available at https://data.mendeley.com/datasets/k3mpgwpyr2/1.

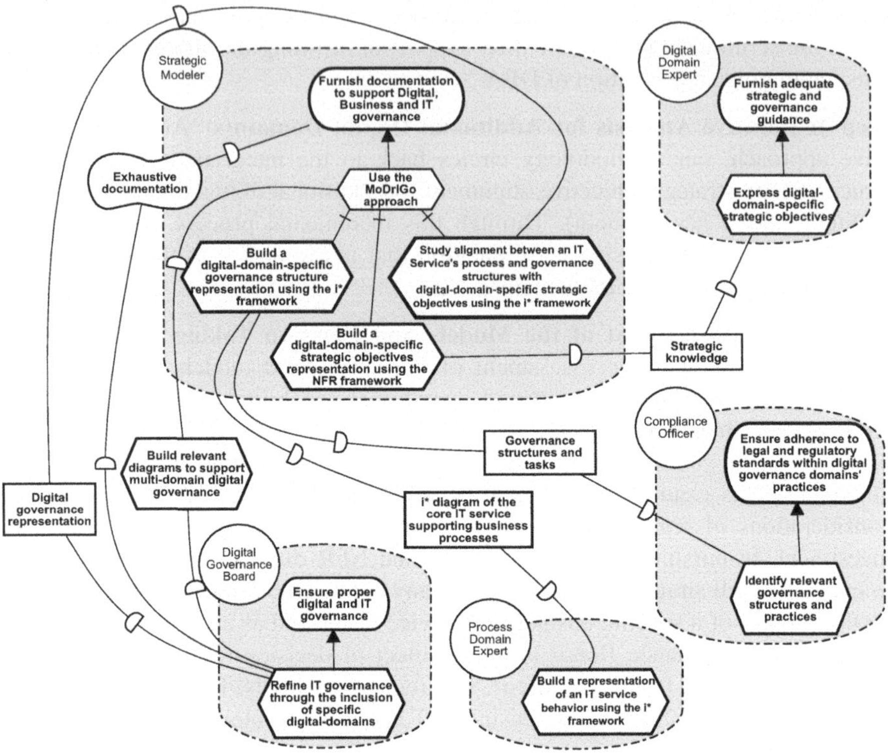

Fig. 3 The digital governance modeling procedure as an *i** strategic rationale diagram

5 Illustrative Example

In this section, we employ a fictive case study to demonstrate the practical application of MoDrigiGo. Using the backdrop of a telemedicine IT service, we illustrate the nuanced integration process of cloud and data governance. Telemedicine technologies have reshaped the way healthcare services are delivered, enabling remote diagnostics and consultations. This case, while hypothetical, serves as a concrete example of the framework's applicability to real-world scenarios.

Step 1: Initial Business Process Description Our modeling journey starts with the telemedicine IT service's business processes. Within the *i** SR diagram, represented in Fig. 4, we define the goals and tasks that are required to the service's operation. These foundational elements are highlighted in the diagram's darkest shade of gray.

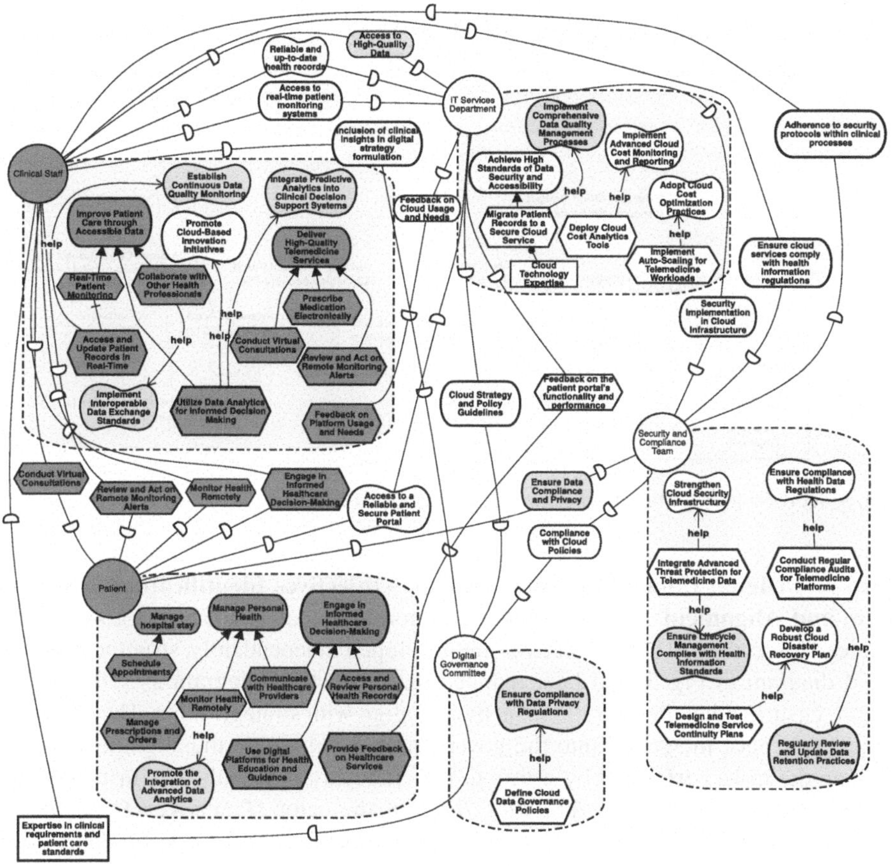

Fig. 4 *i** diagram for the digital governance related to the telemedicine IT service

5.1 Cloud Governance

All the elements (actors, tasks, goals, softgoals, and resources) added for cloud governance are in plain white in Fig. 4.

Step 2.1: Digital-Domain-Specific Governance Structure Identification and Integration This phase introduces the governance structures that are integral to the cloud domain. These structures include the *IT Services Department* responsible for the technical deployment and the *Digital Governance Board* which oversees the broader governance approach. As part of this step, we also establish a *Security and Compliance Team*, whose role is critical in ensuring the telemedicine platform meets all necessary security and compliance requirements. This is especially important for clinical staff who rely on the platform's integrity for patient care.

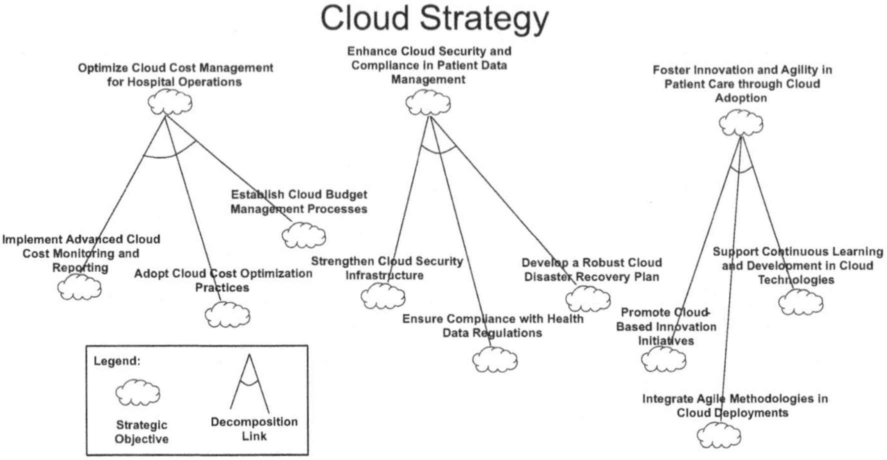

Fig. 5 NFR diagram for the cloud computing strategic objectives

Step 3.1: Digital-Domain-Specific Strategic Objectives Identification, Integration, and Alignment We then conduct a thorough analysis of cloud governance strategic objectives. These objectives are developed independently, structured in the NFR diagram of Fig. 5, and later mapped onto the *i** SR diagram as softgoals in Fig. 4, ensuring that the operational activities align with strategic aims. The strategic objectives, once integrated into the governance model, guide the alignment study, linking the tasks performed by actors to the cloud strategy goals. For instance, the *i** task *Deploy Cloud Cost Analytics Tools* of the actor *IT Services Department* supports the realization of the strategic objective *Implement Advanced Cloud Cost Monitoring and Reporting*.

5.2 *Data Governance*

Step 4: Iterative Analysis for Additional Digital Domain(s)

Step 2.2: Digital-Domain-Specific Governance Structure Identification and Integration We expand our focus to encompass data governance, introducing elements that are denoted in the lightest shade within the *i** SR diagram seen in Fig. 4. This iterative step includes the addition of a key structural component, *Ensure Data Compliance and Privacy*, reflecting the paramount importance of data governance in the telemedicine service.

Step 3.2: Digital-Domain-Specific Strategic Objectives Identification, Integration, and Alignment Due to space limitations, we do not reproduce the sole NFR diagram relating the data strategic objectives here, but it can be visualized

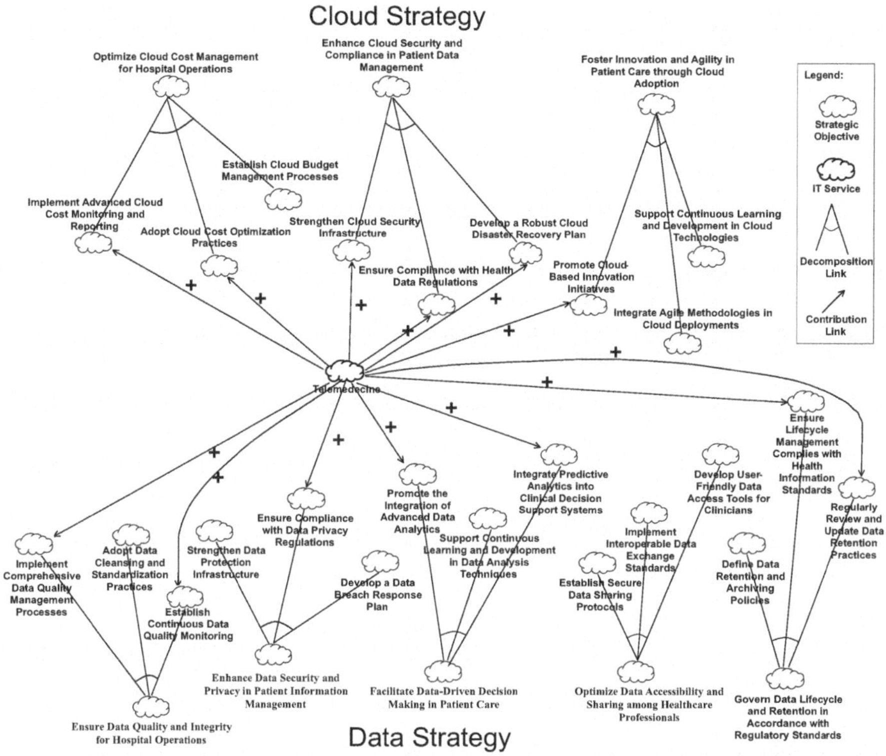

Fig. 6 Cloud and data strategies NFR decomposition model and telemedicine service contributions

in the bottom of Fig. 6. Further strategic objectives tailored to data governance are identified, and a separate alignment analysis is conducted to ensure they are appropriately represented within the service processes (indicated by the softgoals in the lightest shade of gray, distinct from both the white and darkest ones).

5.3 *Digital Governance Analysis and Decision Phase*

Step 5: Full Assessment of the Models and Decision Taking The final phase of our procedure is characterized by a full-scale analysis of the models. In the context of the telemedicine business IT service, the *i** SR diagram serves as a canvas for evaluating each actor, task, and softgoal. This evaluation is not restricted to operational functionality but extends to encompass regulatory compliance, security, user adoption, and return on investment considerations. The Digital Governance Board assumes a pivotal role at this juncture, utilizing insights drawn from both the *i** and NFR models to inform decisions on prioritizing, modifying, or potentially abandoning various IT initiatives.

For a tangible illustration of DBA, an NFR diagram can be constructed to include all strategic objectives from the digital domains in question, juxtaposed with the operationalization of the telemedicine IT service. This approach is visualized in Fig. 6, which synthesizes the strategic impacts at a high level. Decisions emanating from this phase are deeply rooted in a holistic understanding of the digital ecosystem of the organization, ensuring that the governance framework is neither compartmentalized nor static but is both integrated and dynamic. The use of MoDrigiGo to ensure DBA is particularly well-suited for emerging and rapidly evolving fields like telemedicine, where the alignment of business IT services with digital strategy can significantly influence the delivery of healthcare.

6 Discussion

6.1 On the Utility of the Framework Within COBIT and ITIL

The first *Evaluate/Direct/Monitor* (*EDM*) process the *Control OBjectives for Information and related Technology* (*COBIT*) framework [8] (i.e., *Ensure Governance Framework Setting and Maintenance*) underscores the need for a unified governance approach, focusing on analyzing governance requirements and establishing necessary structures and responsibilities. MoDrigiGo enhances this process with its *i** visual modeling language, delineating structures, stakeholders, and dependencies. Similarly, the first *Align/Plan/Organize* (*APO*) process (i.e., *Manage the IT Management Framework*) benefits from MoDrigiGo by systematically defining organizational and governance frameworks, including governance boards, and clarifying roles and responsibilities for the IT personnel, thereby embodying these governance principles.

Also, the second APO process of COBIT (i.e., *Manage Strategy*) prescribes the evaluation of the current and target organizational situations and the creation of a road map to bridge the gap from the former to the second. The direct correlation between tasks and strategic objectives expressed as softgoals within the *i** model provides a mechanism to direct efforts toward desired outcomes, while the iterative nature of the methodology ensures continuous monitoring and refinement. As a parallel of the APO02 process of COBIT, the *Information Technology Infrastructure Library* (*ITIL*) framework [9] proposes *Strategy Management for IT Services*. The latter process would also benefit from the incorporation of our DSR artifact since it helps in strategy generation and execution.

Incorporating both COBIT's APO05 *Manage Portfolio* process and ITIL's *Service Portfolio Management*, our framework enhances IT service oversight through strategic *i** modeling, offering a structured approach for IT service behavior analysis. This method supports APO05's goals for assessing and prioritizing IT investments aligned with strategic objectives. Similarly, it complements ITIL by streamlining the management of service portfolios, ensuring effective planning, implementation, and tracking. The *i** perspective provides stakeholders with deeper insights, bridging strategic and operational facets for optimized organizational support.

6.2 Scalability Considerations

A critical aspect of implementing our proposed framework lies in its scalability, particularly in accommodating multiple digital governance domains or dealing with multiple IT services in study for adoption. From the outset, MoDrigiGo differentiates the alignment process across various business IT services. This stratification aims to facilitate governance-level adoption decisions for entities of substantial size while simultaneously ensuring that *i** modeling efforts remain integrated yet flexible. The incorporation of the first digital governance domain often experiences the most considerable time and resource investment. This is due to the necessity of establishing foundational governance structures and strategic objectives from the ground up. For instance, introducing a "Data Governance" domain requires setting up dedicated compliance and privacy policies, a task that involves extensive planning and coordination. However, once this foundational layer is established, subsequent digital domains can be integrated more efficiently.

7 Related Work

Conceptual modeling frameworks but more precisely *i** have been used for governance-level strategic decision-making in multiple contexts [21].

Sukhwal et al. [16] provide a systematic review of agent-based modeling (ABM) in digital governance research. Their work is essentially focused on governmental functions (and not on individual organizations; digital governance is thus understood in a different way than for MoDrigiGo). It underscores the potential of ABM to address complexities, uncertainties, and heterogeneities in digital governance, identifying gaps in current research and proposing future directions. The review highlights the gradual increase in ABM applications within digital governance over the last two decades, mainly concentrated in non-IS journals, and pinpoints four primary domains of study: *emergency/disaster*, *land use*, *energy*, and *law/policy development*. The authors advocate for expanding ABM applications to unexplored areas and improving model design, implementation, validation, and adoption processes to enhance digital governance and policy formulation. Heng et al. [6] utilize the *i** framework to model the AI ecosystem in Senegal and Cambodia, facilitating an analysis of these countries' digital governance approaches at a global level. This methodology allows for a comparison that highlights deficiencies, especially when contrasted with a Global North country like Belgium, underscoring disparities in digital governance infrastructure and strategy.

Bleistein et al. [2] put forward the *Strategy-Oriented Alignment in Requirements Engineering* (*SOARE*) methodology tailored for e-business systems development. This framework is designed to ensure that the requirements of the supporting systems are in harmony with the overarching business strategies. SOARE employs GORE to articulate business strategy through the identification of long-term goals, with a specific focus on e-business system creation. The evolution of SOARE into B-SCP [3, 4] represents an advancement toward achieving BITA by incorporating three distinct perspectives: *Strategic*, *Context*, and *Process*. Conceptually, B-SCP utilizes *i**-like diagrams for strategizing business models and employs *Role Activity Diagrams* (*RAD*) [25] for the delineation of business processes, alongside *Problem Frames* [10, 11] for the contextual mapping of strategy execution. A noteworthy aspect of B-SCP's approach to conceptual modeling lies in its unified representation of both business strategy and the envisioned system within a singular model, interconnected through designated arrows that bridge the different conceptual layers.

Noel et al. [13] discuss challenges in Model-Driven Development for ensuring strategic alignment of information systems with organizational goals. It introduces a Holistic Model-Driven Development method that integrates three modeling frameworks (*i**, Communication Analysis, and OO-Method) for a comprehensive approach from organizational strategy to code generation. The paper identifies issues in maintaining strategic information through modeling levels, emphasizing the need for traceability and automated transformations. Challenges include integrating strategic goals with business processes, managing information loss, and ensuring models reflect organizational strategies effectively.

Pant et al. [14, 15] use the *i** framework to describe coopetition situations (i.e., simultaneously involving cooperation and competition between two or more organizations). Cooperation in a coopetition context fosters enhanced collective welfare, while competition drives the pursuit of individual organizational gains. The *i** framework allows to map out the coopetitive landscape, detailing the dependencies that exist between organizations. This mapping is crucial for aligning these dependencies with a range of IT design considerations. The essence of coopetition necessitates a harmonization—or, at the very least, efficient communication—among the information systems operated by the participating organizations. This requirement influences various aspects, including data models, integration methods, and organizational workflows. Through conceptual modeling, a nuanced portrayal and assessment of interorganizational ties are facilitated [15], serving as a foundation for informed decisions in IT governance and management strategies. Kolp and Wautelet [12] explore the creation of human organizational patterns with *i** in both generic an instantiated manners. Specifically, structure-in-5 and joint venture organizational styles are ways to organize at strategic level in order to maximize utility within one or more organizations.

MoDrigiGo (like MoDrIGo and StratAMoDrIGo) adopts a more fragmented and detailed approach compared to other methodologies. This means that they break down complex processes into smaller, more manageable components. The benefits of this approach include a more thorough examination of each component, which can lead to more precise alignment of IT services with business, IT, or any kind of digital strategies. However, this fragmentation can also introduce challenges, such as the need for increased coordination and integration among the various components. Justifying this choice, the detailed breakdown enables a nuanced understanding and management of specific elements, ensuring that each aligns closely with strategic objectives. To the best of our knowledge, MoDrigiGo is the only framework that natively allows practitioners to flexibly integrate various domains of digital governance within a single framework, making it the only holistic yet customizable framework for DBA. The introduction of MoDrigiGo represents a genuine contribution of this paper.

8 Conclusion

In our investigation entitled "50 Shades of Digital Governance," we study the research question: *how can an i*-centric framework support DBA within the multifaceted nature of digital governance?* This paper has shown the framework's potential to intricately align digital strategies with the development of operational business IT services, leveraging the capabilities of *i** modeling. This approach underscores the "50 shades" metaphor, reflecting the myriad, evolving domains within digital governance, each with its unique significance and interplay in the organizational context. Through the application of *i** in the MoDrigiGo context, entities gain the ability to clearly delineate and evaluate how well operational practices align with strategic objectives on a rather detailed level. This evaluation is vital for attaining alignment at both organizational and strategic levels within digital initiatives. Looking ahead, we foresee expanding our exploration to encompass the continuously emerging domains of digital governance, embodying the diverse "shades" that characterize this field. For instance, Aghakhani et al. [1] propose a customizable set of strategic objectives for the governance of the digital transformation itself; it is structured around an NFR tree and is meant to be immediately integrated in the framework presented in this paper. Future work will not only validate the framework in broader applications but will also explore its integration with existing governance standards, enhancing its utility in navigating the ever-shifting landscape of digital governance.

References

1. Aghakhani, G., Wautelet, Y., Dijkmans, D., Heng, S., Poelmans, S., Kolp, M.: Supporting digital transformation strategy formulation through a customisable set of objectives: conceptual model and expert opinions. Enterpr. Informat. Syst. **18**, 2300089 (2024)
2. Bleistein, S.J., Aurum, A., Cox, K., Ray, P.K.: Strategy-oriented alignment in requirements engineering: Linking business strategy to requirements of e-business systems using the SOARE approach. J. Res. Pract. Informat. Technol. **36**(4) (2004)
3. Bleistein, S.J., Cox, K., Verner, J.M.: Validating strategic alignment of organizational IT requirements using goal modeling and problem diagrams. J. Syst. Softw. **79**(3), 362–378 (2006)
4. Bleistein, S.J., Cox, K., Verner, J.M., Phalp, K.: B-SCP: a requirements analysis framework for validating strategic alignment of organizational IT based on strategy, context, and process. Inf. Softw. Technol. **48**(9), 846–868 (2006)
5. Chung, L., Nixon, B., Yu, E., Mylopoulos, J.: Non-functional Requirements in Software Engineering. Kluwer Academic Publishing, New York (2000)
6. Heng, S., Tsilionis, K., Scharff, C., Wautelet, Y.: Understanding AI ecosystems in the global south: the cases of senegal and cambodia. Int. J. Inf. Manag. **64**, 102454 (2022)
7. Hevner, A.R., March, S.T., Park, J., Ram, S.: Design science in information systems research. MIS Quart. **28**, 75–105 (2004)
8. ISACA.: COBIT 5: A Business Framework for the Governance and Management of Enterprise IT. ISACA (2012)
9. itSMF: ITIL Foundation Handbook. The Stationery Office (2012)
10. Jackson, M.A.: Problem Frames—Analysing and Structuring Software Development Problems. Pearson Education, Upper Saddle River (2000)
11. Jackson, M.: System behaviours and problem frames: Concepts, concerns and the role of formalisms in the development of cyber-physical systems. In: Irlbeck, M., Peled, D.A, Pretschner, A. (eds.) Dependable Software Systems Engineering *NATO* Science for Peace and Security Series, D:Information and Communications Security, vol. 40, pp. 79–104. IOS Press, Amsterdam (2015)
12. Kolp, M., Wautelet, Y.: Human organizational patterns applied to collaborative learning software systems. Comput. Human Behavior **51**, 742–751 (2015)
13. Noël, R., Panach, J.I., Pastor, O.: Challenges for model-driven development of strategically aligned information systems. IEEE Access **10**, 38237–38253 (2022)
14. Pant, V., Yu, E.: Coopetition with frenemies: Towards modeling of simultaneous cooperation and competition among enterprises. In: The Practice of Enterprise Modeling—9th IFIP WG 8.1. Working Conference, PoEM 2016, Skövde, November 8–10, 2016, Proceedings, pp. 164–178 (2016)
15. Pant, V., Yu, E.S.K.: Modeling simultaneous cooperation and competition among enterprises. Busin. Inf. Syst. Eng. **60**(1), 39–54 (2018)
16. Sukhwal, P.C., Kankanhalli, A.: Agent-based modeling in digital governance research: a review and future research directions. In: Scientific Foundations of Digital Governance and Transformation, pp. 303–331. Springer, Cham (2022)
17. Tsilionis, K., Wautelet, Y.: A model-driven framework to support strategic agility: value-added perspective. Inf. Softw. Technol. **141**, 106734 (2022)
18. Tsilionis, K., Wautelet, Y., Truyers, L., Ding, Y.: Strategic agility in practice: Experts' opinions on the applicability of a model-driven framework. In: Babkin, E., Barjis, J., Malyzhenkov, P., Merunka, V., Molhanec, M. (eds.) Model-Driven Organizational and Business Agility—Third International Workshop, MOBA 2023, Zaragoza, June 12–13, 2023, Revised Selected Papers. Lecture Notes in Business Information Processing, vol. 488, pp. 1–15. Springer, Berlin (2023)
19. Wautelet, Y.: A model-driven it governance process based on the strategic impact evaluation of services. J. Syst. Softw. **149**, 462–475 (2019)

20. Wautelet, Y., Kolp, M.: Business and model-driven development of BDI multi-agent systems. Neurocomputing **182**, 304–321 (2016)
21. Wautelet, Y., Kolp, M.: Conceptual modeling as a tool for corporate governance support: State of the art and research agenda. In: Visvizi, A., Lytras, M.D. (eds.) Research & Innovation Forum 2019—Technology, Innovation, Education, and their Social Impact, RIIFORUM 2019, Rome, April 24–26, 2019, pp. 535–548. Springer, Berlin (2019)
22. Wautelet, Y., Heng, S., Kiv, S., Kolp, M.: User-story driven development of multi-agent systems: a process fragment for agile methods. Comput. Lang. Syst. Struct. **50**, 159–176 (2017). https://doi.org/10.1016/j.cl.2017.06.007
23. Wautelet, Y., Kolp, M., Heng, S., Poelmans, S.: Developing a multi-agent platform supporting patient hospital stays following a socio-technical approach: management and governance benefits. Telemat. Inform. **35**(4), 854–882 (2018)
24. Weill, P., Ross, J.W.: IT Governance: How Top Performers Manage IT Decision Rights for Superior Results. Harvard Business Press, Brighton (2004)
25. Wilson, J.M.: Business processes: modelling and analysis for re-engineering and improvement. J. Operat. Res. Soc. **47**(4), 595–596 (1996)
26. Yu, E.: Modeling Strategic Relationships for Process Reengineering, chap. 1–2, pp. 1–153. MIT Press, Cambridge (2011)
27. Yu, E., Giorgini, P., Maiden, N., Mylopoulos, J.: Social Modeling for Requirements Engineering. MIT Press, Cambridge (2011)

Using *i** to Analyze Ethicality Requirements Following Ontology-Based Requirements Engineering

Renata Guizzardi, Glenda Amaral, Giancarlo Guizzardi, and John Mylopoulos

Abstract New developments on Information Systems (ISs) and especially on Artificial Intelligence (AI) have been posing continuous risks to humans and societies, going beyond problems of security and safety and including many more ethical problems. In this context, ethicality becomes a major requirement for AI systems that prevents them from being biased, making mistakes, or going rogue. Requirements Engineering (RE) is the research area that can support the development of ethical systems by design. However, proposing concepts, tools, and techniques that support the expression, analysis, and operationalization of ethicality requirements remains a great challenge in the RE field. In our work, we rely on Ontology-based Requirements Engineering (ObRE) as a method to elicit and analyze ethicality requirements, defined with basis on the following principles: Beneficence, Nonmaleficence, Explicability, and Autonomy. This chapter presents requirements elicitation and analysis guidelines for each of these principles. The guidelines have been carefully crafted with basis on an ontological analysis effort previously done. In addition, we use a driverless car case to illustrate our work. Based on the guidelines and the ontological concepts, we present the analysis of this case by using *i**, which we consider particularly suitable for the analysis of ethicality requirements. The reason for such suitability comes from the close alignment of *i** with the ontological concepts that serve to define ethicality requirements. This is also discussed in the chapter.

R. Guizzardi (✉) · G. Amaral · G. Guizzardi
University of Twente, Enschede, The Netherlands
e-mail: r.guizzardi@utwente.nl; g.c.mouraamaral@utwente.nl; g.guizzardi@utwente.nl

J. Mylopoulos
University of Toronto, Toronto, ON, Canada
e-mail: jm@cs.toronto.edu

X. Franch et al. (eds.), *Social Modeling Using the i* Framework*,
https://doi.org/10.1007/978-3-031-72107-6_12

1 Introduction

We are facing a time of profound and rapid changes promoted by Information Systems (ISs) and especially Artificial Intelligence (AI) developments. In this new world we are building, there is much more uncertainty than sureness. Every day, we watch astonished the news reporting that a new kind of fraud is becoming common, a piece of fake news has ruined someone's reputation, and a system error or bias has led to a personal or community calamity.

Changes are bound to affect all areas of society. For example, with deep fake generation, law is about to suffer one of the biggest changes in the past 50 years. Suddenly, pictures and videos are no longer viable proof against a given defendant. Is DNA going to become the only unquestionable proof? What is it to come? Many questions like this come to mind in these disrupting times we have been living.

As researchers in Information Systems, we have the duty to act to endow technology developers with the tools they need to face the challenges posed by these new changes. Taking the example above, how can we generate close to 100% accurate deep fake detectors? This is one out of a million examples we can come up with. As a matter of fact, if we want ISs to be carefully and consistently developed, shepherded by ethical and moral principles, it is time we roll up our sleeves and work towards methods and guides to develop trustworthy systems.

Ethics has been the concern of humanity for centuries, having as father no one else but Socrates, from ancient Greece [9]. Since then, many developments and prominent figures have emerged in this area and, more recently, the focus on technology ethics (although not new) has been strengthened [11, 20].

Ethicists and AI researchers have been recently studying the interplay of ethics and AI systems where the subjects of ethical codes are systems that play such roles, e.g., worker or driver. Floridi et al. [12] propose five general principles that underlie ethical codes and are role-independent. These have been adopted by the European Commission in a document concerning trustworthy AI [6]. The principles are *Autonomy* (respect human dignity), *Beneficence* (do good to others), *Nonmaleficence* (do no harm to others), *Justice* (treat others fairly), and *Explicability* (explainability, transparency). But besides being recognized and well-defined, these principles need to be embedded into software engineering practices, in a way that they may effectively guide the design of ethical systems.

Our work claims that Requirements Engineering (RE) is the area of research (within ISs development) more capable of promoting positive impact on the development of trustworthy systems. This is justified by RE's natural purpose of guaranteeing that systems are developed to fulfill their hardgoals (i.e., functional requirements) as well as to manifest particular qualities (i.e., non-functional requirements). RE is not only responsible for eliciting requirements that will guide the design of a system-to-be but also for ensuring that such requirements have been properly met and also for monitoring that these requirements remain valid throughout the life cycle of the system. However, to the best of our knowledge, there is no current Requirements Engineering method to support the development of ethical systems.

In a previous work [19], we presented an ontological analysis of ethicality requirements and showed how Ontology-based Requirements Engineering (ObRE) can support requirements engineers in eliciting and analyzing ethicality requirements.[1] Moreover, ObRE has also been used in previous works focusing on the development of trustworthy systems [3, 4].

In this ongoing work, we use ObRE to propose a method for eliciting and analyzing ethicality requirements. We can categorize ethicality requirements for a system-to-be as *Ecological Requirements* [18], in that they are derived from the ecosystem within which the system-to-be is embedded. After all, it is that ecosystem that determines *values* and *risks* that can lead to ethical behaviors by the system ([18], p. 253). This is aligned with the concerns we manifested about the ethical use of technology, which, although bringing much *value*, also brings many *risks*. And these risks must be accounted for and analyzed in contrast with the values delivered by systems and services applying such technologies.

The focus in this chapter is on the requirements elicitation and analysis guidelines created with basis on the ontological analysis presented in [19]. We aim at showing how these guidelines may support the development of goal models, thus with a special focus on Goal-Oriented Requirements Engineering (GORE) and on the *i** framework [8] in particular. *i** provides many modeling constructs that are aligned with the ontological categories we apply to analyze ethicality requirements, such as agent, goal, and delegation. These and other constructs facilitate the analysis of ethicality requirements, also providing the means for refining goals to arrive at more concrete requirements that must be met by the system-to-be. We believe that the use of *i** in one of the step of the ObRE method may lead to safe gains in the requirements analysis of trustworthy systems.

The remainder of this chapter is structured as follows: Sect. 2 discusses the role of ontological analysis for Requirements Engineering; Sect. 3 describes the ObRE method; Sect. 4 presents the ontology-based guidelines to support the elicitation and analysis of ethicality requirements, created with basis on the ontological analysis conducted in [19]; Sect. 5 presents requirements elicitation and analysis using *i** for a driverless car case; finally, Sect. 6 presents some final considerations and sketches future work.

[1] "Ethicality requirements" is adopted as a name for the class of requirements studied in this chapter by analogy to other quality requirements studied in software engineering, such as usability, reliability, portability, etc. The use of this term (as opposed to "ethical requirements") highlights that they represent requirements for ethical systems, analogous to how "trustworthiness requirements" represent requirements for trustworthy systems. To put simply, the predicates "ethical" and "trustworthy" are not meant to be predicated over the requirements themselves.

2 Ontological Analysis for Requirements Engineering

The notions of *ontology* and *ontological analysis* adopted here are akin to their interpretations in philosophy [7]. In this view, *ontological analysis* (i) characterizes what kinds of entities are assumed to exist in a given domain and (ii) offers a metaphysical account of the nature of these kinds of entities. An *ontology*, in turn, is a system of concepts and their relationships that result from (i) and (ii).

As such, an ontology is neither merely a logical specification nor it is mainly concerned with making terminological and taxonomic distinctions. For example, in addressing the domains of risk, one is less concerned with what specific subtypes of risk exist (e.g., physical, biological, financial, electronic) but instead with what exactly *is* risk. What kind of entity is it? What is its nature? Is it an object? An event? A relationship? A complex property? If the latter, is it a categorical or dispositional property? What is the bearer of such a property? And so on.

Given the nature of this method of analysis, it must be supported by a domain-independent system comprising the most general categories, hence crosscutting several domains (e.g., objects, events, relationships, dispositions, etc.), i.e., what is termed a foundational ontology (aka top-level or upper-level ontology). In [19], we adopt the Unified Foundational Ontology (UFO) [17] and the UFO-based ontology representation language OntoUML [14].

As previously mentioned, a major challenge for requirements analysis today is to propose concepts, tools, and techniques that support Requirements Engineering activities for incorporating high-level societal concerns and goals, such as privacy, fairness, trustworthiness, and ethics, into the software development processes as explicit requirements. Ontological analysis (OA) provides a foundation for the elicitation of such requirements, as it enables a deep account of the meaning of a particular domain. The main idea is to systematize the elicitation and analysis of requirements, by using an ontological account for a class of requirements. By "semantically unpacking" concepts such as trustworthiness ethics, OA can help analysts cope with complex requirements, where the analyst literally doesn't know where to begin in conducting elicitation and analysis, which is the case of ethical requirements.

We emphasize that a key concept to deriving ethical requirements is that of *Runtime Stakeholders* [18]. These include those stakeholders that are using, affected by, or influencing the outcomes of a system as it is operating. Traditional RE often limits runtime stakeholders to just users of the system-to-be. However, for AI systems this needs to be extended to other parties. For example, for a driverless car, runtime stakeholders include passengers—i.e., the users of the car—but also pedestrians, whose path may cross that of the car and shouldn't be hit; bystanders, who shouldn't be scared or splashed as the car drives by; nearby drivers, who, as a courtesy, should be allowed to cut in front in the car's lane; and fellow drivers in general, who might benefit from information about an accident that just happened in the vicinity of the car. This is illustrated in Fig. 1.

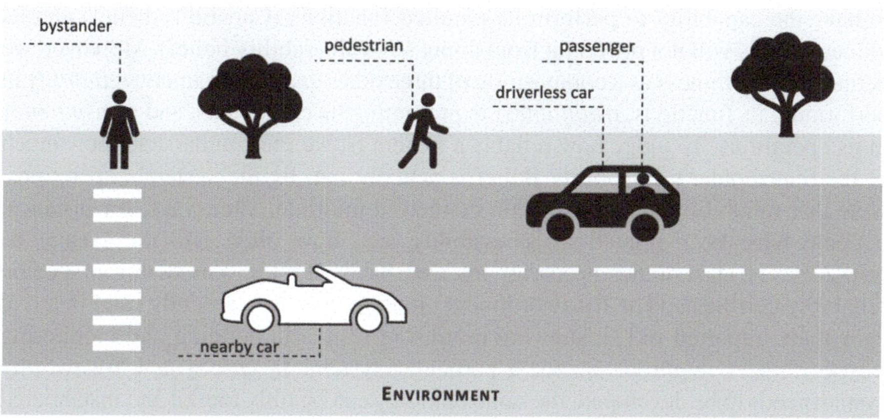

Fig. 1 Driverless car ecosystem

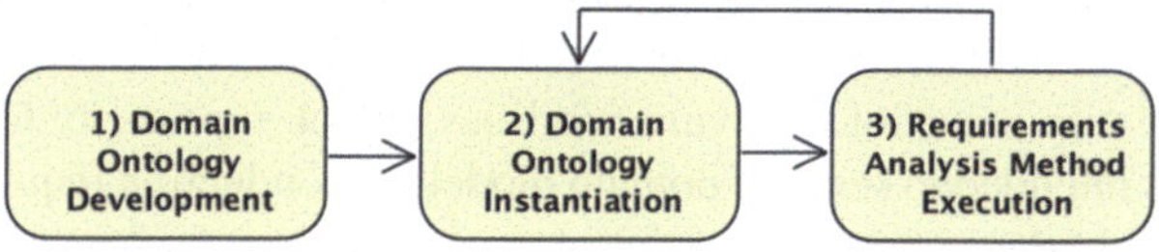

Fig. 2 The ObRE process

Understanding well the ontological concepts underlying a particular domain may be a complex task. To alleviate the complexity of the application of ontological analysis in Requirements Engineering, it is interesting to have explicit guidelines to support the analyst during the requirements elicitation.

3 The ObRE Method

Figure 2 illustrates the process of the ObRE method, showing the three activities mentioned in Sect. 1.

The process starts with **(1) Domain Ontology Development**. Requirements analysts and ontology engineers perform ontological analysis for a class of requirements. We emphasize that ObRE does not prescribe that the requirements engineer is versed in the use of ontological analysis concepts. For that, ObRE assumes the presence of an ontology engineer, and the requirements engineer plays a role of a domain expert in the ontology development process. The outcome of activity 1 is an ontology modeled in OntoUML [14].

This activity is performed once for each class of requirements and doesn't need to be repeated for each new system development project. For example, in [2], we conducted ontological analysis about the notions of *trust* and *trustworthiness*. According to the results of our analysis, a system is trustworthy if it is believed to have the capability to perform its required functions (Capability belief) and its vulnerabilities will not prevent it from doing so (Vulnerability belief). Moreover, we define trustworthiness as a composition of three other qualities, namely, *reliability* in performing its functions, *truthfulness* in presenting its credentials, and *transparency* in its operations. To judge how reliable a system is, we must understand how much of the Stakeholder's Capability Belief is actually met by the system's operations. Note that reliability could have been defined in multiple other ways, for instance, it could have been related to accessibility, i.e., how often will the system be responsive to stakeholder needs, or inferred by the system possessing a specific reliability certificate. The trustworthiness ontology has been recently used in a real case study, reported in [3], showing promising results in defining and monitoring trustworthiness requirements for a particular system. In case a new trustworthy system needs to be developed, the same ontology can be fully reused and instantiated for the new system-to-be.

Having the requirements explicitly defined and understood, the analyst may perform **(2) Domain Ontology Instantiation**. Here, the analysts focus on a particular system and instantiate elements of the ontology. For a security ontology, this step would identify stakeholders, vulnerabilities, attack types, etc. for a particular system. This is intended to serve as domain model for conducting requirements analysis. We highlight the importance of this step, since the same class of requirements may lead to distinct concrete requirements for each system. Thus, instantiating the ontology created in 1 helps identify these particular requirements and opens the way for requirements analysis. This is also the step in which requirements elicitation and analysis guidelines are created, making explicit to the requirements engineer which ontological concepts should be the focus of her attention and how this can support her to elicit and analyze requirements.

In activity **(3) Requirements Analysis Method Execution**, analysts use the domain model and the elicitation and analysis guidelines to define and analyze system requirements. For instance, she may simply define a requirements table, listing the requirements instantiated with the help of the ontology. Or if she prefers a more sophisticated analysis methodology, she may use goal modeling, define the contribution of different choices to accomplish a particular goal (i.e., requirement), and specify how goals relate to each other, as well as to relevant stakeholders' resources and tasks. Or yet, she may create user stories based on the identified ontological instances. From this point on, the requirements analysis may progress as the chosen method prescribes, however, with the benefit of having the ontology and ontological instances as guides. In this chapter, we exemplify this activity using Goal-Oriented Requirements Engineering (GORE).

As depicted in Fig. 2, steps 2 and 3 are intended to be carried out iteratively, as with most RE methods. This supports the analyst in revisiting the previous activities while maturing the requirements elicitation and analysis.

4 Ontology-Based Guidelines to Support the Elicitation and Analysis of Ethicality Requirements

In [19], we apply steps 1 and 2 of ObRE for ethical principles as qualities, and we model ethicality requirements as a non-functional requirements (NFRs) refined into sub-NFRs related to such qualities, following the definitions presented in [16]. In a nutshell, ethicality requirement is a combination of beneficence requirement, nonmaleficence requirement, autonomy requirement, and explicability requirement. The ontological analysis of all these types of requirements is based on the following definitions of principles [12]: Beneficence (do good, i.e., promoting well-being, preserving dignity, and sustaining the planet); Nonmaleficence (do no harm, i.e., avoiding potentially negative consequences of overusing or misusing AI technologies); Autonomy (strike a balance between the decision-making power of artificial and human agents), and Explicability (making the AI decision-making process intelligible and accountable). Floridi et al. [12] also propose the principle of Justice, which remains a future NFR to be incorporated in our work, thus being out of the scope of this chapter.

In the remaining of this section, we present elicitation and analysis guidelines created with basis on our ontological analysis to support the requirements engineer in eliciting and analyzing ethicality requirements. For more detail about the ontological foundation of such guidelines, one must again refer to [19].

4.1 Guidelines Focusing on Beneficence and Nonmaleficence Requirements

The ontological analysis highlights the concepts that are important in defining each NFR. For example, let us analyze *Beneficence* and *Nonmaleficence* requirements, allowing us to contrast these two related NFRs.

Drawing from [19] and [22], Beneficence and Nonmaleficence requirements can be elaborated using the notions of *Value* and *Risk*. In a nutshell, we can say that *Value* can be thought of as the degree to which a value experience satisfies an agent's goals, while *Risk* can be conceived as the degree to which a risk experience can dent that agent's goals. Considering the definition of beneficence as "doing good to others" [12], we can say that Beneficence Requirements are related to "creating value" to stakeholders in the ecosystem in which the system is included. It means that Beneficence Requirements can be seen as goals related to an intention of **positively** impacting the goals of stakeholders in this ecosystem. Analogously, considering the definition of Nonmaleficence as "doing no harm to others" [12], we can say that Nonmaleficence Requirements are related to "not posing risks" to stakeholders. Consequently, Nonmaleficence Requirements can be seen as goals related to an intention of preventing the occurrence of events that may **negatively** impact stakeholders' goals. Events that impact agents' goals, either positively or

Table 1 Guidelines to support elicitation and analysis of Beneficence and Nonmaleficence requirements

Beneficence and Nonmaleficence requirements are elicited together.
Consider the ecosystem of the system under development. Now try to identify important events of the domain surrounding it. If two Agents (i.e., stakeholders in the ecosystem) participate in the same *event*, analyze if this event: (i) *Positively* impacts the agent's Intentions. If so, this event is known as Gain Event and the intentions identify Beneficence Requirements. As a result, the system may this way create value to the ecosystem stakeholders; or (ii) *Negatively* impacts the agent's Intentions. If so, this event is known as Loss Event and the countermeasure to avoid such loss identify Nonmaleficence Requirements. As a result, the system may prevent risks to the ecosystem stakeholders. Ontological concepts: Intention, Gain Event, Loss Event

negatively, are usually known as *Gain Events* and *Loss Events*, respectively. In this sense, Beneficence Requirements intend to create Gain Events, which positively impact stakeholders' goals. Similarly, Nonmaleficence Requirements intend to prevent the occurrence of Loss Events, which negatively impact stakeholders' goals.

As a result, we came up with the following elicitation and analysis guidelines that should usher the work of requirements analyst (see Table 1).

In the sequel, in Fig. 3, we instantiate the ontology with two examples (a Beneficence and a Nonmaleficence Requirement) in the context of driverless cars.

In the first example, the Passenger of a driverless car intends "not to be late." In order to address this, we have the Beneficence Requirement that "the car should choose quicker route towards destination" related to the Intention that the "driverless car arrives on time at destination," which is a Beneficence Intention that aims at creating a Gain Event. The event "driverless car arrives on time at destination" is a Gain Event that positively impacts the Passenger's goal of not being late.

In the second example, the Passenger intends to "feel safe." In order to address this, we have the Nonmaleficence Requirement that "the car should adopt a defensive driving behavior" related to the Intention of "preventing aggressive direction," which is a Nonmaleficence Intention that aims at preventing the occurrence of a Loss Event. The event "passenger feels nervous as the car drives aggressively" is a Loss Event that negatively impacts the Passenger's goal of feeling safe.

4.2 Guidelines Focusing on Autonomy Requirements

Another important ethicality requirement is the Autonomy Requirement, defined by Floridi et al. [12] as the "power to decide." In this chapter, the authors argue that when using AI, people voluntarily delegate some of their decisions to the system.

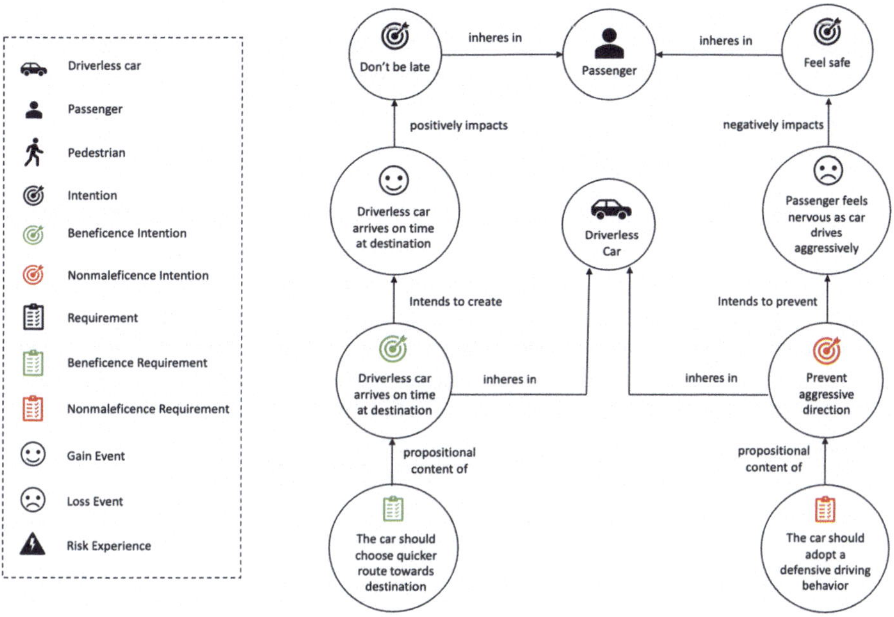

Fig. 3 Ontology instantiation showing Beneficence and Nonmaleficence requirements

Thus, dealing with system autonomy means defining the right balance between what is to be decided by the user and what can and should be **delegated** to the system.

The concept of Delegation has been targeted by the Unified Foundational Ontology since its early days. In a DELEGATION, two agents play the role of DELEGATOR and DELEGATEE. To analyze autonomy, the STAKEHOLDER assumes the role of DELEGATOR, while the SYSTEM assumes the role of DELEGATEE.

Each autonomy requirement is associated to a particular LEVEL OF AUTONOMY to capture the fact that a STAKEHOLDER delegates the decision-making power to an ARTIFICIAL SYSTEM up to a level. In other words, the LEVEL OF AUTONOMY modulates the strength of this delegation relation, i.e., how much is in fact delegated to the system.

To understand AUTONOMY DELEGATION, it is also crucial to consider concepts borrowed from UFO-L, an ontology of legal relations. Considering well-known legal theories, UFO-L defines eight legal relationships, which are grouped in four pairs of legal positions:

1. Right and Duty. If subject S1 has the right to an action A or omission O against subject S2, then subject S2 has a duty to perform action A (or omit O).
2. Permission and No-Right. If subject S1 holds a permission towards subject S2 to an action A (or omission O), then subject S2 has no right to demand that the permission holder S1 omits action A (or refrains from omitting O).

3. Power and Liability. If subject S1 has legal power in face of subject S2 to create, change, or extinguish a legal position (a right, duty, permission, etc.) X for subject S2, then subject S2 is liable towards subject S1 w.r.t. this legal power.
4. Disability and Immunity. If a subject S1 has, in face of subject S2, no power to create, change, or extinguish a legal position X for subject S2, then subject S2 is immune to changes in the legal position that affect her.

We here generalize these notions from UFO-L to consider not only *legal positions* but also *social positions*, i.e., social rights duties, permissions, powers, etc. This way, we use such positions to regulate the relationship between stakeholder and system, regardless if there is currently a law to regulate such relationship.

One of the most important parts of dealing with ethical requirements is handling ethical conflicts. In other words, what happens when two stakeholders have conflicting requirements or when the system needs to make a choice between favoring one stakeholder over another, in face of the same requirement. This is one of the contexts in which it is useful to analyze autonomy requirements.

Let us consider a possible conflicting situation in the context of a driverless car example. It is intuitive that all stakeholders (e.g., passengers and pedestrians) have the same requirement of "being safe." Suppose that in some point in the car's route, there is a tree that must be avoided. But not hitting the tree while saving the passenger means running over some close-by pedestrians. This case illustrates the well-known trolley problem in philosophy. And Fig. 4 illustrates one possible choice to handle such conflict.

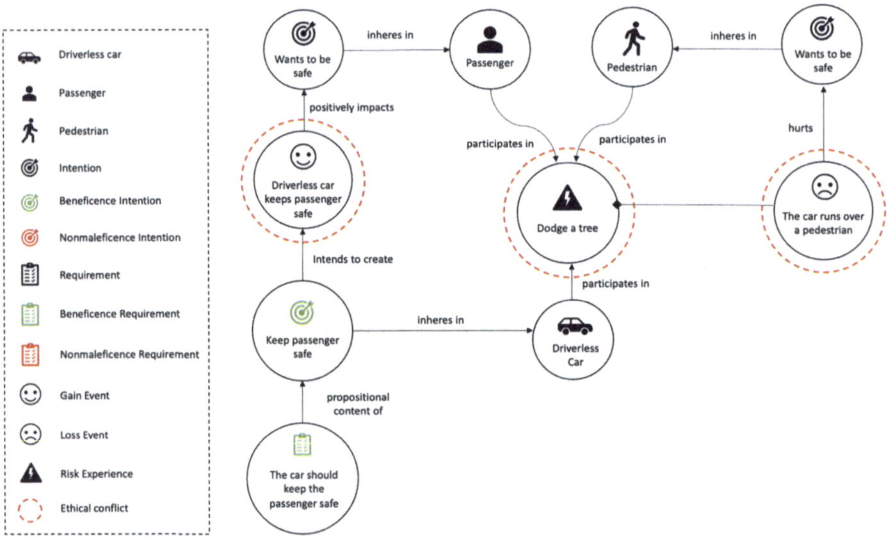

Fig. 4 Ontology instantiation showing a choice the driverless car makes in face of an ethical conflict

Here, dodging the tree is a Risk Experience that has participations from the *Driverless car*, the *Passenger*, and the *Pedestrians*. This is a point of attention for the requirements analyst; whenever two (or more) stakeholders participate in the same RISK EXPERIENCE, it is possible that such experience results in a GAIN EVENT for one stakeholder and a LOSS EVENT for the other. For the tree dodging example, the Driverless Car decides to dodge the tree, leading to a passenger Safe GAIN EVENT and a Pedestrian LOSS EVENT. Ultimately, the car fulfills the Keep Passenger Safe ETHICALITY REQUIREMENT, failing to fulfill the same requirement w.r.t. the Pedestrians.

Note that in the illustrated case, we assumed that the Driverless Car had the PERMISSION to perform that action (the GAIN EVENT) on behalf of the Passenger in face of this particular RISK EXPERIENCE but also that it has the POWER to overrule its *duty to omit* from performing an action that harms the pedestrian (a LOSS EVENT). An AUTONOMY REQUIREMENT referring to an AUTONOMY DELEGATION TYPE for this particular case has been decided a priori. And the AUTONOMY LEVEL was high, allowing the Driverless Car to fully make that decision. Notice that the human stakeholders that are the delegators of that autonomy level to the car be found to bear the corresponding social and legal responsibility for the artificial system's actions and omissions.

Table 2 shows three guidelines to support requirements analysts in eliciting and analyzing autonomy requirements based on ontological concepts.

Table 2 Guidelines to support elicitation and analysis of autonomy requirements

Thinking in terms of pairs of correlative Social Positions (e.g. *Duty and Right*, *Permission and No Right*, etc.) helps the identification of related Autonomy Requirements. Here is an example in the driverless car case: the pedestrian wants to be safe and has the *Right* to cross the street at red traffic light. Consequently, the driverless car has the *Duty* to stop at a red traffic light (an Autonomy Requirement). Ontological concept: Social Position
Consider the ecosystem of the system under development. Now try to identify important events of the domain surrounding it. If two Agents A and B (i.e., stakeholders in the ecosystem) participate in the same *event*, analyze if causes a positive impact on the Intention of Agent A and a negative impact on the Intention of Agent B. If so, there is an **ethical conflict**. Analyze the conflict to identify requirements that create value to Agent A (Beneficence Requirements), and requirements that prevent risks that can cause losses to Agent B (Nonmaleficence Requirements). Ontological concepts: Intention, Impact Event
If two (or more) stakeholders participate in events such as the ones in the previous guideline, we can say that they share a Risk Experience. If that is the case, the analyst should consider if it is possible in such cases, to defer the choice to the system's end user. Ontological concepts: Intention, Risk Experience, Impact Event

4.3 Guidelines Focusing on Explicability Requirement

Explicability has been in the center of discussion regarding AI systems [1, 10]. According to Floridi et al. [12], this requirements should be viewed in the sense of "intelligibility" (addressing the question "how does it work?") and in the sense of "accountability" (addressing the question "who is responsible for the way it works?").

Ontologically speaking [19], an explicability requirement refers to a number of ACTION TYPES (including types of DELIBERATIONS and DECISION-RESULTING ACTIONS) whose trail of provenance has to be made intelligible. In this context, this means reconstructing the chain from DECISION-RESULTING ACTIONS to the DECISIONS they manifest, from those to the DELIBERATIONS that create them, from the latter to the PREFERENCES relation on which they are grounded, from the latter to the CRITERION, i.e., QUALITIES, DISPOSITIONS, INTENTIONS, as well as SOCIAL POSITIONS that constitute the PROSPECT ASSESSMENTS that are the truthmakers of these preferences.

Now, turning to accountability, there are three aspects to consider. Let us first address the notion of moral responsibility. In disposition-based philosophical studies of moral responsibility [5], an agent A is taken to be morally responsible for action X if (1) A has caused X and did that (2) intentionally and (3) autonomously and (4) there is a system of values (and norms) on which the appropriateness of A can be judged. Our ontologies [19] make explicit that there are here at least types of agents that can be considered the bearers of moral responsibility. First and foremost, these are the stakeholders who must form their intentions and preferences taking into considerations a wider backdrop of collective values, values of other stakeholders in the ecosystem at hand (see, e.g., the autonomous car ecosystem in Fig. 1), and who delegate their goals to artificial agents including via the formulation of social positions in autonomy delegations. Second, these are artificial agents (ethically designed systems) to which these intentions and autonomy levels are delegated (refer to the discussion on Autonomous requirements in Sect. 5.3).

In our analysis, we make clear that artificial systems are ethically designed when they have the capacity and (adopted) intentions (1) to perform actions (2) that bring about value to the relevant stakeholders and mitigate their risks (4), when they honor their delegated autonomy agreements, i.e., they act at the appropriate level of autonomy (3) defined by the relevant stakeholders (the prospect beneficiaries). By being able to intelligently recreate the chain of entities connecting actions performed by an autonomous system to the original stakeholder's intentions and delegations, systems designed in conformance to our analysis would be able to explain also moral responsibility (accountability) for these two types of agents [19].

Let us think of an example in the context of the driverless car case. Suppose that the car is driving the Passenger through a highway in a lane of slow traffic speed but fails to overtake the vehicles that are riding in front. When asked by the Passenger why it chooses not to overtake (DECISION-RESULTING ACTION), the driverless car responds that overtaking the car (DEPRACATED BEARER) would take them to a lane which is obstructed by an accident in 500 Km. Given the Passenger's Intention of reaching the destination fast and safely, and the Quality of the lane of being obstructed, the driverless car decided to maintain the current lane, not overtaking the other vehicles. This example shows that the analyzed ontological concepts provide the means to trace the driverless car action to the decision that led to such action, along with the used criteria, making it clear for the stakeholder why that action was executed instead of an alternative one. From the accountability perspective, the driverless car may also point out that it has a high Autonomy Level w.r.t overtaking, based on a specific contract made with the Passenger, who delegates the Decision to overtake or not to the driverless car. Such delegation is composed of a Permission to decide.

If one takes explanation to be "deduction in reverse" and, in particular, if what we are "reversing" is a type of causal chain (thus, enabling a type of *causal explanation*), we have that by providing a representation structure that explicitly models the chain connecting actions performed by an autonomous system to decisions and preferences and, ultimately, to the original stakeholder's intentions and delegations, this approach also supports the design of systems that are able to intelligibly and unaccountably explain and justify their actions by explicitly traced causal processes.

Finally, the notion of Explicability Requirement put forth here can be seen as a special case of *Why-Question* or *Requests for Explanation* in the approach of Pragmatic Explanation [21, 23]. In particular, having Preferences modeled as a comparison between alternative Prospect Ascriptions allows for providing a *contrast class*[2] against which deliberations are made.

In what follows, the reader may find a guideline to help the analyst to elicit Explicability requirements (Table 3).

5 Requirements Analysis Method Execution Using *i**

In this section, we exemplify activity 3 of the ObRE process.

Table 3 Guideline to support elicitation and analysis of explicability requirements

Consider stakeholder A (agent) of the system under development ecosystem. Now verify *conflicting requirements* w.r.t the other stakeholders' requirements and w.r.t. other requirements of stakeholder A. If decision D is taken by the system hurts a requirement (i.e., hurts the intention) of stakeholder A, explain decision D. In this case, this requirement of stakeholder A is an (Explicability Requirement). Repeat the same for the remaining stakeholders in the ecosystem.

Ontological concepts: Decision, Intention

[2] See [23] for the role of contrast classes in Pragmatic Explanation.

5.1 Using the i* Framework to Analyze Ethicality Requirements

The modeling language underlying the i* framework is comprised of concepts such as agent (actor), goal, quality, task, and resource. Moreover, it provides relationships such as refinement, means-end link, and delegation (dependence). These constructs have been considered in the RE literature as very appropriate to analyze requirements in general. In this chapter, we advocate that it is particularly adequate for the analysis of ethicality requirements.

The point we want to make is that the ontological concepts analyzed to define ethicality requirements (Beneficence, Nonmaleficence, Autonomy, and Explicability requirements) are also present in *i**. For instance, to analyze a stakeholder's requirement, our ontology relies on the concept of stakeholder's intention which is associated to a goal of such stakeholder. Stakeholder (an agent in our ontology) is directly represented as actor in *i**. Capturing goals in *i** is a very direct application of such ontological concept. With the help of refinement, goals may become more and more concrete, until a point in which the analyst is satisfied regarding its granularity, in a way that it may be directly implemented in the system-to-be (in case of functional requirements) or serve as a quality to characterize the system (in case of non-functional requirements). Additionally, the relation of delegation adopted to explain autonomy requirements can be directly mapped to the dependence construct in *i**. The ontological appropriateness of i* is not a coincidence. In our early work, we used ontological analysis to provide semantic-based guidelines for the use of *i** [13, 15]. And by doing so, we ended up incorporating many of the concepts related to *i** in UFO.

To sum up, most entities in the goal model can be obtained directly by mapping elements from the **ontology instantiation** (activity 2 in ObRE; refer to Sect. 3). Furthermore, for each of them, more specific goals, qualities, tasks, and resources can be identified and represented. The mapping between the ontology concepts and their representation in the *i** Goal Model is presented in Table 4.

Table 4 Guidelines for mapping ontological concepts to i* Goal Model entities

Ontological concept	Representation in i* Goal Model
`Driverless car`	`Actor, Agent, Role`
`Passenger`	`Actor, Agent, Role`
`Pedestrian`	`Actor, Agent, Role`
`Nearby car`	`Actor, Agent, Role`
`Intention`	`Goal dependence, Quality dependence`
`Beneficence requirement`	`Goal, Quality`
`Nonmaleficence requirement`	`Goal, Quality`
`Autonomy requirement`	`Goal, Quality`
`Explicability requirement`	`Goal, Quality`

Having explained the benefits of using i^* to analyze ethicality requirements, the reader must know that our ontological analysis of ethicality requirements does not prescribe a particular requirements elicitation and analysis method. Each RE approaches has its advantages and limitations. For example, the relation between the relevant ontological concepts for each principle and the ethical requirements is easier to spot in a requirements table than on an i^* model, which is also much easier and fast to create than a goal model. The goal model, however, makes more explicit which intention (and thus which requirement) is related to each of the agents involved in our case. Moreover, it is visual and it allows a much more detailed requirements analysis, in terms of more and less abstract requirements, solutions, and needed resources. User stories are also very relevant as analysis method, since they help create concrete and well-stated cases relating to ethicality requirements. The requirements analyst should ultimately make a choice for the requirements elicitation and analysis method based on their particular preference or skill.

5.2 Beneficence and Nonmaleficence Requirements Analysis

Let us now use goal modeling for analyzing Beneficence and Nonmaleficence requirements for the Driverless car case that we have been using to illustrate our method. Figure 5 depicts a goal model for this case, using the i^* framework [8].[3]

The model considers five stakeholders of the driverless car ecosystem, namely, ***Passenger***, ***Pedestrian***, ***Bystander***, ***Nearby Car***, and ***Environment***. It also depicts the dependency of each of these stakeholders and the ***Driverless Car***. With respect to the **Passenger**, the ***reaching destination on time*** goal dependency relates a positive impact event in which the Passenger participates (*passenger arrives on time at destination*), while the ***feeling at ease*** dependency relates to the negative impact captured for this same stakeholder (*passenger feels nervous when the car drives aggressively*). The i^* model also allows dependencies to be added, for instance, when drawing the model, we realize that avoiding accidents dependency is relevant for the Passenger. Regarding **Pedestrians**, the ***promptly crossing the road*** goal dependency relates a positive impact event in which they participate (*pedestrians waiting by a crossroad have priority to cross it*), while the ***moving safely through traffic*** dependency relates to the negative impact captured for this same stakeholder (*the car runs over a pedestrian*). As for **Bystanders** the ***avoid being splashed*** goal dependency relates a negative impact event in which they participate (*be splashed if the car passes by a puddle of water*). In the case of the **Nearby Car**, the ***avoiding accidents*** goal dependency relates a negative impact event (*be hit*). Finally, for the **Environment** the ***avoid pollution*** goal dependency relates a negative impact event in which this stakeholder participates (*be polluted*).

[3] The goal models in this chapter were drawn using the piStar tool, available at https://www.cin.ufpe.br/~jhcp/pistar/.

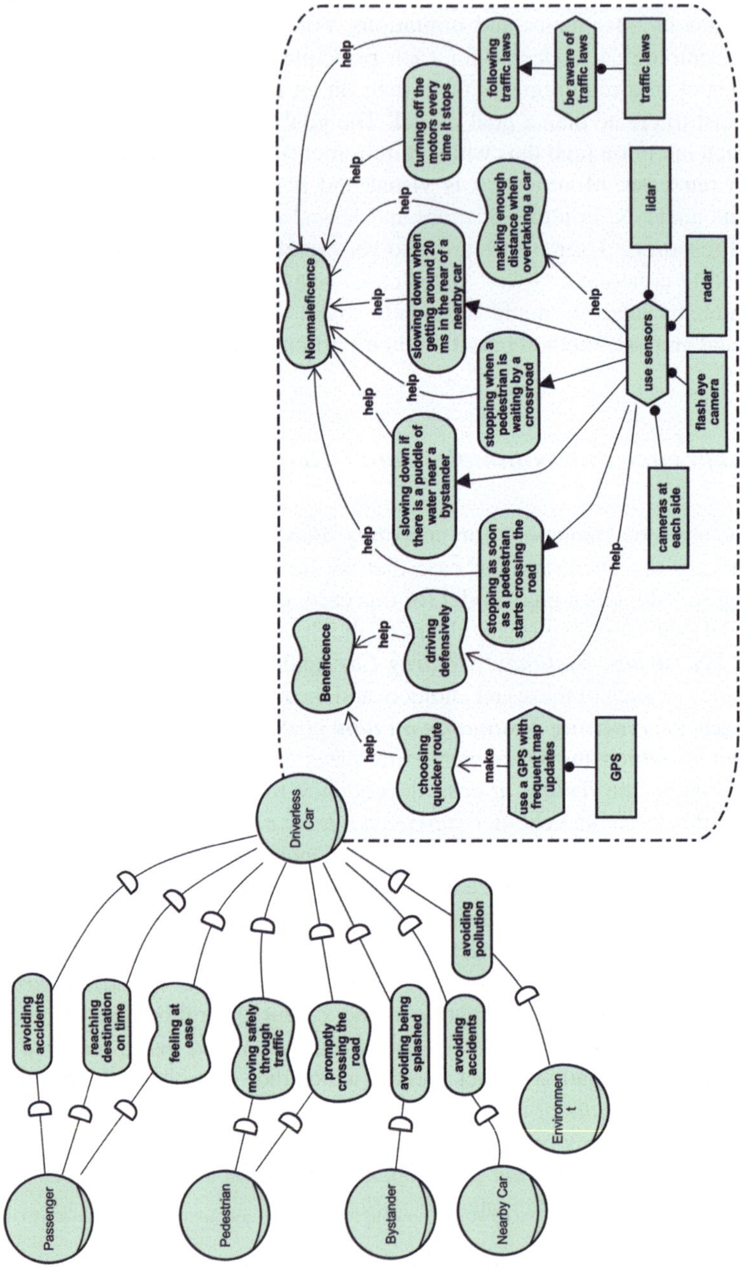

Fig. 5 The driverless car Beneficence and Nonmaleficence requirements model using *i**

Besides dependencies, the goal model of Fig. 5 depicts the internal perspective of the Driverless Car, assisting in the analysis of the system's requirements. Note that the ethical principles of Beneficence and Nonmaleficence are represented there by qualities (consistent with our ontological notion of NFR). Then, for each of these qualities, more specific goals and qualities are identified and related to them by contribution links. For instance, the ***choosing quicker route*** quality helps (i.e., partially contributes to) the achievement of Beneficence. Additionally, ***choosing quicker route*** may be indirectly related to the ***reaching destination on time*** goal dependency of the Passenger.

5.3 Autonomy Requirements Analysis

Figure 6 exemplifies some autonomy requirements for the driverless car case. For autonomy requirements, the stakeholders considered are ***Passenger***, ***Pedestrian***, ***Bystander***, and ***Nearby Car***. Regarding the Passenger, the goal dependencies on the Driverless Car are the same as in the Beneficence and Nonmaleficence requirements goal model (Fig. 5). The goal dependencies for Pedestrian, Bystander, and Nearby Car are, respectively, ***moving safely through traffic***, ***being safe***, and ***avoiding accidents***. Note that, in the conflicting situation illustrated in Sect. 4.2, there is a conflict between the Bystander's goal of feeling safe and the Passenger's goal of avoiding accidents, and its underlying goal of feeling safe as well. By making goal dependencies explicit, the goal model allows the analyst to identify conflicting goals in advance and consequently be more proactive in the requirements specification.

Considering the internal perspective of the Driverless car, the ethical principle of Autonomy is represented as a quality. Then, by analyzing the social (and legal) positions between the stakeholders and the driverless car (see Sect. 4.2), more specific goals and qualities were identified, related to the actions and decisions delegated to the system. For example, ***Duty*** leads to the goal ***following traffic laws***, as the Driverless car has the duty to follow these laws while conducting the Passenger. Similarly, ***Power*** leads to the goal ***take the best course of action in the imminence of an accident***, as the Driverless car has the power to decide the best course of action in the imminence of an accident.

5.4 Explicability Requirements Analysis

Figure 7 exemplifies some explicability requirements for the driverless car case. The stakeholders considered for this requirement are ***Passenger***, ***Pedestrian***, ***Bystander***, and ***Nearby Car***. With respect to the last three stakeholders, the goal dependencies are the same as in the Autonomy requirements goal model (Fig. 6). Regarding the Passenger, his goal of arriving on time has been added to the goal dependencies illustrated model in Fig. 6.

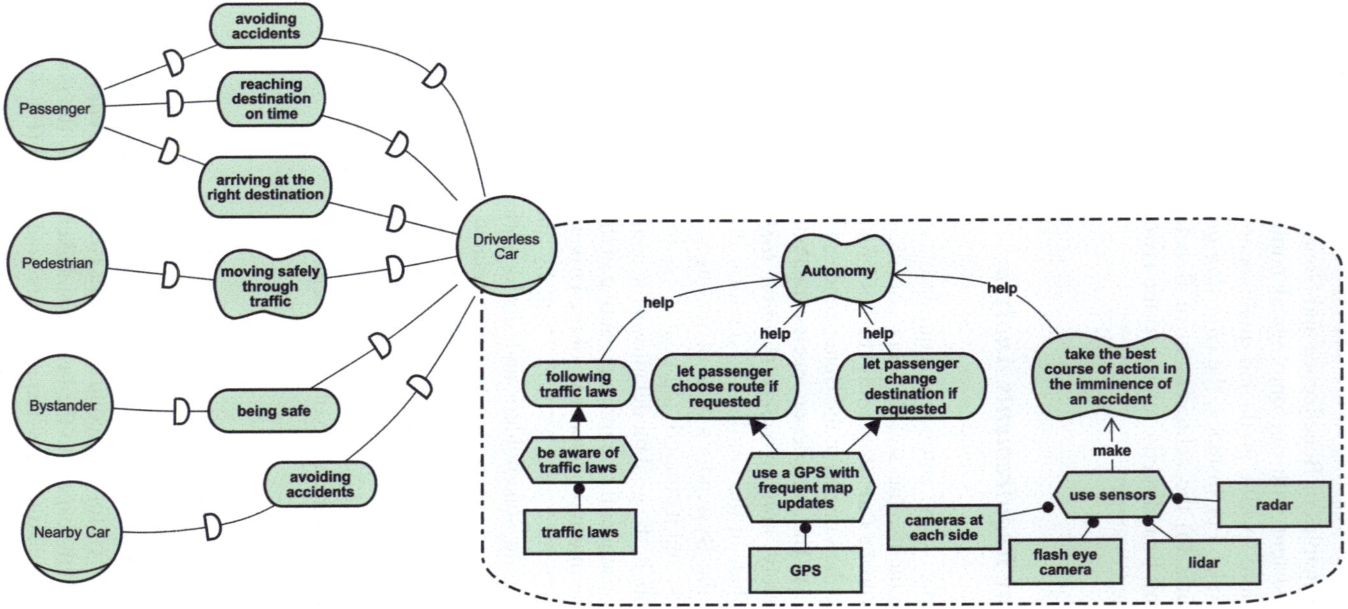

Fig. 6 The driverless car Autonomy requirements model using *i**

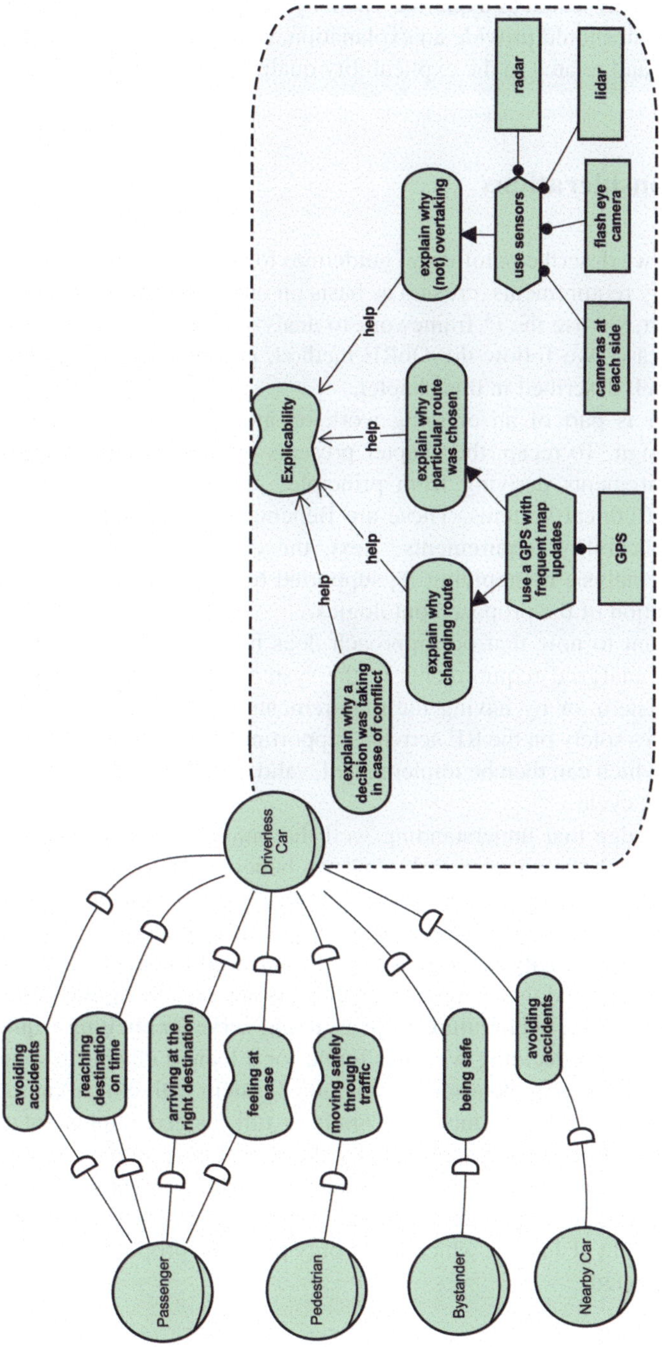

Fig. 7 The driverless car Explicability requirements model using *i**

Considering the internal perspective of the Driverless car, the ethical principle of Explicability is represented as a quality. Then, by analyzing for which decisions and actions the system should provide an explanation, more specific goals and qualities were identified and related to the explicability quality by contribution links.

6 Final Considerations

In this chapter, we describe ontological guidelines to enable the elicitation and analysis of ethicality requirements, created as basis on ontologies presented in previous work. Moreover, we use the *i** framework to analyze ethicality requirements for a driverless car case. We follow the ObRE method, proposed elsewhere but whose activities are well described in this chapter.

This chapter is part of an ongoing work on an RE method to create ethical systems by design. To recap, the chapter presents ontological guidelines for four ethicality requirements deriving from principles previously defined guiding the development of ethical systems. These are Beneficence, Nonmaleficence, Autonomy, and Explicability requirements. Next, the chapter conducts requirements elicitation and analysis by applying *i**, supported by the presented guidelines and by the instantiation of the proposed ontologies.

It is important to note that our approach does not prescribe a specific way to implement the analyzed requirements in the system, for example, by developing a rule-based system, or by having the requirements hardcoded. Our ObRE-based approach focuses solely on the RE activity, supporting the elicitation and analysis of requirements, which can then be implemented, validated, and monitored throughout the system's life cycle.

We acknowledge that understanding well the ontological concepts underlying our approach may be a complex task. And we believe this complexity is actually given by the challenge of designing systems that exhibit ethical behavior. That is why we find it important to come up with practical guidelines to conduct the work of requirements analysts, so that they do not need to deeply understand the ontological concepts and their relations. In this chapter, we exemplified our method for a driverless car case, but in future projects, it may serve for eliciting requirements for a financial system deciding who is eligible for a loan, a chatbot responding to user queries based on large data sets, or any other system with ethical implications.

Our agenda for the future includes, firstly, a full-fledged implementation and validation of our ObRE-based approach, by doing real case studies in the domain of ethical systems and having experts evaluate the results. Moreover, we intend to deepen our analysis of ethical conflicts, and to propose an ontological analysis of the ethical principle of Justice, which is the only principle proposed by [12] that we have not yet targeted.

References

1. Adadi, A., Berrada, M.: Peeking inside the black-box: a survey on explainable artificial intelligence (XAI). IEEE Access **6**, 52138–52160 (2018)
2. Amaral, G., Guizzardi, R., Guizzardi, G., Mylopoulos, J.: Ontology-based modeling and analysis of trustworthiness requirements: Preliminary results. In: International Conference on Conceptual Modeling, pp. 342–352. Springer, Berlin (2020)
3. Amaral, G., Guizzardi, R., Guizzardi, G., Mylopoulos, J.: Ontology-based requirements engineering: The case of trustworthiness requirements. In: 40th International Conference on Conceptual Modeling, pp. 257–267 (2021)
4. Amaral, G., Guizzardi, R., Guizzardi, G., Mylopoulos, J.: Trustworthiness requirements: The pix case study,. In: International Conference on Conceptual Modeling, pp. 257–267. Springer, Berlin (2021)
5. Anjum, R.L., Lie, S.A.N., Mumford, S.: Dispositions and ethics. In: Powers and Capacities in Philosophy, pp. 231–247. Routledge, Milton Park (2013)
6. High-Level Expert Group on Artificial Intelligence, E.C.: Draft ethics guidelines for trustworthy ai, draft document (2018)
7. Berto, F., Plebani, M.: Ontology and Metaontology: A Contemporary Guide. Bloomsbury Publishing, London (2015)
8. Dalpiaz, F., Franch, X., Horkoff, J.: iStar 2.0 language guide. arXiv:1605.07767 [cs.SE] (2016). dalp-fran-hork-16-istar.pdf
9. Dhillon, N., Lim, J.: Socrates: The Father of Ethics and Inquiry. Rosen Publishing, New York City (2016)
10. DW, G.D.A.: DARPA's explainable artificial intelligence program. AI Mag **40**(2), 44 (2019)
11. Floridi, L.: The Ethics of Artificial Intelligence: Principles, Challenges, and Opportunities. Oxford University Press, Oxford (2023)
12. Floridi, L., Cowls, J., Beltrametti, M., et al.: AI4people–an ethical framework for a good ai society: opportunities, risks, principles, and recommendations. Minds Mach. **28**, 689–707 (2018)
13. Gomes Jr., R., Guizzardi, R., Franch, X., Guizzardi, G., Wieringa, R.: An Empirical study to validate the use of ontological guidelines in the creation of i* models. In: 7th Brazilian Seminar on Ontologies (ONTOBRAS 2015). CEUR (2015)
14. Guizzardi, G.: Ontological Foundations for Structural Conceptual Models. Telematica Instituut/CTIT (2005)
15. Guizzardi, R.S.S., Guizzardi, G.: Ontology-based transformation framework from TROPOS to AORML. In: Social Modeling for Requirements Engineering, pp. 547–570. The MIT Press, Cambridge (2010)
16. Guizzardi, R., et al.: An ontological interpretation of non-functional requirements. In: Proceedings of the FOIS, vol. 14, pp. 344–357 (2014)
17. Guizzardi, G., Wagner, G., Almeida, J.P.A., Guizzardi, R.S.S.: Towards ontological foundations for conceptual modeling: the Unified Foundational Ontology (UFO) story. Appl. Ontol. **10**(3-4), 259–271 (2015)
18. Guizzardi, R., et al.: Ethical requirements for ai systems. In: Proceedings of the Canadian AI 2020, pp. 251–256 (2020)
19. Guizzardi, R., Amaral, G., Guizzardi, G., Mylopoulos, J.: An ontology-based approach to engineering ethicality requirements. Softw. Syst. Model. **22**, 1897–1923 (2023)
20. Luppicini, R., Adell, R.: Handbook of Research on Technoethics. IGI Global, Pennsylvania (2009)
21. Romanenko, E., Calvanese, D., Guizzardi, G.: Towards pragmatic explanations for domain ontologies. In: Knowledge Engineering and Knowledge Management: 23rd International Conference, EKAW 2022, Bolzano, September 26–29, 2022, Proceedings, pp. 201–208. Springer, Berlin (2022)

22. Sales, T., et al.: The common ontology of value and risk. In: Proceedings of the 37th International Conference on Conceptual Modeling (ER), vol. 11157, pp. 121–135. Springer, Berlin (2018)
23. Van Fraassen, B.: The pragmatic theory of explanation. Theor. Explanat. **8**, 135–155 (1988)

Part V
Visions

Agent-Oriented Modeling for the Age of AI: Nine Pivots Toward a Reconceptualization of Requirements Engineering

Eric Yu

Abstract Modeling techniques have been instrumental for conceptualizing and architecting complex systems. Since the early days of requirements engineering (RE), concepts such as *process* and *object* have served as core abstractions undergirding many modeling languages and have seen extensive application in all kinds of domains. Today, software systems are engaging with humans in ever deeper, more intricate, sometimes even intimate ways. They leverage pervasive digitalization to learn from data, acquiring increasingly humanlike characteristics. An abstract concept of *agent*, proposed much earlier in AI for characterizing artificial agents, suitably extended and generalized, could potentially serve as a core abstraction for requirements modeling for today's complex sociotechnical environment. In this chapter, we outline a modeling ontology by elaborating on the sociotechnical actor concept originally proposed in *i**. The proposal also suggests shifting the focus of RE from the specification of a target technology system to one of assisting stakeholders to explore how they might augment their "selves." A personal wellness app is used as a motivating example.

1 Introduction

Digital technologies have vastly transformed everyday life in recent years. Today, further advances in machine learning (ML) and artificial intelligence (AI) offer promises of dramatic benefits yet could pose serious threats to lives and livelihoods.

For requirements engineering (RE), the challenge is to provide methods and techniques to help stakeholders explore the space of potential technology solutions so as to identify those that offer desired benefits while minimizing potential negative consequences.

E. Yu (✉)
University of Toronto, Toronto, ON, Canada
e-mail: eric.yu@utoronto.ca

X. Franch et al. (eds.), *Social Modeling Using the i* Framework*,
https://doi.org/10.1007/978-3-031-72107-6_13

Most RE techniques in use today were conceived in earlier eras and are ill-equipped to respond to today's much richer and faster-moving environments. In the past, most software and information systems offered solutions that are task-oriented and narrowly confined, often in work or business-related settings where users were trained to use the system. Requirements techniques aimed to define intended functions and interactions precisely and in great detail.

Today's "smart" machines are increasingly general purpose and aim to respond flexibly to a wide range of user needs. With advanced machine learning algorithms and models, machines are able to recognize human behavioral characteristics and adjust their own behavior accordingly. As systems today incorporate more advanced ML and AI components, we can expect them to engage with humans in increasingly humanlike ways.

From a modeling perspective, RE techniques need to be able to adequately describe and analyze the kinds of services and capabilities that today's systems offer and how problems, issues, and concerns that arise can be addressed. They need to map out the space of potential technology solutions and to analyze their implications and consequences, so that stakeholders can make informed decisions.

The agent concept had been used as an abstraction for characterizing machine behavior since the early days of AI [1]. The *i** framework [2] adapted the concept for the purpose of requirements modeling and analysis. In this chapter, we argue that an agent-orient modeling approach is well suited to address the RE challenges in the age of AI. We put forward a vision for extending the agent-oriented modeling approach as initially proposed in *i** [3, 4]. The proposal is presented in terms of nine "pivots," together constituting a transition from the prevailing way of thinking about RE to a new conceptualization.

2 A Motivating Example

Consider a health and wellness app that can be personalized to help you stay healthy and fit [5, 6]. By emphasizing prevention, it has the potential to reduce healthcare costs, overcome shortages of health professional, and improve outcome for an entire population. It draws on personal health records and population health data, as well as ongoing advances in medical knowledge and expertise. It taps into live data on your wearable and mobile devices and gives you timely advice on your dietary choices and suggestions on how to stay active. To make effective suggestions, it adapts to your predilections and inclinations and can sense and help you manage your emotions. Your healthcare team is kept up to date on your conditions and will take proactive action when necessary. Your health insurer will reward you for avoiding expensive procedures.

What features of such an app would you want or not want? What aspects of your daily life would you be willing to expose to the app in return for what benefits? If you are the family physician, how would you want the app to participate in the care of your patient, and how would your experience and expertise contribute?

If you are the regulator, how would you ensure that the service would not be harmful to individuals and would serve the public interest? If you are the developer or service provider, how would you balance the various interests to achieve a viable and sustainable business model? How would you ensure that the system is functioning properly as intended and whether it is living up to various stakeholders' expectations? [7].

There are numerous opportunities to incorporate AI into the app and supporting platform, from statistical ML to generative AI using foundation models. During requirements analysis, stakeholders would want to assess the potential benefits and pitfalls of various technology options.

3 From Process to Objects to Agents

Models are necessarily simplified representations of reality. They simplify by omitting unnecessary details while capturing essential aspects. Requirements modeling languages typically offer a small number of concepts (comprising the modeling ontology [8]) based on abstractions that are considered sufficient for the purpose of requirements analysis while "abstracting away" the rest.

In the early days of computing, the concept of process served as a powerful core abstraction for requirements modeling [9, 10]. In the era of interactive and distributed computing, object orientation became the dominant modeling paradigm [11]. Today, as software systems interact with the world in increasingly humanlike ways, the concept of agent holds promise for modeling how machines relate to the world and to each other.

The agent concept was first proposed as an abstraction for AI by Allen Newell [1]. It offered a higher-level characterization of the behavior of a machine, in terms of the goals that it can achieve. It served as a specification for building AI agents and for reasoning about how agents behave at a high level independently of software implementation mechanisms.

The *i** framework adapted the agent concept for the purpose of requirements modeling and analysis, for reasoning about how machines are situated in the world in a social setting. *i** actors relate to each other at an intentional level. They depend on each other for goals to be achieved, tasks to be performed, resources to be furnished, and quality goals (softgoals) to be satisfied. When an actor is depended upon to achieve a goal, it has the freedom to choose among alternative ways for achieving the goal.

Intentional relationships allow for a high-level way of describing how actors relate to each other. This is well suited to the age of AI, where machines increasingly have the ability to do what is expected, without prior specification of every interaction in detail.

While the *i** framework could serve as a foundation for requirements analysis, it abstracted away aspects that have become important today, particularly concerning rich humanlike behavior such as learning. In the chapter, we outline how we might extend the agent-oriented modeling approach to meet today's challenges.

The transition from process to object to agent orientation can be viewed as a natural progression of requirements modeling paradigms [4]. Each paradigm relies on abstractions that make simplifying assumptions about the world. Each step in the progression can be seen as an incremental removal or relaxation of earlier assumptions so as to be able to cope with the increasingly complex ways that today's powerful technology systems engage with the world.

In the process modeling paradigm, the analyst/designer has a full view of the entire end-to-end process, has control over how any parts of it is to be redesigned, and can globally optimize. In the object-oriented paradigm, behavior is distributed and localized. Local information is encapsulated and hidden. Prior assumptions of the omniscient and omnipotent analyst/designer are replaced by localized decision-making. The criteria for decision-making, however, are not captured in process models or object models. Intentionality resides in the analysts/designers. In goal-oriented requirements modeling [12, 13], intentionality is made explicit in the model and becomes available for analysis. In agent-oriented modeling, such as in *i**, intentionality is distributed and localized to each actor. Each actor is autonomous, although their freedoms are constrained by dependencies among them.

4 Nine Pivots Toward a Reconceptualization of RE

The proposed vision is premised on an ontology[1] of the world revolving around strategic actors and their relationships, rather than processes, objects, or user stories or scenarios that are the mainstay of current RE practices [14, 15]. The first two pivots recall the central ideas behind *i**. Each of the subsequent pivots elaborates and extends the agent-oriented modeling paradigm to encompass a richer ontology and a broader vision of RE. The proposal is meant to stimulate further developments in requirements modeling concepts and languages, agent-oriented or otherwise.

4.1 Pivot 1: From Unidirectional Stipulations to Multilateral Relationships

Requirements are often thought of as "shall" statements about what users and stakeholders want from a target system and how the system should behave, to serve as guidance and objectives for developers to meet [16]. To arrive at such statements,

[1] The term ontology is used in this chapter to refer to the set of concepts underlying a modeling framework [8]. The chapter outlines a skeletal ontology, leaving issues of language design open for future work.

the various parties would want to explore different options to gain understanding about the implications of the choices they make. As technology systems offer new and unfamiliar functionalities and venture into new application areas, this exploratory stage of requirements analysis becomes more important [3], as there are greater uncertainties about potential benefits as well as vulnerabilities and pitfalls.

*i** thus shifts focus from the usual understanding of requirements as prescriptive or optative statements directed from the client to developers to the analysis of the multilateral relationships among stakeholders and machines and the changes to those relationships arising from new technology solutions. Stakeholders aim to advance or protect their strategic interests as technology proposals are considered. The relationships are expressed at the intentional level, leaving detailed interactions to be specified during the later stages of requirements definition. With highly flexible and general-purpose AI applications, specification of detailed behavior may not be possible or necessary.

In *i**, stakeholders are modeled in terms of Actors.[2] Actors achieve goals by performing tasks with available resources. Alternative ways for achieving goals are differentiated by how they contribute toward quality goals (softgoals). By depending on others, an actor can take advantage of opportunities beyond its own capabilities. At the same time, it becomes vulnerable to potential failures beyond its control.

Actors are intentional—their actions are motivated by goals and softgoals. They are autonomous in that they have the freedom to choose among alternative ways for achieving goals. They are social in that their freedoms are constrained by dependencies with other actors. They reason about alternatives as best they can and seek to advance their strategic self-interest by leveraging opportunities while mitigating vulnerabilities [3].

In the wellness app, each of the stakeholders—the wellness seeker, the physician, etc.—would aim to benefit from the technology while avoiding negative consequences. They would have dependencies on the machine, but the machine also depends on the people around it if it is to function as intended. During requirements exploration and negotiation, each stakeholder would assess whether a proposed configuration of relationships is to its advantage and will seek to advance or at least protect its position. They would assess the viability of goal achievement by analyzing how success or failure would propagate across the network of dependencies and rationales.

4.2 *Pivot 2: From AI Agents to a Generalized Actor Abstraction*

In AI, the term "agent" refers to a computational entity—a machine [17, 18]. In humanistic disciplines, agent often refers to a human individual. For RE, we seek

[2] In this chapter, terms such as Actor, Role, and Agent are capitalized when used as defined in i*. When uncapitalized, their meanings are as in common usage.

abstractions that allow for decisions about the automation boundary to be made during RE, not as prior givens. In process modeling as well as object-oriented modeling, processes and objects can be analyzed at an abstract level[3] independent of implementation considerations so that allocation of responsibilities to humans or machines can be determined as a result of the RE process. The same principle is also recognized in the goal-oriented RE approach [19].

In *i**, the Actor is an abstraction that is independent of the medium or mechanisms of its eventual realization.[4] The abstraction adopts an external view and attributes intentional properties to an entity regardless of its internal makeup or mechanisms [22]. It is therefore equally applicable to humans and machines, or any combinations thereof, of any size or complexity. Machines are attributed intentionality and agency because they embody design intents and rationales. By explicitly representing intents and rationales in requirements modeling, the impact of design options on stakeholders can be explored and analyzed.

While analysis at an abstract level allows design options to be explored with the greatest flexibility, the abstract entities ultimately need to be related to their potential realizational counterparts. *i** modeling provides for abstract Actors[5] (called Roles) as well as realizational[6] Actors (called Agents) to be included in the same model so that dependencies among them can be recognized and analyzed. In the age of AI, where many automated systems operate based on probabilistic principles, one can expect that Agents may not fully meet the expectations defined in Roles. In traditional programmed software, even where functional requirements are fully met (sometimes supported by proofs of correctness), the non-functional or quality requirements may be met only up to a certain degree [23]. In the case of humans, roles often serve as aspirational guidance for actual behavior.

[3] In the structured analysis method based on process modeling [9], the abstract level is referred to as the logical model, in contract to the physical model. These are analogous to abstraction levels in data modeling.

[4] Although the i* Actor abstraction was partly inspired by the concept of agent in multi-agent systems and agent-oriented software engineering [18, 20] and appear to share some of the same properties, e.g., autonomy, sociality, etc., these terms have different connotations in their respective contexts [21]. An autonomous agent in AI is a machine that has the ability to act intelligently on its own without human intervention. Sociality refers to machines cooperating and acting collectively. In i*, these terms refer to properties of abstract Actors regardless of their realizational mechanisms.

[5] The terms *agent* and *actor* are used with a variety of connotations in various disciplines, with different degrees of abstraction. In the human and social disciplines, an agent or actor often refers to a human individual but can sometimes refer to a larger social entity, such as an organization or a nation state. In AI, an agent is an artifact to be implemented in software. In i*, Actor, Role, and Agent are concepts for use in modeling and so are therefore all abstractions. In i* models, they generally refer to classes but can also appear as instances of classes. The Actor is the generic concept, with Role and Agent being specializations. They can be further specialized into subclasses.

[6] We refer to an Agent as being realizational rather than realized, since it is still an abstraction. When a Role is PLAYed by an Agent, the relationship takes the Role one step closer toward realization.

In *i** modeling, the realization relationship from Agent to Role is denoted by the PLAYS association link. An Agent can depend on another Agent for achieving its goals, but those dependencies can be mediated by a Role so that different candidate Agents for PLAYing that Role can be considered. Note that since Roles and Agents are autonomous Actors, they can have mutual dependencies, unlike in conventional software architectures where intentionality flows one way along the realization relationship.[7] By using IS-A hierarchies to distinguish among different types of Agents, classes of machines and humans with various capabilities and characteristics can be defined, e.g., those with and without learning, different types of learning, etc.

4.3 Pivot 3: From Unitary Actor to Composite of Multiple Autonomous Actors

It is commonplace to think of a person as having one or more roles at work—project lead, software developer, etc., in addition to multiple roles in personal and social life, such as parent, citizen, fitness club member, etc. We learn to manage the competing demands from these roles, each representing different sets of interests and values. Different individuals may live up to the expectations of these roles to varying degrees. In simpler times, when software applications were narrowly focused, each stakeholder could be treated as a unitary actor with a single set of more or less coherent goals and strategic interests. In the age of AI, we are increasingly dealing with broad-based open-ended applications, possibly trained on all-encompassing data sources, as in the case of large language models (LLMs). Social psychologists have studied in great depth how humans manage multiple identities and conceptions of selves [24, 25]. In any given context, one or a small number of one's selves may be salient, i.e., dominate over others.

For RE, we propose to model multiple identities by treating any Actor as potentially composite, with each constituent Actor being a full-fledged Actor like any other (i.e., has all the properties of intentionality, autonomy, sociality, etc.). RE analysis could then be as fine-grained as desired. The wellness seeker, in addition to a StayingHealthy Role, may have other Roles such as BecomingWealthy. The wellness app may well be discerning among these multiple identities (the healthy versus the wealthy person) and targeting them selectively to effect behavioral change. It may offer an AI agent that nudges the StayingHealthy role to adhere to an exercise or diet regime.

We use the PART association link to denote the part-whole relationship between the composite Actor and its constituents. An Actor could be a Role or an Agent capable of realizing a Role. Goal analysis is conducted by propagating goal

[7] Top-down in a layered architecture. Lower-layer components are used to meet the objectives of higher-layer components.

satisfaction values through explicitly defined intentional dependencies between any kind of Actor, including between Agent and Role, between a part and the whole, as well as among the parts. By including a Role and the Agent PLAYing that Role as constituent Actors within a composite Actor, we are able to analyze the mismatches between Role and Agent, which appear as unsatisfied dependencies.

Beyond the human individual, we apply the composite autonomous Actor concept to sociotechnical structures of any size and complexity, comprising of Agents and Roles that may or may not yet exist, and which in turn may be composite.[8] The composite Actor concept can therefore be used to model an organization normally thought of as being made up of human and technology elements.

By considering the Roles that the human and machine Agents are PLAYing, one could explore whether those Roles, or some of its subparts, can potentially be realized through different combinations of humans and technology. In the wellness app, the LoggingPhysicalActivities Role, previously played by the human, can now be played by the wellness app equipped with sensors. Whether the Nudging Role would be better played by the app or by another human may depend on the context and could be assessed empirically.

4.4 Pivot 4: From Separate to Intertwined Development and Use

In the past, software took years to develop and, once delivered, would be updated infrequently. Development processes were modeled and analyzed separately from the processes in which the systems are used, such as business processes, and typically using different modeling languages and analysis techniques, e.g., SPEM [26] vs. BPMN [27]. In the digital age where usage is constantly monitored to inform developers, there is a much tighter coupling between development and use. Users' expectations on functionality and quality evolve continuously. There are numerous decisions and choices during development that can result in success or failure during usage. When systems do not behave as expected, users often adapt the system or devise work-arounds to fit their own processes.

RE modeling can be used to expose and analyze how choices made throughout development and use affect each other. Following the agent-oriented approach, we model development and usage in terms of strategic Actors, with dependencies that can crisscross among development and use. With a generalized Actor concept, we aim to cover a notion of development that is applicable to human development as well as the development of machines.

---

[8] By conceptualizing the Actor as a generalized abstraction, it can be recursively refined or composed, as in the generalized abstractions of process and object. Note however that compositionality of the generalized intentional Actor is a more complex concept, as each Actor is autonomous and has agency.

We introduce an association link A DEVELOPS-THRU B to mean that Actor A develops through the efforts of Actor B. The direction of the link suggests that even though A is the beneficiary of the development efforts of B, it is A that wants to be "developed," to acquire new or enhanced capabilities. This is consistent with the notion of a person going through development, e.g., through professional training programs. Both A and B are autonomous actors and would assess the relationship strategically in terms of opportunities and vulnerabilities. This is in contrast to the conventional view in systems development, where A, normally thought of as the user, is a passive recipient of the development efforts.

We refer to A as the Developient and B as the Developier (words coined to dissociate from the conventional concepts of user and developer but to rhyme with recipient and developer for mnemonic aid). The terms refer to the two ends of the association relationship, rather than special kinds of Actors. This leaves the specifics of the "development" process in B and the "usage" process in A entirely open, so as to accommodate any kinds of development methods. Similarly, the usage process is unconstrained and can include unintended use cases and even misuse. RE analysis would aim to uncover issues and alternative solutions from the strategic viewpoints of stakeholders. A and B can be refined into sub-Actors for detailed analysis.

In the digital age, we as users of technology frequently evolve our own practices in our various Roles, as we integrate various systems and services into our lives, which themselves are evolving all the time. By modeling development and use within the same framework, RE analysis can examine and reconsider the allocation of responsibilities and decision rights between development and use. For example, in considering alternative design for personalization, a wellness app that automatically detects and infers user preferences may be simpler to use but renders the user feeling less in control.

4.5 Pivot 5: From Separate to Intertwined Learning and Doing

Recent dramatic advances in AI are achieved by applying machine learning algorithms on massive amounts of data. It is essential for RE to offer suitable abstractions that will enable stakeholders to assess technology systems today as they incorporate AI. As these systems become deeply embedded in human lives, it is equally important to include human learning in RE analysis.

We take the same approach for modeling learning as for development (Pivot 4), in order to support analysis of strategic relationships among autonomous Actors capable of learning.

We introduce LEARNS-THRU as an association link from A to B to mean that B contributes to the learning of A. We refer to A as the Learnient and B the Learnier (mnemonically rhyming with recipient and learner but distinct from them in meaning). The link indicates a relationship between two Actors relative to each other, without presupposing the properties of A or B. Analysis is conducted through intentional dependencies explicitly defined between the two Actors. This approach leaves the specification of how learning takes place entirely open, so as to accommodate all kinds of human and machine learning.

The Learnient can be thought of as the user of the results from Learnier, integrating the learning into its own activities, the "doing." Both Actors, being strategic actors with agency, make choices according to their own best interests. The Learnient would assess how Learnier's way of learning would be beneficial or problematic, while the Learnier may adjust its practices to respond to Learnient's needs and concerns if that suits its own interests.

A wellness app that learns from user behavior to improve its effectiveness could be modeled as having a learning Role (the Learnier side) separate from the doing Role (the Learnient side) so that their dependencies to and from other actors can be separately identified and analyzed.

As in the case of development, RE analysis can help redistribute the kinds of choices open to each side. For example, the Learnier may restrict what is learned to a narrower context or leave more room for interpretation or adaptation by the Learnient. More detailed analysis can be conducted by elaborating on sub-Actors on each side. A drill-down into learning can reveal where biases originate and how they might be mitigated by other Actors during development or use. Elaboration on the doing or usage side might uncover how what is learned could be misused.

We treat learning as similar to development in that in both cases, the beneficiary, the Learnient and the Developient, gain capability. We provide the two links (LEARNS-THRU and DEVELOPS-THRU) to correspond to the distinction between software systems gaining capabilities through machine learning from data versus through explicit programming of encoded knowledge, respectively. The former is inductive and relies on instances and examples. The latter is deductive and relies on concepts and theories. In the case of humans, they correspond to learning through experience versus through descriptions or instructions. A person who follows a fitness exercise regime based on explicitly articulated instructions and schedule would be considered to have undergone "development," whereas if he acquires a pattern of regular workouts through the habituation, we would consider that to be "learning."

The LEARNS-THRU and DEVELOPS-THRU links can be used together and can also be applied to humans and machines in any combination. This allows software systems created through a mix of machine learning and programming to be analyzed in their human social context, including, for example, human-AI collaboration in a business process or AI-enabled enterprises. They can also be used to examine alternative methods and associated tools for creating ML and AI solutions, compare their relative strengths and shortcomings for different types of applications, and trace problems and issues to their contributing sources through the network of dependencies and to locate Actors that are responsible or capable of remedial actions. Such analysis would be important for achieving trustworthy and responsible AI.

For instance, to generate effective reminders to nudge a busy user to get active from time to time, the wellness app could use ML models learned from that user's activity patterns, combined with best practice heuristics developed by health experts. The Reminding function (a Role PLAYed by WellnessApp) LEARNS-THRU Reminder-ML-process and DEVELOPS-THRU AppDevelopment process, which has a dependency on HealthBehaviorExperts for knowledge about effective nudging.

4.6 Pivot 6: From Detached to Empirically Grounded Actors

In the age of AI, systems rely heavily on diverse types and sources of data to respond to changing conditions in the world. Many software systems are created by observing actual results from repeated experimentation, rather than by applying well-worn techniques with predictable results. These include online experiments like A/B testing and algorithm selection and hyperparameter tuning in machine learning [28].

We introduce the concept of Sensors and Actuators in an Actor's intentional model so that it can refer to what happens to the world. They are tagged as such in the literals (names) of intentional elements (Task, Resource, etc.) and serve as interface points to the non-intentional, causal world.

A Sensor variable is an input to an Actor from a causal world, i.e., the Actor can decide what to do based on the value of the sensed variable. They may appear as a Resource in an *i** model or as a Situation or Indicator following BIM [29].

An Actuator variable is an output to the world. The Actor can manipulate the value of the variable, through an *i** Task.

In cases where models about the causal world exist to complement the intentional models of strategic Actors, Sensors and Actuators would refer to named elements that are variables in those models, e.g., in causal loop diagrams of system dynamics or in systems of differential equations.

During RE, one would analyze vulnerabilities and opportunities in the ways that an Actor interacts with the non-intentional world, in addition to the intentional relationships it has with other Actors. Feedback and adaptive architectures are important in many contexts, including for example, continuous software engineering, DevOps, MLops, and the data-driven enterprise [28]. Observations and interaction with the non-intentional empirical world are also essential for human learning.

The wellness app could sense and respond to its application context (health results, healthcare team actions, user behavior, etc.) in many different ways. By extending intentional modeling with sensors and actuators that interact with the causal world, the RE analyst would be able to analyze the implications of alternative sense-and-respond configurations from the viewpoint of strategic interests of various stakeholders.

4.7 Pivot 7: From Atemporal to Temporally Contextualized Actors

When Actors make choices and face trade-offs, they do so within a temporal context. Short-term decisions may be less well informed and hurried. Decisions for the longer term may face greater uncertainty and psychologically feel more distant. Trade-offs may need to be made between short-term effects and long-term consequences.

When multiple Actors relate to each other intentionally, it is important to recognize that each Actor may operate on a different time scale or specific time frame. One might respond differently to an urgent complaint from a long-standing customer, compared to an inquiry from a new customer about a possible project next year. Decisions made in the context of the Project Manager Role may be in the time frame of each project, whereas the Agent playing the Role may include career-long considerations in its decisions. The wellness app user and various healthcare team members, in their multiple roles, would each be making choices and trade-offs in their respectively different temporal frames.

For the purpose of RE modeling and analysis, we associate each Actor with a temporal frame. A temporal frame may define a finite time horizon or a recurring cycle with a certain frequency. It may be delineated in absolute time or by start and end conditions. It may also define a granularity so as to filter out high-frequency noise and exclude variations that are too slow to be considered significant. Iterative cycles may aim to converge toward a terminating condition, based on sensing and actuating within each cycle.

4.8 Pivot 8: Beyond Goals—Values, Norms, and Emotions

The goal-oriented agent abstraction from early AI [1] provided the inspiration for the *i** Actor. This exclusive focus on goal-guided behavior is an oversimplification that is no longer adequate for today's RE modeling needs.

In the age of AI, software systems increasingly aim to appear to behave in humanlike ways, for smoother interactions and to achieve desired effects and to gain acceptance. Software systems not only can recognize human emotions and values and respond accordingly, many applications aim to trigger emotions and shape values. Furthermore, as AI derives its behavior by learning from humans, they will embody human biases and emotions.

Humans also need to be modelled much more richly than in the past, since we interact with machines increasingly on humanlike terms. For humans, the default mode of interaction is reactive and intuition based, which is fast and automatic, rather than deliberative goal-oriented thinking, which is slow and effortful [30, 31]. Values, which are deeply held beliefs, can override strategic interests.

We further extend the Actor abstraction that we have proposed so far to include behaviors that are driven by values and emotions, besides goals and interests. As before, this extension applies to the generalized Actor, encompassing humans and machines on any scale, with development and learning abilities, and so on.

In the age of AI, while considering technology solutions, stakeholders want to know whether and how their values and emotions will be detected and exploited or manipulated and for what purpose and whether their interests will be enhanced or compromised. They would want to explore alternative options for leveraging values and emotions for positive gains while minimizing vulnerabilities.

By modeling sociotechnical configurations in terms of strategic dependencies among Actors with values and emotions, RE analysis can assess the implications of alternative configurations for various stakeholders. They can explore opportunities and inquire how and where things can go wrong and what mitigation strategies might be sufficient. The effectiveness of wellness and healthcare applications could be significantly affected by differences and variations in cultural and professional values, as well as in emotional responses, among the many roles and participants.

How values and emotions can best be represented for the purpose of RE modeling will need to be explored. While values might be treated as a kind of goal [32], one would also want to be able to analyze how values get transmitted across Actors. Values could potentially be treated as a kind of belief that gives positive or negative support to different ways for achieving goals, as in the concept of Claim in the NFR framework [23], and similar to other argumentation frameworks. By extending *i** with a Belief Dependency, the effects of beliefs can be propagated across Actors using the same qualitative reasoning procedures as for goal reasoning [33, 34].

4.9 Pivot 9: From Requirements on Machines to Augmentation of Selves

In the conventional view, requirements specify the relationship between the target machine and its environment [35]. In Pivot 1, we proposed to shift perspective to think of RE as guiding strategic actors in their search for reconfigurations of relationships that would advance their strategic interests. In that process, we had assumed that the Actors themselves remain unchanged. A target technology system is treated as a newly introduced strategic actor in their midst, resulting in reconfigured relationships among all Actors.

Today's AI-enabled systems have the potential to engage with humans much more deeply and can have far-ranging impacts. We thus propose to take a further step, to think of the requirements process as guiding Actors to examine and transform their selves, incorporating technology into the self where appropriate. We will refer to this vision of RE as aa*I** (or aaIstar), short for "Augmenting Aspiring Selves," to highlight the RE task as that of helping stakeholders to examine and augment their selves and to search for or create Agents that aspire to realize the ideals defined by Roles. The term "augmenting" rather than "augmented" is used to suggest an ongoing and possibly never-ending process.

Augmenting the self by "incorporating" another autonomous Actor (such as a black box AI agent) is analogous to a company acquiring another company and is subject to similar integration challenges, including alignment of interests and values, and dealing with potential third-party allegiances of constituent actors.

An analysis of the self, as applied to all relevant stakeholders, regardless of how they are constituted, is part of the journey in self-transformation, and so is the exploration and search for technology solutions. The notion of "self" is applicable to each Actor, which, being a generalized abstraction (Pivot 2), can be abstract (Role) or realizational (Agent), can be any combination of humans and machines, and can be composite and potentially analyzable in terms of constituent Actors (Pivot 3).

During RE inquiry, each Actor would ask of itself: (From Pivot 1) How are my possibilities for action enabled and/or constrained by strategic dependencies with other Actors? (From Pivot 8) How are my values and beliefs influenced and shaped, and by whom (belief dependencies)? Am I attempting to shape other Actors beliefs or manipulate their emotions? (Pivot 4 and 5) How did I come to be? Who and what do I depend on for my development and learning? (Pivot 6) How am I acting on the causal world and sensing the outcomes? (Pivot 7) What temporal frames do I operate in? How am I situated temporally in relation to other Actors?

This self-reflection provides the basis for exploring alternative configurations of relationships with other Actors and the boundary of the self—How else can things be? What would be a more desirable self? The notion of agency refers to the ability to make choices to respond to or control the environment [36]. Given the opportunity, Actors would seek to strengthen or augment their agency, leveraging technology if necessary.

Taking advantage of the generality of the Actor abstraction (Pivot 2), the analysis of self and exploration of potential future selves can be conducted at an abstract technology-independent level (in terms of Roles), avoiding the common pitfall of favoring particular technology solutions prematurely at the expense of considering further alternatives. Envisioning possibilities at an abstract level transcends material limitations inherent in realizational Agents, such as humans and specific classes of machines. Technology alternatives can be considered in terms of various specialized classes of Agents capable of PLAYing the Roles.

The general Actor abstraction also allows the examination of self to be conducted at multiple levels of granularity. A composite Actor (Pivot 3) can be examined as a single autonomous actor. The same analysis can be applied to each of its constituent Actors and so forth recursively. Opportunities for self-transformation and augmentation may exist for many of these Actors, sometimes at the expense of others.[9] RE methods are needed to help navigate and manage the analysis, as in

[9] As each actor seeks to augment its self, it may be considered harmful or malevolent by some other actors. The modeling framework makes no assumptions about which goals are beneficial or deleterious. The analysis is conducted from the viewpoint of each stakeholder.

the case of complex organizations of human and technology elements. In the age of AI, RE processes are ongoing cycles of transformation, resulting from dialogue and negotiation between what is desirable (Roles) and what is possible (Agents).

In the case of the wellness app, Actors to be considered might include the health conscious person's Roles and realizational Agents pertaining to his health and fitness, family and social life, work life, and those pertaining to persons he interacts within these roles, Actors associated with his healthcare providers, the developers and service providers of the app and platform, and perhaps regulators and policymakers. The RE analyst would work with stakeholders to determine the breadth and depth to which the network of dependencies and associations among Actors should be pursued, to the extent that their decisions would be affected. The characteristics of these Actors may depend on the local culture, demographics, and regulatory and competitive environments.

5 Discussion and Related Work

Requirements engineering bridges the needs and wants of users and stakeholders on the one hand and the capabilities of technology systems on the other. Much attention is currently being paid to how RE techniques can encompass the distinctive characteristics of recent AI technologies, under the rubric of RE4AI [37]. As AI becomes widely incorporated into all kinds of systems, RE techniques must be able to analyze how systems made up of technologies of all sorts, AI or otherwise, affect people's lives, so that stakeholders can make informed choices.

We have proposed to model complex sociotechnical systems using a unified concept of Actor, sufficiently abstract and generalized to encompass sociotechnical actors of any composition while specializable through IS-A hierarchies to distinguish among humans and machines of various types and characteristics.

The Actor abstraction can be seen as a further evolution of the object abstraction. Objects localize and encapsulate data and behavior, whereas Actors localize intentionality and choice. Objects collaborate by exchanging messages. Actors, through intentional dependencies, expand the space of options for each other but also constrain each other's freedom.

The social science literature provides an extremely rich reference source for developing and refining the Actor abstraction. The concept of agency has been extensively explored (e.g., [36, 38]). Social psychologists distinguish among individual self, relational self, and collective self [24]. Many theories of identity have been developed [39]. The concept of role appears in many forms in various theories. The Role concept in *i** is a simplification. The imperfect realization of a Role by an Agent may be compared to the concepts of identity standard and identity verification in identity theory and affect control theory [40]. William James [41] distinguished between the self as subject (I) and as object (me) and hinted at a notion of extended self that can include artifacts. The "extended self" concept has been applied to modern marketing [42] and has been discussed in the context of virtual assistants [43].

Psychologists recognize that emotion is a more fundamental driver of human behavior, whereas deliberative thought and conscious decision-making is cognitively demanding and slow [30]. It has been proposed that the fast and slow thinking of Systems One and Two [31] be viewed as separate minds [44]. RE researchers have drawn attention to the importance of including values and emotions in requirements analysis [45, 46]. Values have been treated as goals [47]. Emotions are especially important in RE for security [48], gaming, gamification, persuasive technology, and affective computing.

Time frames and horizons are important factors in organizational decision-making [49]. Technical debt in software engineering is a manifestation of intertemporal choice and trade-offs [50].

There is much work on RE for adaptive systems, including goal- and agent-oriented approaches [51, 52]. The current proposal suggests to provide only interface points to dynamic models, allowing for different types of system dynamics modeling to be used to complement the intentional modeling of sociotechnical Actors.

The proposal to model learning and doing, as well as development and use, as intermingled processes draws inspiration from the modeling of DevOps [53] and from the treatment of variability in software engineering, where the binding time of variants can be allocated to different points along the multiple stages of development [54]. The proposal is distinctive in aiming to encompass both machines and humans and learning and development together in a single modeling framework.

Reconceptualizing RE as self-reflection and reinvention can be seen as a generalization of the call for businesses to rethink who and what they are as they pursue digital transformation and business model innovation [55, 56]. By asking themselves repeatedly—"what business am I in?" [57]—an online book seller could end up becoming an e-commerce platform and a technology company, a DVD rental company could become a streaming service then a major movie producer, and an athletic footwear company can also become a fashion leader. RE using a generalized Actor abstraction would suggest self-inquiry and prospecting for opportunities at multiple levels at the same time, from individuals to groups to organizations, each constituting of multiple selves, with interactions and dependencies among them and across levels.

The notion of augmented intelligence has been a long-running theme in connection with AI, advocating the use of machine intelligence to complement and amplify human capability rather than to compete with or supplant human intelligence [58, 59]. The proposal of the augmenting self, as articulated in Pivot 9, may be seen as a generalization of the notion of augmentation adapted for the purpose of RE. When applied to a generalized Actor abstraction, augmentation refers to the strengthening or expansion of the agency of an Actor, without prior assumptions about eventual realization, and applicable to Actors of any size or scale (Pivot 2). Agency may be interpreted as the capacity of the self to control the environment [36]. The proposed notion of the augmenting self thus does not rely on any conception of intelligence and is independent of prior assumptions about human or machine capabilities. Using this abstraction for requirements modeling avoids prejudging relationships among humans and machines, allowing alternative configuration of human and machine elements to be explored and determined during RE.

The current proposal aims to benefit from the extensive and diverse literature on these topics to contribute toward a unified requirements modeling framework centered around the core abstraction of Actor.

6 Conclusions and Future Work

As AI continues to gain ground in the computing landscape [60], further accelerating the already massive transformations of the digital era, many brace for the oncoming onslaught of the new technology with anticipation and trepidation. Will I become more productive and valuable, or will I become redundant? How will I share responsibilities and credit with my AI coworkers? Will I have meaningful relationships with others when interactions are mediated through AI? Will my agency be diminished if my life is increasingly taken over by technology? As a business leader, will my investments in advanced technologies continue to be complemented by human ingenuity for continual organizational renewal and sustainability?

RE does not aim to answer the question—will AI be a boon to humanity, or will it diminish human agency in general? But RE techniques can guide each stakeholder to ask, for a specific application setting—which of my constituent selves will a proposed technology intervention augment or compromise? RE can guide the systematic search for alternative configurations of relationships that can best advance overall interests while mitigating against potential vulnerabilities.

This proposal has suggested the Actor abstraction as a core ontological construct for modeling humans and machines alike, through a generalized concept of Actor. The skeletal ontology outlined in this chapter is only a first step in a vision, toward a modeling-based RE framework and methodology. The ontology serves as a basis for developing a language notation and semantics, reasoning techniques and algorithms, and supporting tools. The framework will also need to be supplemented with catalogs of reusable knowledge, such as classes of commonly seen Roles and technology Agents, as well as patterns and anti-patterns of sociotechnical configurations of Actors.

There are many technical issues to be considered, including, for example, whether association links among Actors such as PLAYS, DEVELOPS-THRU, and LEARNS-THRU should include intentional semantics to support reasoning and whether structuring relationships well developed in conceptual modeling for objects—generalization-specialization (IS-A), classification-instantiation (instance-of), and aggregation/ composition (part-whole)—need to be adapted for intentional autonomous Actors. Beyond expressiveness and analytical power, there are issues of cognitive complexity and learnability for eventual practical adoption. One might consider, for example, incremental or selective adoption of pivots for different application settings.

Great strides have been made in recent years in advancing RE concepts and techniques. This proposal builds on foundations in goal-oriented and agent-oriented RE. There is much opportunity to consider how to take advantage of existing research results to give substance to this current proposal, including the considerable bodies of work in applying, adapting, and extending the *i** framework, e.g., [2, 23, 61–64].

When a technology is first introduced, it tends to be used to automate familiar tasks, for greater efficiency, lower costs, and higher productivity [65]. As we gain better understanding of the capabilities and limitations of the technology, we begin to recognize the different ways in which it can reshape our lives and relationships, eventually enabling us to reconceptualize who we are and what we can become [66–69].

Acknowledgments I would like to thank all those who provided invaluable suggestions and feedback during the preparation of this chapter. I particularly want to thank Gerhard Lakemeyer, Alistair Sutcliffe, Alexei Lapouchnian, and anonymous reviewers for their detailed reviews and constructive suggestions to improve the manuscript. Any errors, omissions, or shortcomings in this chapter are entirely my own responsibility.

References

1. Newell, A.: The knowledge level. Artif. Intell. **18**(1), 87–127 (1982)
2. Yu, E., Giorgini, P., Maiden, N., Mylopoulos, J.: Social Modeling for Requirements Engineering. MIT Press (2011)
3. Yu, E.S.: Towards modelling and reasoning support for early-phase requirements engineering. In: Proceedings of ISRE'97: 3rd IEEE International Symposium on Requirements Engineering, pp. 226–235. IEEE (1997)
4. Yu, E.: Agent orientation as a modelling paradigm. Wirtschaftsinformatik. **43**, 123–132 (2001)
5. Benis, A., Tamburis, O., Chronaki, C., Moen, A.: One digital health: a unified framework for future health ecosystems. J. Med. Internet Res. **23**(2), e22189 (2021)
6. Callaghan, S., Lösch, M., Pione, A., Teichner, W.: Feeling Good: The Future of the $1.5 Trillion Wellness Market, p. 8. McKinsey & Company (2021)
7. Hermes, S., Riasanow, T., Clemons, E.K., Böhm, M., Krcmar, H.: The digital transformation of the healthcare industry: exploring the rise of emerging platform ecosystems and their influence on the role of patients. Bus. Res. **13**, 1033–1069 (2020)
8. Mylopoulos, J.: Information modeling in the time of the revolution. Inf. Syst. **23**(3–4), 127–155 (1998)
9. DeMarco, T.: Structure analysis and system specification. In: Pioneers and their Contributions to Software Engineering: SD&M Conference on Software Pioneers, Bonn, June 28/29, 2001, Original Historic Contributions, pp. 255–288. Springer, Berlin (1979)
10. Ross, D.T., Schoman, K.E.: Structured analysis for requirements definition. IEEE Trans. Softw. Eng. **1**, 6–15 (1977)
11. Coad, P., Yourdon, E., Coad, P.: Object-Oriented Analysis, vol. 2. Yourdon Press, Englewood Cliffs (1991)
12. Mylopoulos, J., Chung, L., Yu, E.: From object-oriented to goal-oriented requirements analysis. Commun. ACM. **42**(1), 31–37 (1999)

13. Van Lamsweerde, A.: Goal-oriented requirements engineering: a guided tour. In: Proceedings Fifth IEEE International Symposium on Requirements Engineering, pp. 249–262 (2001)
14. Méndez Fernández, D., Christiansson, M.T., Wieringa, R.: Naming the pain in requirements engineering: contemporary problems, causes, and effects in practice. J. Empir. Softw. Eng. **22**, 1–41 (2016)
15. Palomares, C., Franch, X., Quer, C., Chatzipetrou, P., López, L., Gorschek, T.: The state-of-practice in requirements elicitation: an extended interview study at 12 companies. Requir. Eng. **26**, 273–299 (2021)
16. IEEE/ISO/IEC 29148–2018 International Standard - Systems and Software Engineering – Life Cycle Processes – Requirements Engineering
17. Russell, S., Norvig, P.: A modern, agent-oriented approach to introductory artificial intelligence. ACM SIGART Bull. **6**(2), 24–26 (1995)
18. Wooldridge, M.: An Introduction to Multiagent Systems. John Wiley & Sons (2009)
19. Feather, M.S.: Language support for the specification and development of compo-site systems. ACM Trans. Program. Lang. Syst. **9**(2), 198–234 (1987)
20. Jennings, N.R.: On agent-based software engineering. Artif. Intell. **117**(2), 277–296 (2000)
21. Yu, E.: Agent-oriented modelling: software versus the world. In: Wooldridge, M.J., Weiß, G., Ciancarini, P. (eds.) Agent-Oriented Software Engineering II. AOSE 2001 LNCS, vol. 2222. Springer, Berlin (2002)
22. Dennett, D.C.: The Intentional Stance. MIT Press (1989)
23. Chung, L., Nixon, B.A., Yu, E., Mylopoulos, J.: Non-functional Requirements in Software Engineering. Springer Science & Business Media (2000)
24. Sedikides, C., Brewer, M.B.: Individual Self, Relational Self, Collective Self. Psychology Press (2015)
25. Turner, J.C., Reynolds, K.J.: Self-categorization theory. Handbook of Theories in Social Psychology. **2**(1), 399–417 (2011)
26. Object Management Group Inc. (2008). Software & systems process engineering meta-model specification. Version 2.0, OMG Std.
27. Object Management Group Inc: Business Process Model and Notation (BPMN) Version 2.0. OMG Specification (2011)
28. Fabijan, A., Dmitriev, P., Olsson, H.H., Bosch, J.: The evolution of continuous experimentation in software product development: from data to a data-driven organization at scale. In: 2017 IEEE/ACM 39th International Conference on Software Engineering (ICSE), pp. 770–780. IEEE (2017)
29. Horkoff, J., Barone, D., Jiang, L., Yu, E., Amyot, D., Borgida, A., Mylopoulos, J.: Strategic business modeling: representation and reasoning. Softw. Syst. Model. **13**, 1015–1041 (2014)
30. Evans, J.S.B., Stanovich, K.E.: Dual-process theories of higher cognition: advancing the debate. Perspect. Psychol. Sci. **8**(3), 223–241 (2013)
31. Kahneman, D.: Thinking, Fast and Slow. Macmillan (2011)
32. Thew, S., Sutcliffe, A.: Value-based requirements engineering: method and experience. Requir. Eng. **23**, 443–464 (2018)
33. Amyot, D., Ghanavati, S., Horkoff, J., Mussbacher, G., Peyton, L., Yu, E.: Evaluating goal models within the goal-oriented requirement language. Int. J. Intell. Syst. **25**(8), 841–877 (2010)
34. Horkoff, J., Yu, E.: Interactive goal model analysis for early requirements engineering. Requir. Eng. **21**, 29–61 (2016)
35. Bennaceur, A., Tun, T.T., Yu, Y., Nuseibeh, B.: Requirements engineering. In: Handbook of Software Engineering, pp. 51–92 (2019)
36. Bandura, A.: Social cognitive theory: an agentic perspective. Annu. Rev. Psychol. **52**(1), 1–26 (2001)
37. Ahmad, K., Abdelrazek, M., Arora, C., Bano, M., Grundy, J.: Requirements engineering for artificial intelligence systems: a systematic mapping study. Inf. Softw. Technol. **158**, 107176 (2023)
38. Emirbayer, M., Mische, A.: What is agency? Am. J. Sociol. **103**(4), 962–1023 (1998)

39. Owens, T.J., Robinson, D.T., Smith-Lovin, L.: Three faces of identity. Annu. Rev. Sociol. **36**, 477–499 (2010)
40. Finch, J.K., Stryker, R.: Competing identity standards and managing identity verification. In: Identity and Symbolic Interaction: Deepening Foundations, Building Bridges, pp. 119–148 (2020)
41. James, W. (1890). The Consciousness of Self
42. Belk, R.W.: Extended self in a digital world. J. Consum. Res. **40**(3), 477–500 (2013)
43. Mirbabaie, M., Stieglitz, S., Brünker, F., Hofeditz, L., Ross, B., Frick, N.R.: Understanding collaboration with virtual assistants–the role of social identity and the extended self. Bus. Inf. Syst. Eng. **63**, 21–37 (2021)
44. Alós-Ferrer, C., Strack, F.: From dual processes to multiple selves: implications for economic behavior. J. Econ. Psychol. **41**, 1–11 (2014)
45. Iqbal, T., Anwar, H., Filzah, S., Gharib, M., Mooses, K., Taveter, K.: Emotions in requirements engineering: a systematic mapping study. In: 2023 IEEE/ACM 16th International Conference on Cooperative and Human Aspects of Software Engineering (CHASE), pp. 111–120. IEEE (2023)
46. Sutcliffe, A., Sawyer, P., Bencomo, N.: The implications of 'soft' requirements. In: 2022 IEEE 30th International Requirements Engineering Conference (RE), pp. 178–188. IEEE (2022)
47. Perera, H., Mussbacher, G., Hussain, W., Shams, R.A., Nurwidyantoro, A., Whittle, J.: Continual human value analysis in software development: a goal model based approach. In: 2020 IEEE 28th International Requirements Engineering Conference (RE), pp. 192–203. IEEE (2020)
48. Yasin, A., Fatima, R., Liu, L., Wang, J., Ali, R., Wei, Z.: Understanding and deciphering of social engineering attack scenarios. Secur. Priv. **4**(4), e161 (2021)
49. Orlikowski, W.J., Yates, J.: It's about time: temporal structuring in organizations. Organ. Sci. **13**(6), 684–700 (2002)
50. Becker, C., Chitchyan, R., Betz, S., McCord, C.: Trade-off decisions across time in technical debt management: a systematic literature review. In: Proceedings of the 2018 International Conference on Technical Debt, pp. 85–94 (2018, May)
51. Anda, A.A., Amyot, D.: Self-adaptation driven by SysML and goal models—a literature review. e-Inf. Softw. Eng. J. **16**(1), 220101 (2021)
52. Morandini, M., Penserini, L., Perini, A., Marchetto, A.: Engineering requirements for adaptive systems. Requir. Eng. **22**(1), 77–103 (2017)
53. Colantoni, A., Berardinelli, L., Wimmer, M.: DevOpsML: towards modeling DevOps processes and platforms. In: Proceedings of the 23rd ACM/IEEE International Conference on Model Driven Engineering Languages and Systems: Companion Proceedings, pp. 1–10 (2020)
54. Svahnberg, M., Van Gurp, J., Bosch, J.: A taxonomy of variability realization techniques. Softw. Pract. Exper. **35**(8), 705–754 (2005)
55. Majchrzak, A., Markus, M.L., Wareham, J.: Designing for digital transformation. MIS Q. **40**(2), 267–278 (2016)
56. Teece, D.J.: Business models, business strategy and innovation. Long Range Plan. **43**(2–3), 172–194 (2010)
57. Porter, M.E., Heppelmann, J.E.: How smart, connected products are transforming competition. Harv. Bus. Rev. **92**(11), 64–88 (2014)
58. Engelbart DC (1962) Augmenting human intellect: a conceptual framework SRI Summary Report AFOSR-3223
59. Raisch, S., Krakowski, S.: Artificial intelligence and management: the automation–augmentation paradox. Acad. Manag. Rev. **46**(1), 192–210 (2021)
60. Maslej, N., Fattorini, L., Perrault, R., et al.: The AI Index 2024 Annual Report. AI Index Steering Committee, Institute for Human-Centered AI, Stanford University, Stanford (2024)
61. Amyot, D., Akhigbe, O., Baslyman, M., Ghanavati, S., Ghasemi, M., Hassine, J., et al.: Combining goal modelling with business process modelling: two decades of experience with the user requirements notation standard. Enterp.Model. Inf. Syst. Architect. **17**, 2–1 (2022)

62. Franch, X., Susi, A., Annosi, M.C., Ayala, C., Glott, R., Gross, D., Kenett, R., Siena, A.: Managing risk in open source software adoption. In: International Conference on Software Engineering and Applications, vol. 2, pp. 258–264. SciTePress (2013)
63. Gonçalves, E., Castro, J., Araújo, J., Heineck, T.: A systematic literature review of iStar extensions. J. Syst. Softw. **137**, 1–33 (2018)
64. Ingolfo, S., Jureta, I., Siena, A., Perini, A., Susi, A.: Nomos 3: legal compliance of roles and requirements. In: Conceptual Modeling: 33rd International Conference, ER 2014, Atlanta, GA, USA, October 27–29, 2014. Proceedings 33, pp. 275–288. Springer International Publishing (2014)
65. Venkatraman, N.: IT-enabled business transformation: from automation to business scope redefinition. Sloan Manag. Rev. **35**(2), 73–87 (1994)
66. Bingley, W.J., Haslam, S.A., Steffens, N.K., Gillespie, N., Worthy, P., Curtis, C., et al.: Enlarging the model of the human at the heart of human-centered AI: a social self-determination model of AI system impact. New Ideas Psychol. **70**, 101025 (2023)
67. Carter, M., Grover, V.: Me, myself, and I (T). MIS Q. **39**(4), 931–958 (2015)
68. Hernández-Orallo, J., Vold, K.: AI extenders: the ethical and societal im-plications of humans cognitively extended by AI. In: Proceedings of the 2019 AAAI/ACM Conference on AI, Ethics, and Society, pp. 507–513 (2019)
69. Jarrahi, M.H., Kenyon, S., Brown, A., Donahue, C., Wicher, C.: Artificial intelligence: a strategy to harness its power through organizational learning. J. Bus. Strateg. **44**(3), 126–135 (2023)

SPRINGER NATURE

GPSR Compliance

The European Union's (EU) General Product Safety Regulation (GPSR) is a set of rules that requires consumer products to be safe and our obligations to ensure this.

If you have any concerns about our products, you can contact us on ProductSafety@springernature.com

In case Publisher is established outside the EU, the EU authorized representative is:

Springer Nature Customer Service Center GmbH
Europaplatz 3
69115 Heidelberg, Germany

The manufacturer's authorised representative in the EU is Springer
Nature Customer Service Centre GmbH, Europaplatz 3, 69115 Heidelberg,
Germany. If you have any concerns regarding our products, please
contact ProductSafety@springernature.com

Printed and bound by CPI Group (UK) Ltd, Croydon, CR0 4YY
01/10/2026
02225954-0017